hi concept - lo tech

hi concept - lo tech

Theatre for Everyone in Any Place

Barbara Carlisle and Don Drapeau

Heinemann
Portsmouth, NH

Heinemann
A division of Reed Elsevier Inc.
361 Hanover Street
Portsmouth, NH 03801-3912

Offices and agents throughout the world

Library of Congress Cataloging-in-Publication Data

Carlisle, Barbara.
  Hi concept - lo tech : theatre for everyone in any place / Barbara Carlisle and Don Drapeau.
    p.   cm.
  Includes index.
  ISBN 0-435-07001-0
  1. Amateur theater—Production and direction.   I. Drapeau, Don.
II. Title.
PN3155.C293   1996
792'.0222—dc20
                                                                95-51736
                                                                CIP

Editor: Lisa A. Barnett
Production Editor: Renée M. Nicholls
Cover Designer: Jenny Jensen Greenleaf
Manufacturing Coordinator: Louise Richardson
Front cover: Set for *Esemplastic* created and performed by Pontine Movement Theatre. Design and photograph by Co-Artistic Director, Gregory Gathers. Back cover: Author photo by Nic Fantl.

Printed in the United States of America on acid-free paper

99 98 97 96 DA 1 2 3 4 5 6

*For
Fred
and
Libby*

Contents

Acknowledgments

We have been able to write this book because of the continued support and stimulation of many colleagues. We would like to thank the faculty and students of the Department of Theatre Arts at Virginia Tech, especially Bob Leonard, Bill Barksdale, and Patty Raun, who read the manuscript and offered comments, and David Wedin, who did the drawings in the appendix. All the faculty continue to inspire us with their extensive repertoires of classroom and rehearsal techniques and with their insights into design and production concepts. The collaboration with Ann Kilkelly and the students who created the production *Such Stuff* helped strengthen our work.

We are grateful to the teachers who have attended the summer Hi-Lo workshops, particularly those who have returned for a second or third time and have taken the manuscript with them to their classrooms. Among the latter we single out Katherine Baugher, who has been with the project for five years and has explored the exercises with her high school students.

Barbara Carlisle wishes to thank Ginny Foster and Polly Friend and the students and teachers of Muskegon Intermediate School District and West Bloomfield, Michigan, for inviting her to develop these ideas in school classrooms and with community theatre directors. The book owes a great debt to dancer Shawn Womack and the collaborative work she and Barbara have done with teachers in the summer institutes of the Education Enchancement Partnership of Stark County, Ohio.

Don Drapeau wishes to acknowledge the work of Jane Hinson La Motte, who, as a graduate student in the Department of Theatre Arts at Virginia Tech, designed the system for rehearsal furniture represented in the appendix.

We both are grateful for the excellent advice of our editor, Lisa Barnett.

Introduction

*W*e dedicate this book to the essential theatre act. We believe theatre can come out of any group of people, at any time, in any place. We know that theatre is pliable and resilient, and, if we use it well, it can serve to capture our fullest imaginings. We believe that theatre is not a formula but an art, an art centered on the encounter between the performer and the audience and the work they make together. We have seen that theatre can draw from the richness of many literatures, from tiny incidents in individual lives, from accidents of imagination and spontaneous insights. We have learned to trust the art for what it can bring to our lives, and we have written a book to remind both ourselves and the readers of that power.

This is a practical handbook to making theatre that is rich in thought, energy, passion, artfulness, excitement, and commitment, and intentionally poor in spectacle and technical trappings. This is a handbook for learning and teaching theatre in the simplest settings, with all age groups. It is filled with exercises and examples, diagrams and ideas.

We have written this book for theatre artists in many settings—in communities of amateurs, in professional companies, in schools, in clubs, in camps and campuses, in theatre workshops —artists who believe in the art and search for better ways to harness its energy. We know our book is not sufficient in itself for a lifetime of making theatre, but we think it can provide seeds for beginners. And we hope it will also be a spark for experienced performers who need to rekindle fires that have cooled from too many pale imitations of predigested and threadbare scripts.

Our book owes debts to many ancestors. Its deepest roots are in storytellers who have kept the tales of gods and heroes alive from age to age. It has cousins in elocution classes for children and the recitation of verses for Sunday school circles. It salutes the world's street performers and traveling players, who have carried their theatres on their backs.

Every person who ever took a tale and turned it into theatre, from Aeschylus to Shakespeare to the Kabuki performers and the shadow-puppet players of Southeast Asia, has helped write this book. They represent the impulses that have created great theatre in the first place. We are determined to help theatre in the studio, workshop, classroom, and church basement rediscover that original connection.

We must acknowledge a number of writers whose works are still in circulation and should be used by anyone who is inspired to go on. We urge you to read Viola Spolin's groundbreaking text, *Improvisation for the Theatre*; John Dietrich's step-by-step guide, *Play Direction*; Charles McGaw's *Acting is Believing*, which has made four decades of acting students understand their job; and Robert Edmond Jones' *The Dramatic Imagination*, which showed the twentieth century how to reinvent the theatre's visual world. We were taught by Paul Sills' "Story Theatre" to appreciate the theatricality of our favorite tales. In the more theoretical realm, we have been informed by Richard Schechner's *Performance Theory* and Bert States' *Great Reckonings in Little Rooms*, two important investigations into the phenomenology of theatre and the interaction of performer and audience. You will find the influence of Dorothy Heathcote and Brian Way, pioneers in creative drama, and teachers of creative dance like Anne Green Gilbert and Ruth Murray. An elegant book, *The Art of Making Dances* by Doris Humphrey was for us a primer for using movement and space. And more recent works, Joseph Chaikin's *The Presence of the Actor*, Augusto Boal's *Theatre of the Oppressed*, and John McGrath's *A Good Night Out*, have expanded our thinking about the essential purposes of theatre.

We will not be able to trace all of the histories of specific exercises or processes because ours have evolved and melded, intermarried, and spawned their own offspring in years of working and learning. We hope this book inspires you to borrow ours and invent your own.

We wrote this book to make us all bolder. We want to give confidence, to provide starting points and stepping stones, and to lead theatre makers, whether they are children or adults, to their own sources of inspiration.

Four Basic Principles

We set ourselves four basic principles. They act as warning lights for us and as measures by which we all can judge our projects and our choices.

1. We must understand the nature of the theatre art and ask ourselves if what we are trying to accomplish is best accomplished in the theatre. Are we using the essence of theatre as the center of our work?

2. In the theatre of children and the classroom, the most important question must always be, "What are the students learning?" Does it have anything to do with the nature of the theatre art? Is it positive, constructive, and useful? This may be a fair question for any groups of artists who hope to grow with experience.

3. The quality of the material we choose to put on stage must deserve the time and attention we give it. Does it have its own value, its own truth, its own voice?

4. There must be a guiding aesthetic or point of view that drives each work. Theatre, on whatever scale we create it, is art. Unlike life, art requires a set of integrated aesthetic choices. Have we thought through the approach we are taking? Are we communicating our point of view among ourselves as we work? Is our point of view clear in the final interaction with the audience? Is our work artful?

(We use "artful" in its first and original meaning, "full of art and skill," even though its secondary meaning, "deceitful," has come into common use.)

These four principles are demanding taskmasters. But whether we are guiding kindergarten children in a presentation of nursery rhymes, a group of teenagers in the development of their own writing, or a group of adults in a realization of *Macbeth*, it is these principles that will help us make effective choices along the way.

Within these four principles are many questions:

When theatre takes so many shapes across the world, how can we arrive at its fundamental nature? How well do we understand theatricality? How do we help others understand it, especially when their environment is full of film and video? What can the theatre do that the literal reality of film and video cannot? What is the nature of time and space in the theatre? What is real in the theatre?

If we are teaching, how do we know what students are learning at any given time? How do we pose the questions to ourselves to discover that learning? What evidence do we look for? How do we reconcile the need to teach, learn, and grow, and the need to produce artful theatre?

How do we know when a work is high quality? If it has been tested by New York, London, and academia, is that not enough? If we make work from poems or stories, if we make theatre from our own writing, how can we be sure it will be theatrical?

How do we best match form and idea to arrive at an artistic point of view? Can little children, or untrained adults, understand sophisticated concepts like "a driving aesthetic?" Do they really need to? What does it mean in practical terms?

What role do considerations like the size of the theatre, casting limitations, vocal or physical skills, building a set, and making costumes play in our work? Is smaller always better?

We hope to help you find the answers to these questions. We will also consider those day-to-day quandaries, such as what to do with seventy-five kids in two English classes who want to be in a play? Or how to produce a season of work if no men come to tryouts? Or what to do with only four girls in the drama club, or a company of five women who must work at other jobs and juggle child care with their art? Or how to produce contemporary work when we fear our audience will boycott, cancel, or censor it?

We have tried to set forth a way of thinking to create a variety of interesting theatre. We have drawn from experiences working in schools, professional theatres, and community settings with teachers, students of many ages, and both professional and nonprofessional performers. We imagine the discussions can be used as a fresh start for seasoned professionals, or as a guide to raw beginners who know only that they want to do something in drama and are not sure what that might be.

We should tell you about ourselves. Barbara Carlisle, who has written most of the sections about acting, writing, and directing, has been a teacher, writer, choreographer, and theatre professional for three decades. She has worked in community theatre, professional theatre, public schools, teacher workshops, and camps for talented children. She now writes, teaches play writing and acting to university students, and choreographs and directs her own plays and works from the conventional repertoire. A dozen years ago Barbara began to ask herself, "How can I help teachers or community theatre people who feel that what they learned in a couple of classes in college or past productions is not giving them guidance for working today? How can I help them improve the quality of the performances, and, more important, the depth and breadth of what the participants are learning in the drama work? And how can I help anyone who would like to introduce drama into the classroom or community center but is afraid of the trappings it seems to bring?"

With these questions in mind, Barbara began a one-person crusade, doing workshops and residencies, offering everything from how to make inexperienced performers more responsible, to

exploring the nature of the art, to helping people write and produce their own material, to helping teachers use theatre as a way
of understanding literature. In the process she began to combine
exercises from acting technique, creative drama, creative dance,
writing and directing, Story Theatre, and improvisational games.
Her workshop participants—some of them teachers, some children,
others directors and actors in community theatre—responded with
enthusiasm. A set of processes began to unfold.

In the summer of 1990, Barbara teamed with Don Drapeau,
Head of the Department of Theatre Arts at Virginia Tech, to offer a
summer workshop they called "Hi Concept - Lo Tech." Don, who
wrote most of the design and technical theatre sections, has acted,
designed, and taught theatre history, theatre management, and
introduction to theatre for the past thirty years. He has been a
leader in national theatre organizations and has visited dozens of
college programs across the country as a reviewer for the National
Association of Schools of Theatre. For years before Barbara came to
Virginia Tech, Don had been offering summer workshops to high
school drama teachers, emphasizing ways to use simple materials,
simple ideas, and simple processes to improve their productions.
He found that many teachers are isolated, the only ones doing
drama in their schools. They have little access to professional theatre of any kind, and few people who are interested in their problems. As models they often have only unsophisticated community
theatre productions, where people without experience rely on imitations of imitations of outdated Broadway examples.

As he answered the questions from teachers, Don began to
question the perpetuation of a form of school drama that is based on
re-creations of a tired repertoire, produced with old textbook techniques. He questioned whether these productions teach anything to
students about what is really possible in the theatre. He became
discouraged about the high school star systems that create "theatre
junkies," young people who have become so narrowly focused on
performing, mostly in musicals, that they fail to prepare themselves
for any other pursuits. He questioned goals for secondary theatre
education that are based in a stilted and uncreative form. Don also

saw his concerns about school theatre reflected in community and university theatre, and even in the regional professional theatre.

As a team, we committed ourselves philosophically and practically to changing the idea of "putting on a play" to the idea of "making theatre." Instead of simply following a recipe of what everyone else has done before, we urge making theatre that is personal, inventive, and suited to the people, time, and place of its creation. We believe that putting on a play with the cookie-cutter method takes all the meaningful encounter out of theatre and deals only with the thinnest veneer of the process. Doing plays in the formulaic way is costly in time and energy. It may be flashy on the exterior but it lacks any fundamental exploration of the art from which it springs.

"Making theatre," on the other hand, invests energy in high conceptual thinking instead of expensive materials and excessive hours of meaningless labor. High conceptual thinking is hard, but low technical demands leave the mind and body free to do the creative work. Our book is committed to its title, *hi concept - lo tech*. We are offering a means for revitalizing a tired theatre environment. We hope to infiltrate the English class as well as the drama class, and to fuel a revolution in community theatres, universities, and even professional theatres. We are talking to people who want to lead theatre groups in studios, classes, clubs, community centers, or workshops. The book is a compilation of ideas, organized with exercises, tasks, lists of useful materials, and, in many cases, step-by-step instructions in how to do it. It is also a collection of experiences, observations, and commentary derived from a combined sixty years of experience.

We want this book to be two things: a useful handbook, with specific practical exercises and procedures, and a philosophical guide to rethinking the theatre process. We would like to feed a hunger to re-engage with art making, to allow theatre to spring from the community itself, to cross race, class, and gender barriers, and to free artists young and old to speak with their own voices to new and more responsive audiences.

Discovering the Essence of Theatre

Our basic premise is that theatre lives in many forms and in many places but everywhere its essence is the same. However, the details and conditions of its appearance change constantly.

One morning, before the bell had rung at the Fragrant Grasslands Elementary School in Beijing, a second-grade boy was entertaining his classmates with his animated description of a bicycle collision he had seen on the way to school. Ordinarily, Chinese children come into class and take their seats, sit stiffly, their arms behind them, their eyes focused on the doorway for the entrance of the teacher. Not so this morning. Their classmate had them completely enthralled. Apparently, two old men had crashed into one another, narrowly missing the boy as he darted into the street. The whole class laughed in delight as he impersonated each of the riders and dramatized his own role in the event. When the teacher came into the room, the children did not even see her. She was so amused by his performance that she let him finish his story before she put her hands gently on his shoulders and brought the classroom to attention. It was a moment of theatre, capturing all the essential qualities in the simplest form: an actor, an audience, and a shared set of illusions and assumptions.

He was himself, and then each rider, and we saw it all with him as he set up the moment of the crash.

In Osaka, Japan, three men costumed in black operate the half-life-sized puppets of the Bunraku Theatre. While the story is recited and sung by a chorus and orchestra, the puppets perform the actions. The stage settings are detailed and the puppets wear costumes of Samurai warriors, peasants, wives, and concubines, the personae of traditional Japanese tales. The three puppeteers required for each puppet are exquisitely coordinated: one man operates the head and right hand, one the body and left hand, and one, moving along the floor in a trough below the stage level, operates the feet. Although the puppeteers are in view of the audience, it is not long before they become invisible to the mind as the story unfolds and the puppets become real.

In Stratford, Ontario, a single actor takes on the double roles of identical twins, Antipholus of Ephesus and Antipholus of Syracuse; another single actor plays both the Dromios, identical twin servants to the twin masters, in Shakespeare's *Comedy of Errors*. The audience knows before the play begins that these two actors will be playing double roles. Never forgetting that the same actors are running around switching bits of costume to make their speedy changes, the audience delights in both the plot complications of mistaken identities and the sheer virtuosity of the performers. Suddenly the play is twice as funny because we share in the means by which the illusion is created, even while we accept the reality of it.

You can see that each of these performances is theatre. Each illustrates in its own form the essence of the theatrical encounter: the mutual agreement between the audience and the performer to the conventions of the presentation. Together we accept for the moment that certain things exist for both of us, and based on these assumptions, we will present ourselves a case within these temporarily altered circumstances. The cases are infinite: a story, a series of amusing confusions, a meeting of powerful forces, a complicated plot of protagonists and antagonists, a feeling unveiled, or a new look at people we might know. The key is our collaboration in the moment: what we tacitly agree to accept. The theatrical event exists when together we embark on a metaphorical journey—the performer leading, the audience following—and we arrive at a mutual discovery. The discovery may be a new look at a familiar thing or it may be a revelation of something utterly unknown. This journey can be led by any performer of any age who can capture the audience's imagination and make it accept the conditions of the invention.

Thus, the second-grade Chinese boy that Barbara saw in Beijing created a vivid picture of the crowded city street. His audience participated in the drama of the event, playing along until the expected crash filled them with laughter. Another audience accepts the reality of the puppets or the existence of the twin Shakespearean characters. For us, the most interesting feature of the theatrical encounter is that we all preserve ourselves throughout. I never doubt that I am in an audience and the performer never mistakes himself for the puppet or the character. But we accept the condition that, for a time, we can exist on more than one level of reality. The performance defines that reality.

We believe it is the establishment and maintenance of these new realities that give theatre its power. What is created by the performer and agreed to by the audience can be simple or complex, with all the subtleties of the two Antipholuses and the two Dromios or the simplicity of the Chinese second-grader telling his story. It can be a traditional play with all the conventions of character, plot, rising action, climax, and resolution. But theatre can also consist of magic tricks, stories, poetry, jugglers enticing us with patter, dance that captures our imagination, or any combination of these. The key ingredient is the engagement of the performer and spectator and the establishment of that special space and time in which new realities convene. We learn to manipulate the mutual journey, the suspension of selves, the joint endeavor, when we become artists of the theatre.

Shared Illusion: The Fundamental Theatre Magic

It took us a long time to realize that people often ascribe this fundamental theatrical magic to irrelevant things. They think it is the setting that creates the illusion, or the complications of the plot that carry us along, or the play of lights, or the rising of a curtain, or illusions of sound that make the theatre work. But the essence of theatre is in none of these trappings, as much fun as they may be. It is the interaction of audience and performer that invests theatre with its ability to move and entertain us. What links theatre around the world, from its most modest to its most lavish manifestation, is the confrontation of the performer and the audience and the bond that is created between them.

First Steps in Making Theatre

One of the first things a beginning group must do is to discover for themselves the power of the theatrical moment, that period of engagement when the performer and spectator are one, suspended together in their own time, bound and connected. They need to experience it as both performers and audience in a number of different ways. They need to be on both sides of it in order to learn to manipulate it themselves. They need to discuss it and critique it, to know when it is happening and why, and when it is not happening and why. With this understanding they become empowered to make theatre.

The Role of the Leader

We know that leading theatre exploration involves guiding a group toward both experiencing and studying the process, and finally, creating within it. The leader is part of the exploration, setting up tasks, encouraging involvement, facilitating individual development, and discovering along with the participants. We have learned that the more a leader works with a group, the more obvious it is that the group can help itself. The goal is empowerment, helping individuals discover their ability to make theatre and making them better and better critics of their own process. What the two of us have discovered from teaching is that real growth happens when people are able to see where they are and what they need to do better.

The leadership role we propose is very different from that of the director or teacher who feels bound to be the resource for all artistic decisions. It is different from the role of a person who has a compelling idea and wants performers to realize it. Our leadership role assumes that in most creative groups, whether they are children or adults, artistic ideas will flow from different sources at different times, and that once people understand what they are doing, they can help each other realize their work and become more sophisticated in doing it.

This leader poses problems, listens for solutions, guides processes, provides resources, sets the atmosphere, offers support, and maintains forward movement. The leader does not need to have all the answers, but he or she needs to have many questions and should recognize a good answer when it appears.

With help from resources like this book and others we mention, a beginner who is a willing learner and has a passionate curiosity about theatre can be a leader, learning along with the group.

Finding the Artistic Leadership

In our experience, artistic ideas flow in a variety of patterns. They will not all come from any single leader. A group may brainstorm until one idea catches their imagination and the originator of that idea takes charge. That person may take the idea as far as it will go; others comment and contribute mainly as the realizers until another takes up the role. Leadership may come in pairs of people or in a core of the group. There is no absolute pattern. But leadership is important. Theatre requires a sense of direction and a critical eye and ear. A teacher may supply it in a large measure, but gradually the group must develop its own critique. When a process begins to flow automatically, when people immediately fall in with appropriate contributions to a central notion, when good choices are quickly recognized by others, then the group has evolved its own aesthetic. The official leader just keeps it going. That is where you are headed.

Leadership Style

We know that in the early stages of getting underway, the style of the leader is critical. In each of the exercises that follow, the leader sets a task with certain conditions and then facilitates the execution of the task, always allowing for a great deal of individual freedom in the solution to the problem. The leader encourages, guides, explains, and presses the group for analysis and articulation of concepts. The leader does not become the arbitrary judge of good and bad. It is not the goal of the group to please the leader. But the leader will help the group develop its own aesthetic sensibilities and its own artistry.

The Simultaneous Process

A premise of all the exercises we do is that everyone is active all the time. Exercises are done by all, simultaneously, so everyone is engaged in the problem solving. There is little standing around and watching. This means everyone is learning and practicing all the time, and people do not have time to disengage. Even when people are performing for each other, we ask the audience to be active, to listen, to critique, to applaud, and to be aware that their turn is next.

✳ *Dividing into Effective Work Groups*

If you are working with teenagers or children, the group division can be an important dynamic. It is even true with adults. Here is a simple strategy.

The leader is beating a tempo on a dance drum or other rhythmic instrument, or playing music on a tape.

Leader Dialogue

Everyone walk around the room, covering all the spaces. Don't bump into anyone. Concentrate on moving and eliminate talking. Try very hard not to say anything. Just move around the room. Try to keep the tempo of the rhythm you hear. Avoid walking in a single circle. Cut across the room in different directions. Now, without any conversation or spoken language, form a big circle. Good. Now, without discussing it at all, just moving as you need to, form two circles. Good. Now form groups of four or five. No talking, just look and see. (Or, form groups of two or three, whatever is needed for the exercise.)

Advice to the Leader

If you do this a few times, groups become used to forming themselves into work groups for any exercise. Then they can do it quickly without preliminaries. Since much of the work we will do will involve small groups, it is important to divide into many different ways and to get people used to the idea that they can function in any combination for any given exercise. You may deliberately group males and females separately, or mix gender groups, or mix heights and weights, or ages—as exercises vary. With some age groups it may be useful in the very first exercises to use clusters that have automatically formed.

Noise and Concentration

Small groups can work simultaneously, even though they might create a lot of noise. Noise is good when it represents everyone's contribution to the work. People working have an amazing capacity to focus. If the noise represents confusion or distraction, the leader may need to pull the group back as a whole. We borrowed Viola Spolin's word "freeze" as our trigger to stop the group in order to listen to a new instruction. When groups are working, the leader can move around among them providing individual assistance as needed. Both distracting noise and silence from a group can indicate a need for a little outside help.

Side Coaching to Ensure the Quality of the Experience

A second premise of this approach is the role of the teacher/leader as a *side coach*. We borrowed the term from Viola Spolin, author of *Theatre Games for the Classroom* and *Improvisation for the Theatre*. Side coaching consists of instructions given to the group *during the exercise,* loud enough for all to hear, guiding people to stay with the goals of the exercise, keeping the experience on track or modifying it as it progresses. Side coaching keeps people focused, is not personal, and informs everyone of things to keep in mind.

Follow-up Discussion

A third premise of our work is that people are more likely to learn from an experience if they can talk about it and understand why they did it. Doing the exercise is important, but knowing why you did it is also critical. This is how you empower individuals to be in charge of their own growth.

✳ *The First Experience: Telling Another's Story*

With this first exercise, the leader helps the group establish some basic premises for working in theatre. This exercise can be introduced in the first session with adults or teenagers, after the most rudimentary opening protocol. Children may need more warm-ups and group games before doing this exercise.

Leader Dialogue

Please find a partner. Each of you must tell your partner a story of something that happened to you that had some emotional content. It might have embarrassed you, or frightened you, or made you laugh, or hurt your feelings. It must be a true story, but it must be something that you are willing to have told in public, so it should not be so personal that it cannot be shared. The truth matters because, in telling your partner, you will be committing to something that is real for you, and your partner will need to commit to that reality as well. It does not have to be a monumental experience. It can be something so simple as getting a gift you always wanted, or getting one you hated, getting scolded, getting lost, getting hurt. We have all had experiences that affected us emotionally. Both partners tell one of these to the other person.

When you have heard your partner's story, and he or she yours, then each of you will tell your partner's to the group as if it happened to you. You will tell it in first person, and it will be your story. You will have a few minutes to tell each other your stories. It can be anything from any time in your life. It just has to be true, and have some feelings attached to it, good or bad.

Advice to the Leader

Allow six to seven minutes for the story exchange. Watch to see if everyone is talking and get a feeling for when they seem to be finished. Ask if they are ready. Give the group a one-minute warning. Set up a place at the front for the storytelling with a chair or a bench where the storyteller will be separated from the space of the audience. Do not use a podium, because it is important that the performer not hide behind something. Tell the participants to volunteer, and to keep the stories going. It should not be necessary to call upon anyone, if you tell them it is *their* responsibility to keep the stories going.

Side Coaching

Try not to refer to your partner or acknowledge him, or have eye contact with her. You don't want to be distracted by the original teller and you want us to believe it is your story. As a good audience, we will listen carefully and applaud when a story is over. Stay in the moment, keep up the belief in what you are saying.

Advice to the Leader

Some may start to exaggerate for comic effect. When it appears that the experience is being distorted for that purpose, you may want to control it. Give this critique between stories. "It is not necessary to make the audience laugh. Some stories won't have that effect. It is not wrong, but it isn't necessary."

Beginners often have trouble finishing a performance. You may need to tell them: "When you are finished, pause, then go sit down. Don't slide away before you have finished. It is not necessary to check with the leader or anyone else when the story is over."

The leader may have to start the applause and can keep up people's courage by saying something positive after each one: "good story," "very moving," "very touching," "thank you."

Depending on the composition of the group, this exercise may require that a male tell a female's story and vice versa. To avoid gender stereotyping or inappropriate gestures, suggest that it is permissible to change the gender of a character in the story in order to adapt the story to the teller. In a very specific case, such as "when I had my first baby," it is permissible to alter any feature or angle of the story if that alteration will make the story more the property of the teller. The illusion of truth is the most important goal. Tellers can also be encouraged simply to adopt the other gender as their own and go with the story as themselves. That takes a little courage, and it will be up to the group leader to make the environment friendly to that kind of choice. Encourage the audience to "go along," to avoid laughter and to let the story unfold, and congratulate individuals when they are brave.

In this storytelling exercise are all the basic elements of a theatre experience. Without really knowing it, the performers are being actors and writers and they are interacting with an audience. The teller has done everything an actor does: take on a persona and, through him or herself, tell someone else's story, commit to it, and capture an audience's belief. This is powerful stuff. Beginning theatre practitioners need to articulate what happened for themselves as both audience and performer.

Follow-up Dialogue

Did you believe that the stories had really happened to the person telling them? Why? As you were telling your story, what were you thinking?

How many of you made up something in telling the story? Why? (Ask specific people.) *How close did you get to believing that the story had happened to you? As an audience member, what kinds of things really made you want to listen? What held your interest?*

The leader can expect people to observe that the details in one story were believable; that the person telling acted as if it had really happened; they could easily feel the same feelings that the person had felt. Whether or not the participants in this discussion are clear about their reasons for liking or disliking something, they are creating a set of theatre criteria for judging all of their work. To assure that the experience is widely understood, it is important to call upon many individuals, even those who don't speak up, to answer questions about their own participation.

Deepening the Understanding

After you have done the storytelling, ask some of the more confident performers to go back up on the stage. Ask them to reassume the character and let them spontaneously improvise details on the skeleton that they have. *What happened after that? Did you ever tell anyone about it? Who? Did it hurt/bleed/smell funny/last long*—whatever is appropriate to the story. Let others try this with the participants asking the questions. You will discover quickly that the power of belief leads to the capacity to improvise within a given set of circumstances. These are more skills for the actor and writer. The improvisations can quickly become dialogue within an embryonic play.

Another Step

The storytellers may take either their own story or their partner's story and write it as a monologue. They can elaborate upon it, add detail. Here is a ready-made, meaningful experience that can be the center for a piece of personal writing.

Have pairs or small groups set up a situation on the stage telling the monologues to each other as if they were characters in a play. They may choose to tell one story as an "aside" to the audience, and another to the group on stage. Or they may choose to comment to the audience on what is being said, as if the people on stage could not hear.

✳ *Making Theatre Out of Personal Experience*

One important thing everyone has learned from the storytelling exercise is that an individual's own experiences are a source for creating theatre. When people discover that, they have found a starting point for a life of creativity.

Leader Dialogue

If we go back to the stories people have told, let's look at what held your interest. What would you include in a list of qualities they have in common? What kinds of stories in general hold your interest? What kinds of shows do you watch on TV? Or what movies do you see? Why do you watch them? What are the characteristics of things you think are good?

Their lists may include such things as suspense, humor, good endings, believable characters, good dialogue, and good action; really emotional; sounded like something that could really happen to me; really wondered how it was going to come out; you always know the way a certain character is going to act; the characters are true to life; the stories are good; the characters are sexy—or clever, or witty.

Qualities That Make for Good Theatre

We have our own list for you to consider, you might have your own. But as we think about good theatre, we have come up with these ingredients: suspense, surprise, predictability and familiarity, action, humor, empathy and truthfulness, aesthetic distance, and theatrical convention. In each theatre piece they exist in different proportions, with different emphases and different combinations. Each one is worth talking about.

Suspense

Through years of directing and designing for theatre we have figured out that, in one sense, all good theatre is a mystery. There is something in every good piece of theatre that makes us want to know more, to find out how this whole thing comes out. We may want to know if a person is going to be all right, or how a difficult situation is going to end, or whether or not a person is going to find what they are looking for. We may wonder whether this situation is as familiar as we think it is, or whether a person's feelings are similar or different from our own. We can even wonder if a particular costume idea will be repeated, or how a multiple-unit set will be used in the next scene. Suspense is the tension between the expectations that we create in the audience and the question of *how* or *if* those expectations are going to be met.

In telling the individual stories, there is always some suspense. The basic question "What happened next?" is, in itself, suspenseful. Theatre suspense, however, is not as much in the story as in how it is told. Some performers will create suspense because of the way they set up the details one by one so the audience can see the story happening. Some will create suspense with the rhythm of their storytelling—stretching something out, looking around to see if people are following, laughing to themselves because they can remember the situation even though they haven't described it yet, beginning to feel melancholy, frightened, disgusted because they can recollect the feelings strongly, even before the events are described. Storytelling is one of the theatre's oldest devices— messengers describing tragic deaths, heroes boasting of exploits, lovers seducing with tales of woe. Its theatricality is in the engagement of the audience in the unfolding of the story. And there is always suspense, both in the story and in the effect of the telling on the audience.

In analyzing the effectiveness of theatrical material, the important questions to ask are: What is the mystery here? What do I want to know?

Surprise

Surprise is a dependable ingredient of good theatre. The audience thinks someone is one kind of a person and they turn out to be another. We think events will go in one direction and they go in another. We think a certain word will be used, but a better, more apt one comes instead. We think a set device is going to turn around but it unfolds instead. Sometimes surprise is funny. Sometimes it is sad, even tragic. Often it is pleasurable without being either. It makes us feel good to be in on a discovery of a new thing, a new way of looking at something or somebody.

Predictability and Familiarity

Are we contradicting ourselves? We just talked about suspense and surprise. The fact is, many great dramas and theatrical performances have little surprise. Sometimes we are interested because we know the entire routine by heart and we want the pleasure of experiencing it again. We can laugh a hundred times at a Laurel and Hardy piece of comedy or a Monty Python sketch. We like knowing the behavior of stock characters and predicting exactly how they will react. Sometimes we like being reminded of our own lives by seeing ourselves in others. We might be intrigued because, even though we know exactly how this is going to end, we want to find out how these characters feel about it. We feel we can listen to what is going on inside someone's head, and we care about that person because we know exactly what they will say. The suspense comes from wondering how we ourselves are going to feel when it is over.

Action

The oldest definitions of drama describe conflicts of forces that must be played out with human action. Because these definitions were formulated when major theatre works took up the lives of heroes and gods, the actions tended to be on a large scale—murders and suicides and revelations of past evils. One thing we learn from telling each other's stories is that *actions can be very small and still capture our imagination*. We may even redefine action to be intellectual or emotional action, the revelation of attitudes and feelings that have shaped human lives. Our television and movie screens are full of violent action and physical passion. That fact tends to make us think that live theatre must compete with the sensations of the screen. What we learn in our story experiment is that *the center of the theatre event is not in the elements of the story, but in the drama of revealing it, directly, in person, to a live audience*. This interaction has much to teach us about the nature of theatre.

Humor

We have read our share of books and essays about humor and comedy. Here is a simple version of a very complicated analysis: Comedy is based on being able to distance oneself sufficiently from an event to see the basic incongruities among things. Painters might call it a figure/ground distinction. That is, what is in the foreground is not consistent with what is in the background. A person in a tuxedo is not inherently funny. A person in a tuxedo at a football game could be. Another way of thinking about it is point of view. It is hard to laugh at slipping on a banana peel if you are the one slipping. It is easier to laugh later on if, on thinking about it, you can see yourself as someone else must have seen you, gliding along unaware, then suddenly, legs flying out in front of you, landing on your backside. Familiarity, expectations, surprise, even suspense, all play a role in comedy. It is almost impossible to find humor in a set of totally unfamiliar conditions because you cannot identify the incongruities. That is probably why slapstick comedy transcends time and cultures. The physicality of the human body, faced with pain, annoyance, fear, the elements, or in combat with nature in some form, is free of the particularities of language, time, and custom. Thus, a woman annoyed by a bee buzzing around her head or a man frustrated by a crying baby can be a subject of comedy understood by many.

The fact that human beings like to laugh seems to be anthropologically indisputable. How to make them laugh is the topic of many years of study and discipline, and is the province of particular people with the gift not only to see the ridiculous but also the ability to communicate it to us. While being funny, or making things funny, is not the primary topic of our discussion, it will continually inform our sense of the theatrical.

Empathy and Truthfulness

We have already introduced the issue of belief. As an audience member I want to believe what I see. I want to believe, for the moment at least, in the pretended conditions. Empathy takes us another step. When we can identify a common humanity with what is going on, we are more satisfied with our experience. This empathy was identified by Aristotle in his Poetics, and it still serves us as a feature of the theatrical contract. At a performance of Mummenschanz, the German mime and puppet theatre troupe that works with nonhuman objects, it is startling to discover how quickly a great piece of pipe, a huge balloon, or a box begins to take on human characteristics. One box is afraid of the other, one ball is chasing the other, two pieces of carpet fall in love, little dramas are created with movement alone—no sound, no dialogue. By the theatrical contract, the audience agrees to accept these skillfully executed movements as the willful acts of sentient beings and we laugh, smile, even weep at their stories. The essence of what Mummenschanz has done is to create empathy, to draw us into believing these creatures and to engage our feelings with theirs. When things seem true, when the audience believes them, the empathic response is profound.

Whatever the scale of the event, the theatre audience demands that it be taken up by truth. Truth is not defined here as something that really happens to friends or neighbors, but *theatrical truth is what we are able, for the moment, to believe is real*. The reality is based on the ability to engage us in feelings, in caring about what is happening. Señor Wences, a comedian of the fifties, used to make a fist, draw lipstick around the space made by his thumb and forefinger, dot two eyes on his hand and wrap a hand-kerchief around it as a scarf. The bodiless character he created spoke with the comedian's ventriloquist voice and became a sharp, irreverent critic of Wences' entire life. There, at the end of the man's sleeve, lived another creature, full of vitality, whom we believed to be real. It was the commitment to the moment, the honesty of the performance, and the real emotions the floating head seemed to have that caught us up.

The Truth Test

In every theatrical encounter we will need to apply these tests: Was the moment real? Did we believe it? Did the performer believe it? Did it engage our emotions? Was it true to the situation it attempted to establish? Was it sustained throughout? Did we care about what happened? Even in the most bizarre extensions of con-ventional reality, the truth test applies. The theatre must draw us in with its own momentary truth and allow us to empathize with what happens on the stage.

The Need to Practice

There are some people who have a natural gift for capturing the truth of the moment. More people have to learn it. We have col-lected activities that your group can practice to heighten their abil-ity to intensify their honesty in performance. Everyone can grow from practicing with the human tools of body and voice, gesture and language, to create theatrical truth.

✴ Aesthetic Distance and Theatrical Convention: The Other Half of Theatre

Understanding the essence of theatre demands some understand-ing of the psychic phenomena that characterize the theatrical con-tract. Here is a discussion.

Follow-up Dialogue

Let's talk about theatre space and the relationship of the audience and the performer in this storytelling exercise. We arbitrarily declared that up there was a space for the performer and over here is a space for the audience. The theatre encounter is based on mutually agreed upon conditions. They may not be spoken, but they are understood. There is a contract here, a set of agreements that we stick to. In this storytelling exercise, what were the contracts we made as either audience members or performers? What did you agree to believe? As performer? As audience? The contract elements are actually so basic that you might not notice them if we didn't call attention to them. Because they are basic, they are very important.

The audience had to:

Accept the performers as the ones who had the experience, even when we knew they did not.

Let the performer speak uninterrupted by us, as if there were a barrier between us that did not let us interact directly.

Acknowledge the performance with the gesture of applause.

Stay within our audience space and respect the space of the performer.

The performers had to:

Commit to the story as their own experience.

Stay within the performance space.

Believe that they spoke to an "audience," not just a group of people; that is, treat us not as individuals that they knew, but as a group gathered for their performance.

Believe that we would accept the story as their own even though we all knew it was not.

These contracts create what writers have called aesthetic distance. Aesthetic distance is the implied assumption of the roles of audience and performer. It is part of what separates theatre from other situations where someone is talking to others. A teacher and a class, a minister and a congregation are operating within shared space and a palpable reality of their situation. They are who they are. In theatre there is a new reality agreed to that assumes the inviolability of the performance space and a new persona for the performer. That change goes into effect when the performance starts, no matter how simply it is accomplished. Within the basic theatrical encounter is always some measure of aesthetic distance. It can be established on many levels. We can sit in a dark room and watch a play on a lighted stage with three realistic walls and a cast of characters who are costumed and talk only to each other. Or we can see a classmate turn a dowel rod into an umbrella and make us believe she is walking in the rain. When Peter Pan asks the audience to applaud in order to bring Tinkerbell back to life, the aesthetic distance remains intact—we know what our contracts are—but it includes the audience's clapping. When audiences are asked sing along, a similar thing happens. Both the audience and the performers establish a new identity, a persona, a theatrical space, and a set of appropriate behaviors.

The appropriate behaviors of performer and audience are also referred to as conventions. There are conventions—consistent appropriate behaviors in a given situation—for both audience and performer, and they are interactive. Later, we will play with conventions and explore their possibilities. For now, it is important to say that *a theatre convention, such as whether I speak directly to the audience or only with those on stage, works only when it is agreed to and participated in by all parties.*

Elementary school children may not be able to articulate all these issues even when they honor them. Children often have an intuitive understanding of aesthetic distance and convention. You will hear children say, "You can't go in there because that's a wall," or "You can't talk to me because I'm invisible," and other children instantly play along. All theatre requires this childlike playing. We make use of it as a basic ingredient. From junior high on, young minds are capable of discussing this difference between theatre and life. When they understand it they can exploit it more fully. Even adults who have worked in theatre for a long time enjoy deconstructing their experience. We have watched them become more inventive at creating within old conventions and more ingenious at establishing new ones.

Making convention your friend is a goal of Hi Concept - Lo Tech Theatre. It is the conventions, the aesthetic distance, that matters in the theatre, and not the actual space in which theatre takes place. We can prove that theatre can take place in the room where you are working because you have just done little pieces of theatre there. We know from history that theatre takes place in opera houses, old movie theatres, banquet halls, palaces, on the street, in churches and temples, at fairs, on puppet stages, in tents and amphitheaters. We can create a stage simply by indicating that here is the audience and here is the performer. A sleight-of-hand magician can create a tiny theatre as he performs for a couple at a table in a crowded restaurant. A rock band may require a stadium. A pyrotechnical performance may take up an entire riverfront or mountainside. For the moment, we will pay closest attention to theatre that works in the intimacy of the ordinary room, and use it to explore theatre in general.

The Performer at the Center of Theatre: Strengthening Acting Skills

*I*f we reduce the capacity to make theatre to its sine qua non —without this we have no theatre—we have the actor, the audience, and some space in which they meet. Let us begin with the actor, or we might say "performer," since the cult of acting of the twentieth century has more narrowly defined the art than we propose. To place the actor/performer at the center of the art, we must focus on the process of transformation. Acting is transforming, finding the persona necessary to capture the quality of the moment.

Acting and Life: Understanding Transformation

Once we arrive at the teenage years, our ability to transform ourselves has taken some deep and narrowly defined paths. We are one person with our friends, another with our parents, another with our teachers, and perhaps, in the private time we are alone, still another. As we become adults, these different personas may fuse and separate in new ways, but they still exist. We take on our various personas so automatically that we rarely analyze them, even while we are careful not to mix them up. They exist because we need different people to perceive us differently. This need to be perceived in a certain way both aids and interferes with the ability to transform ourselves for the making of theatre. We know we are able to do it, but we worry about what people are going to think! To overcome this self-consciousness, it is necessary to get ourselves into an easy habit of becoming something other than ourselves, to get bolder and bolder in our changes, and to make a deeper and deeper commitment to the transformations.

Sometimes the persona we seek is a specific character, a complete personality with a history in the work being done. Sometimes the persona is a performer—not precisely the individual one would meet at home or for lunch, but the personality the performer takes on to become what is required for the performance. Sometimes the performer must be both character and performer simultaneously, and sometimes the performer moves between the two or among several characters. *Transforming oneself is a key acting ability.* It requires making decisions about who I am, what is my attitude about any number of things, why am I here, to what do I respond, and what do I intend to do with the others who are around me.

Presentation: The Other Side

Whatever we say about theatre seems to have two opposing sides: make-believe and truth, audience and artist, pretending to be someone else while always knowing who one is, empathy and aesthetic distance. Theatre lives on the tension of simultaneously held oppositions. The excitement of performing comes from its fundamental duality.

Theatre requires the performer both to transform herself and to present that new person to an audience. She takes on a persona. She works at being that other person as fully as possible. However, she does it for an audience, knowing herself that she is doing it. The transmission of the transformation to an audience is the act of theatre. We come to see Maggie Smith play Rosalinde. We don't come to see Maggie Smith or Rosalinde independently. It is Maggie Smith *playing* Rosalinde—transforming herself into someone else—that is essential to the art. It doesn't matter whether we know the actress apart from the role or not. The playing is part of the event, even as we lose ourselves in the performance. In fact, we want both to lose ourselves in the event and to keep alive our knowledge of the performance. The actress wants to become the character fully and still gauge the effect she is having on the audience. A pair of supporting dualities!

The same is even true for stand-up comedians who perform as "themselves." They are "on" when they perform, and in interviews they will talk about being someone else in front of that mike. As audience members, we can see they are "playing" someone who is very much like them, but someone who is performing for our benefit, exaggerating certain characteristics, taking on certain attitudes for their comic value. Simultaneously we believe the person we are hearing is wholly real. Theatre performance rides on this sharp edge of two realities.

The observation of acting has taught us, at least since Stanislavsky and probably long before, that acting requires internal transformation if it is to be believed. What gets presented to an audience, the external part, appears true because the actress has found the truth of it for herself. This building of a bond between the inside and outside of the performer takes time and care.

We need, in short, to practice. We think it is essential to practice on both transformation and presentation, and to work on the physical and psychological dimensions of performing. They all are interconnected: a physical action gives rise to a state of mind, a state of mind gives rise to an action, an action gives rise to a perception, a perception gives rise to an action or a state of mind.

If your group wants to become more truthful, more spontaneous, and more forceful in making theatre, you must work on both the body and the mind, the transformation and the presentation, the inside and the outside of performing.

The exercises we recommend have been inspired by voice lessons, dance and creative movement classes, visual art, theatre games, creative dramatics, and acting classes. They are designed to help people be adventurous. Because they lead to making little works of theatrical art, they are also building the confidence needed to be more and more expansive in making theatre. Gradually you learn to use theatre to explore your own lives, to discover the lives of others, and to present your discoveries on a journey with an audience.

Vocal and Body Warm-ups: Loosening, Relaxing, and Stimulating Nerves and Muscles

Any group of adults or children needs to allow itself a transition from the preoccupations and distractions of daily life to the focus needed for artistic life. The first step in the transition is to escape the normal. Art consists of conscious aesthetic choices. It requires a particularly acute state of mind. Warm-ups help condition the body and the mind to a special set of assumptions. We need to be spontaneous. We need to be expansive. We need to be responsive. We need to shed our constraints and censors.

The warm-up also helps prevent injury to muscles and vocal chords. It mediates between the routine of daily life and the shock of unusual physical and psychological demands.

✳ Hang and Bounce/Uncurl

Leader Dialogue

We are going to find ways to relax the tensions in your mind and body. Find a spot in the room where you can move your arms freely without bumping into anyone. Stand with your legs slightly apart, your feet firmly squared under your hips and shoulders. Find the center of your weight. Let your arms drop loosely at your sides. Now: Drop your head, shoulders, arms, and torso, and let them hang down from the waist. Let your knees bend and your hands brush the floor. Release the tension in your neck. Let the full weight of your head and upper body hang free. On a slow count of eight, bounce gently in that position, relaxing arms, hands, neck, head, face, shoulders. The purpose is to relax, and to increase the flow of blood and oxygen to the upper body. Waggle your tongue, drop your jaw. Say "aaahhhh." Shake your head to see if it is loose.

Advice to Leader

A hand drum greatly assists these exercises. You can keep a rhythm. A set of claves or sticks will also work. If you have no drum or claves, you can clap your hands or snap your fingers. As you work, talk in a soft, soothing manner. Your goal is to loosen people up and relax them. Watch for people who are still holding their heads tensely. Put your hand on the backs of their necks and tell them to release the head. Let everyone hang for as long as it takes to get the whole group into a relaxed position. They should be quiet. Talking and laughing indicates tension. The relaxation works only if you give in to it.

Demonstrate all the exercises as you lead them. That is the quickest way to introduce them, and it allows you to warm up as well. However, you will need to monitor the exercises and to encourage people to give over to the relaxing power of the weight of their own bodies.

Leader Dialogue

Now we are going to uncurl the spine slowly. Think of your spine as a series of building blocks. As you stand up slowly to the count of eight, pile one vertebra on top of the other, one at a time. Let your head stay heavy and drooping. Take the whole eight counts and bring the head up last on the count of eight. At the top, drop your shoulders into place. Ready, and, one. . . .

Advice to Leader

The "ready, and" prepares people to start the exercise together. Doing things together in time to a beat is a fundamental skill of performing. These warm-up exercises should also be thought of as rhythmic practice.

Leader Dialogue

When you get to the top we are going to go back down as slowly as we came up. Curl your vertebrae, head dropping first and going down, taking the full eight counts to curl back down. Ready, and one. . . . When you reach the bottom we will bounce eight counts and then come up again, uncurling for eight counts.

Side Coaching

Listen to the beats, take all eight counts, and keep the head, neck, arms, hands, and shoulders relaxed. Relaxing takes concentration. This is also a beginning exercise in concentration. No need to check to see if you are getting it right. There is no need to watch anyone else in this exercise so you can let your head drop over. Even close your eyes if you want. And don't worry, no one is watching you. This is a silent exercise so there is no need to comment. The silence lets the mind relax along with the body.

✳ Stretching and Yawning: Letting Oxygen Reach All Parts of the Body

Leader Dialogue

Stretch your hands over your head as you do when you wake up in the morning. Open your mouth wide into a big yawn. Repeat that until you feel all the joints are opening up. Reach to the ceiling with your right hand. Stretch up to the ceiling with a full body reach, from the heel of your foot. Feel the stretch all along your side. Let your head hang down to the side. Stretch right for four slow counts, and then switch to the left for four slow counts. Ready, and: Right, two, three, four. Left, two, three, four . . . repeat.

Now stretch both arms over your head and drop your head forward; put your hands on the back of your head and stretch the upper muscles of your neck; now look straight forward, arms stretched over your head. Slowly, open your arms out and bring them half way down extending to the sides, relaxing your shoulders. Extend your arms out to the sides, palms up, and release your shoulders, as if you were holding a huge tray. Relax into your breathing. Let yourself take deep breaths and exhale slowly. Hold that for a moment, and then slowly let your arms drop all the way to your sides. Breathe deeply and easily. Release the shoulder tension.

Advice to the Leader

Be sure people are not holding their breath as they exercise. Deep, relaxed breathing is essential to effective voice production and good circulation. Repeat the stretching, especially if the group is sluggish or sleepy. When the arms are outstretched to the sides, look at the participants to see if they are standing squarely over their legs, centering their weight, relaxing their shoulders. This is a very open position. It is strong yet vulnerable. Many people feel strange if their arms are very far from their bodies. This exercise helps make that open position feel normal.

✳ Shoulder Rotation and Arm Swings: Opening the Chest, Gaining Flexibility

Leader Dialogue

With your arms down at your sides, move the shoulders to the front, upward, back, and down in a slow rolling motion. Breathe. Rotate four times. Forward, up, backward, down. Reverse the direction: Rotate backward first, then up, then forward and down—four times. Swing your right arm in a huge figure eight—be sure you have room around you. Feel the weight of the arm as you swing it four times on each side. Bend your arms at the elbows and raise them to chest height. Cross them in front of your body and then swing them behind your body, as if you were going to make the elbows meet behind your back (you won't). These exercises open up your chest and loosen the upper body.

✳ Neck Rotation

Leader Dialogue

Drop your chin on your chest and rotate the head slowly to the right, to the back, to the left, and to the front. Now reverse: left, back, right, and front. Four times in each direction. As your head goes to the back, drop your jaw open. Keep your jaw relaxed. Let the weight of your head pull on your muscles. Breathe.

✳ Finger Stretch and Wrist Rotation

Leader Dialogue

Arms out front. Make a tight fist. Now stretch your fingers as widely as you can. Fist. Stretch. Fist. Stretch. Repeat. Now shake out your hands, fingers loose. Rotate your hands on your wrists, in and out, making a figure eight.

✳ Feet and Legs Warm-up

Leader Dialogue

Rock on your feet, using all the muscles in your toes and instep. Put your weight first on the left foot, bring the right foot up so only the ball of the foot is touching the floor. Now shift the weight to the right foot and bend the left foot; like walking in place, right, left, right, left for eight counts. Now bring one foot off the floor so just the tip of the toe touches the ground and the toe is pointed; put it down and shift your weight to the other foot. Right, left, right, left. Now pick up each foot off the ground and run in place for eight counts easily, small steps. Shake your hands, shake your arms, shake your head, loosen your jaw, waggle your tongue. Now be sharp. Get some height. Breathe. Shadow box with your hands as you run. Run in place as fast as you can, pounding the floor. Get your pulse rate up a little, move the blood through your body.

Advice to the Leader

This simple list of physical warm-ups can be varied. You can borrow from dance and exercise classes and acting handbooks. Everyone has favorites. The purpose is to loosen the body and get the blood circulating. All parts of the body should be warmed up. The procedure should go from slow to fast and allow for relaxation and focusing. Inasmuch as this is not a dance class, there is no need to do extensive stretching. If a group can become familiar with a set of warm-up exercises, they can take the lead and then get started efficiently with other activities. Good breathing is essential throughout. So is commitment and concentration.

✳ Face and Voice Warm-up: Building Facial Muscles, Vocal Chords, and Breath Support

Leader Dialogue

Your voice is one of your most important sources of expression. We need to expand and develop its capacities. Make a big face. Stretch your eyes and mouth open as widely as you can. Now make a small face. Squeeze your face like a prune, then a big face, then a small face. Move all of your face to the left. Move it all to the right. Using all the muscles in your face, say slowly: eeeee *and grin widely. Change to* aaay, *rounding slightly; change to* aaaah *and make a square with your mouth. Feel your throat opening. Change to* oooh *and feel your head opening and your face speaking into a long tube. Change to* uuuu (or ooooo) *and feel your tongue dropping and your throat opening still wider in the back. Repeat slowly, observing the changes in your face, mouth, head, and throat. Let your lips gently form an* mmm *between the vowel sounds, and say slowly,* me, may, ma, mo, mu. *Now more quickly in succession, accenting the first sound and counting four syllables to a beat:*

Me, may, ma, mo
me, may, ma, mo
me, may, ma, mo
mu.

Repeat. Change pitch. Start low and go higher. Change the vocal sound to a musical pitch, starting with a low, soft tone. Move up by half-steps on the "U" sound.

Using the tongue, say la, la, li, li, la, la, li, li, lo, lo, lo, lo, lu. *Say them slowly. Now speed up, two syllables to a beat. Exaggerate your mouth and tongue movement.*

Repeat this sentence slowly, articulating every vowel and consonant. Exaggerate with your lips and mouth muscles; feel your throat opening up: "The lawyer's awfully awkward daughter, ought to be taught to draw." *Repeat three times. Now speed it up and say it as fast as possible.*

Put your fingers on the muscle connecting the jaw to the skull. Press and massage that muscle to release the tension we collect there. Work your massage around your cheeks and jawbone and across your face.

Try this: Tommy told tattle tales.
Sondra sings simple songs.
Daddy dangles dimpled dumplings during Donny's dinner.

Advice to the Leader

Americans typically speak with very lazy mouths. For the sake of being understood in performance, they must practice articulation constantly. That means watching faces to see a good deal of exaggeration in the use of mouth, cheeks, lips, and tongue. After a time, the exaggeration begins to feel natural and the speech will be clearer.

✳ Vocal Warm-ups for Strength, Variety, and Breath Support

Leader Dialogue

Drop your jaw as low as it will go in a relaxed position. Put your hand on your abdomen below your stomach. See if you can feel your body receiving and releasing air as you breathe through your mouth. Take a deep breath and release it slowly saying ho. *Repeat, breathing through your nose. Say slowly with me:* Ho, ho, ho, ho. *Now faster:* Ho, ho, ho, ho, ho, ho, ho. *Repeat. Now, starting low with a continuous sound, make a drone and keep it going as long as you can. Take another deep breath and continue the sound. Bring your voice from its lowest speaking pitch to its highest, slowly:* Hooooooooooooooooooooooiiiiiiiiiiiiiiiii. *Now start at the top and go back down:* Iiiiiiiiiiiiiiiii-iooooooooooooooooooooooooo. *Repeat bottom to top. Repeat top to bottom. Not too loud.*

Using the sentence: "The lawyer's awfully awkward daughter ought to be taught to draw", stand up straight, feet square. Speaking from as deep in your torso as you can reach, say the sentence to a spot on the wall far across the room. Don't shout, just find the volume to project your voice. Now speak it in a stage whisper—whispering loud enough to be heard by the same spot. Now say it in your highest voice. Now say it in your lowest voice. Keep your articulation clear.

Advice to the Leader

Vocal chords can be strengthened and stretched, like other muscle tissue. Although a person's vocal character is unique, its flexibility can be improved. It can become more pleasing, richer, expressive. To do so requires a great deal of attention and study. Kristin Linklater's *Freeing the Natural Voice* is one resource for a program of vocal development. Another is Arthur Lessac, *The Use and Training of the Human Voice*. People can also injure their vocal chords by misuse or overuse, by shouting and screaming, even by singing out of their range or singing without warming up. On the other hand, measured practice over time can result in a strong vocal instrument. The purpose of these warm-up exercises is to make people aware of their voices, to begin to imagine a better vocal instrument, and to recognize the value of practice.

Specialized study will be needed for individual development. None of the warm-ups described here is designed to do the work of a regular class in voice production, singing, acting, ballet, Tai Chi, or modern dance. Serious amateurs and professionals will do more specialized study as they develop their performance instruments. These exercises are intended to set a framework for productive work in the art of transformation.

Moving Through Space: Warm-ups for the Mind and Body in Space

One of the basic tools we have for making believe is the body. Our bodies can pretend to be crawling animals, trees in the wind, floating leaves, waves in the ocean, books on a shelf, parking meters, or washing machines—any endless number of things. They can also abstract themselves into states of mind, into conditions of circumstance. Our bodies can place us in other worlds, specific and real. Not only can we transform ourselves into other things and other people, we can also make people believe that we are, indeed, what we have become. We can act like a parking meter. We can even think like a parking meter. Once we have become something other than ourselves, we inhabit another world. We can have parking meter wars, parking meter families, parking meter courts, or parking meter restaurants. And in this transformation of theatre, we bring the audience to accept the parking meter world we have created.

Our task is to get ourselves in the habit of using the body to express ideas and images. We want to work in the abstract and the literal. The body can seem simply to grow, to be free, to be constrained, to be angular or rounded, or it can be a wolf or a bird, or an electric drill. Or by extrapolating and adopting an element from something outside itself, the body can be a person who has wolf-like qualities. We start by exploring the body in space.

✳ Walking in Space

Leader Dialogue

This is a body and space exercise. Your task is to walk around the room, walking across every floorboard, and through every corner. Your responsibility is to keep walking, keep moving, but not to bump into anyone else. Keep your movement in time to rhythm I give you. You will all take different paths. Remember not to bump into anyone, and listen to the rhythm. If it gets faster, you get faster. When the rhythm stops with a strong beat, freeze where you are. Avoid making circles. Change directions. Work across spaces. Weave in and out. Discover your body in space. Become aware of each other and the space you occupy. Become aware of your body in relation to the beat.

Advice to the Leader

Keep the rhythm steady until you can see that people are really working at walking all around the room. Then speed it up. Slow it down. Discourage the group from walking in a circle. Remind them about respecting other people and avoiding contact. This exercise begins to make people keenly aware of themselves and others in space. It takes concentration to keep going, to find different places to explore, and not to bump into anyone. When they are walking smoothly, go on to the next task.

The word *task* is used throughout our work. The word *problem* also is useful. What you avoid is "I *want* you to do such and such." The leader should not become the guru. That takes away all the power of the participants. We suggest you give tasks that the group can accomplish, through which they can learn about themselves and about the art of theatre. If they do not understand the purpose of the task when it is completed, or if they have no idea what they have learned, they risk being mere puppets in the hands of a master. Puppets have no life of their own. *Our* task is to make them all masters of their own artistic lives. You need to explain what you do, and then all talk about it afterward. If it didn't work for some, that is fine. But explaining, processing, and discussing is critical throughout the work.

✳ Levels and Shapes

Leader Dialogue

Now, on the sharp beat, your task is to stop, take a body position full of angles, and freeze. If I call out "freeze low," you take a low position, near or on the floor. If I call out "freeze middle," it should be at seat height, knees bent; if I call out "freeze high," your pose should be up high. Each time you are to find a new body position. Let's practice. Show me an angular position at the middle level. Go. What parts of your body can make angles? Now, each time, make something different, thinking of your elbows, back, knees, neck, hands, hips, wrists, feet, waist. Go. Keep walking until the sharp beat and silence. Listen for the level. Discover your body and its shapes. Experiment. Try something new.

Advice to the Leader

Alternate the walking, the "freeze high," "freeze low," "freeze middle," until people begin to get inventive. Encourage them to get as low and as high as possible. Encourage them to use their elbows or knees, and to use the angle of their heads. Say "nice choice" or "good idea" to people with especially inventive poses in order to prompt others to use more expansive gestures. We learn in this case by seeing other possibilities. Borrowing or imitating is a legitimate step to self-discovery.

Try having them go directly from a low to a high position without any walking in between. You can warn people as they are walking to prepare for the next freeze. "The next time I call freeze, take an angular pose and be in a different level from the people around you." You can always substitute loud drumbeats for the word "freeze."

To make it more challenging, make it the task to choose their own level each time, and each time to change. If they have been high, they must change to a medium or low the next time. Then ask them to change from an angular shape to a curved shape. On the next change, ask them to "support yourself on something other than your two feet. You can use your torso, your knees, one foot, and a hand. But support yourself on something other than your two feet." After they freeze, ask them to move at the level at which they froze. Suggest new locomotor possibilities—crawling, sliding, creeping, skipping, leaping.

✳ Adding Physical Contact to the Experience

Leader Dialogue

The next time you freeze, be in contact with another person. Negotiate this silently. Be respectful of each other, but do not be afraid to touch. Remember you can touch with knees, elbows, head, and back, as well as hands and feet. Freeze. OK. Shake it off and walk again. This time when you freeze, be in contact with another person using something other than your hand. This is silent work. Your talking will be through the actions of your body. Freeze. Shake it off. This time when you make contact, be sure you are at a different level from the person you are contacting. Freeze. Shake it off. Now, as a whole group you have a responsibility to fill up the largest volume of space that you can occupy and still be in contact with each other. Think about height and breadth and depth. When I say freeze, occupy that large volume of space. Freeze. Shake it off. This time you are to occupy the greatest possible horizontal space, still remaining in contact. Freeze.

Deepening the Experience

As the participants become more inventive with their body shapes, draw the floor plan of a movement sequence on a blackboard or piece of cardboard: an S shape, or a line, a curve and dashes to indicate jumps, and the words "low, medium, and high" to indicate where they take a stationary pose and at what level. Have the participants choreograph a set of moves to correspond to the floor plan. Ask them to change the speed or level or character of movement between points. They can crawl, hop, slide, skip, roll, or whatever they imagine. Let them draw and exchange floor plans with each other. Divide them into small groups to create their own floor plans, more elaborate designs, a different pattern for each performer with points of contact. Suggest that they try working in parallel or unison movement. Have them record what they did, memorize it, and perform it for the rest of the group.

Follow-up Dialogue

What did you have to do to go through this sequence? What happened inside your head? What did you think? What did you become aware of? Let people try to remember various moments in the work. Let them comment on their own watching, feeling, their comfort or discomfort, their discoveries. Give people time to respond. Listen for awareness of different physical relationships in their own bodies and with others. Let them comment on differences in thinking with the body and with the head. *How spontaneous did you become? When did you begin to feel comfortable in crazy positions? Talk about the thinking you do to imagine a sequence of the body in space.*

✸ Introductions—Claiming the Stage Space

There are a number of ways to get members of a group to know each other. Even if they have already been together for a while, this exercise serves to deepen their understanding of each other. The real purpose, however, is an introduction to the space of the stage and to using the space as a performer. Even to the most experienced theatre artist, performing has its intimidating elements. Because the intimidation of the stage never goes away altogether, it is important to confront it and learn to use it.

Delineate spaces for the stage and for the audience. On the stage space, place a couple of chairs or boxes and a table, spread apart so they have no particular relationship to each other but so that someone could use them to sit, stand, or lie on to speak to the audience. Determine where the entrances and exits for this stage will be. The audience can sit on three sides or on one side.

Leader Dialogue

Your task is to select an entrance to come on stage. Enter. Go to a spot on the stage. Tell us your name. Go to a different spot on the stage and at a different level, tell us something about yourself in one sentence. Choose something we might not know if you didn't tell us and something that will help us know you. It must be a true thing, because we are working on the power of our own stories to make theatre. It can be a very tiny thing, or a big thing, but something you are willing to share. Then exit. The entrance and the exit are part of the task. Start off stage and finish off stage. You may use any entrance or exit we have set up.

It is the responsibility of all of you to keep this going. When one person is finished, another should go right ahead. Take a minute to decide what you want to tell us. Someone volunteer to be first. Be sure to use the full entrance and exit.

Advice to the Leader

It is useful to start this off by introducing yourself to set up the model. In any case, the leader should be part of the introductions. To keep the exercise going, get the group to applaud, and you say "thank you" or "good" or offer other encouragement after each introduction. If people are a little adventuresome—choosing unusual poses, you can add "nice choice," or "very brave."

Side Coaching

Go all the way off stage before you enter. Go all the way out before you go back to your seat. Don't let the group wait. Keep the introductions coming.

Deepening the Experience

Ask the group to do the exercise again. The task the second time is to keep the experience fresh, maintaining the illusion that we don't know what they are going to say. The illusion of freshness and spontaneity is a constant concern of performing.

Leader Dialogue

This time, vary the speed of your movement. If you enter slowly, go very fast to your second space. If you run on, then use slow motion to exit. Be inventive in your use of speed. Vary your levels as well.

Follow-up Discussion

After the second round, ask the group to discuss both experiences. Listen for observations about evaluating the first round, borrowing others' ideas, the problem of self-consciousness, the difficulty of making it seem real the second time. Ask them about the feeling of waiting to go on stage, passing through the stage space, how it feels to exit, and the difference between being on stage and not being on stage. Ask them to comment on what they observed of others in those situations. This is a good time to talk about the magic of the stage space and its unique demands on performers. People may want to discuss their stage fright. They may talk about the huge amount of space the performer feels, and about the desire to go quickly and get it over with. These alterations of perceived distance and time are common performance phenomena. Others may comment on adrenaline and its highs—heart racing, sweaty palms, breathlessness—or the similarities between athletics and performing on stage.

✳ Expanding the Use of the Body in Space

When you are working with teenagers or children, the group division can be an important dynamic. As we mentioned earlier, this preliminary activity can eliminate some of the group-making struggle while it teaches nonverbal interaction.

Leader Dialogue

Go back to walking around the space. Trace your own pattern. Move in large arcing movements. Do not bump into anyone. Now move in straight lines only, making only sharp turns. Imagine a grid on the floor running parallel with the walls. Walk only on the lines of the grid. You may walk backward, forward, or sideways. Now, add stopping to your movement. You may pause, reverse, or turn, but stay on the grid. Do not let anyone bump into you. You may only follow the lines of the grid. Vary your movement choices but stay on the grid.

Now, release the grid and form two circles. Say nothing, just quickly make two circles. Good. Now make three circles. Quickly, silently, join whatever group needs you. Now each circle forms a square. Silence. Just see where you are needed to go and go there. Good. Now break up and walk independently with large arcing movements. Now form groups of four or five persons. With your group create a capital I. Now make a triangle.

Side Coaching

Negotiate silently, just with your body. Let people make their own decisions. Move where you are needed. Try to take in what the group is doing. We will wait until each group achieves its purpose. Resist the impulse to tell people where to go. Let them discover where they are needed, or change your own body in order to inform someone else.

Advice to the Leader

Take plenty of time to let each step happen. You may use soft drumbeats or music in the background. You will have to remind people to work silently and not to direct each other. Let individuals see what is happening and where it is going. You can keep them going with various tasks until you see them beginning to understand silent, physical group negotiation. The idea is to get the group to begin to negotiate space, to enjoy the work of responding to a verbal/physical impulse, to become part of a group action, to make physical decisions quickly.

You can vary the directions any way you like. The first time you do it you may get only moderate success. But you will want to repeat this activity through many sessions. It is a good warm-up and people enjoy getting quicker and more inventive in solving problems. It leads eventually to skillful spontaneous physical improvisation.

We have found this exercise easily leads to small groups that are accidental. Say, "Make groups of four or five," and the job is done. If you open with the group movement process on various occasions, it will be easy later on to say, "Find a partner who is distinctly different in either height or weight from you" or "Form groups of three or four that are gender-mixed."

✳ Positive and Negative Space

As we continue exploring stage space, it will be more and more apparent that we occupy it in relation to other things: furniture, the audience, other people, or other space. One of the important concepts in the visual arts is the interaction of positive and negative space: space that is occupied by an object and space that is occupied only by space. Visual artists, including photographers, videographers, and filmmakers, use the interplay of positive and negative space as major tools of composition. They manipulate our attention and perceptions by the way objects interact with the background and with each other. They are keenly aware of the distance between objects and the white or black space around them. We have seen a magazine ad with a tiny name on a blank page, or a dense collage packed with hundreds of images. We have seen a blank screen contrasted with a talking head, or a single figure walk onto an empty plaza. Positive and negative space in a performance area function in the same way. Stage space is active, even without anything in it. All negative space has potential force. Performers learn to exist with that force and to use it. They learn to understand their own bodies as both solid objects and creators of spatial relationships.

To begin the positive/negative space exercise, ask the group to divide itself into clusters of four or five people.

Leader Dialogue

Thinking about positive and negative shapes, your task is to create a sculpture. A positive shape is one occupied by a solid—in this case, your body. A negative space is occupied by space. Where I am is the positive shape; the unoccupied shapes I create around me are the negative space. If I hold out my arm, there is a negative shape underneath it. One person starts by creating a shape. The shape will have positive and negative spaces. The second person joins into the shape occupying one of the negative spaces, creating more negative spaces where another person can join. One at a time, each member of the group joins the sculpture. You may be in contact with another person, but you may not discomfort another person or cause them to fall. All these decisions are to be made silently. Someone needs to volunteer to start by creating the first shape. Now another person join. Remember, no talking, just think with your body. All groups will work simultaneously. If I call out "freeze," hold what you are doing.

Side Coaching

Remember to use different levels. Remember to look for negative space to fill and create more negative space for the next person. Take time. Wait for the last person to finish making their choices. As soon as you have finished one, freeze it for a few seconds and then break it up and start another one. Look for tiny negative spaces. Look high and low for opportunities. Be careful not to disturb another person's balance, but don't be afraid to make connections.

Advice to the Leader

Keep the groups working constantly. If necessary, designate a starter. With statements like "nice variety, nice tension, good choices, good use of the floor, good contact idea," encourage groups and individuals when the shapes are varied or interesting. Call out "freeze" and have groups look at each other to discover the visual effects. One of the purposes of this exercise is to get people comfortable with physical contact and unusual relationships. They will need this comfort later as they work in theatre collaborations. They will also need to think imaginatively and to think three-dimensionally with their bodies. If you are concerned about inappropriate behavior from someone, you may need to include in the instructions: "You understand that you are not to be rude or crude, either in your gestures or your contact with your group members."

Follow-up Dialogue

Ask the group to talk about what they experienced doing the sculptures. *What happened in your head? What did you see in the sculptures that made them interesting?* Look for recognition of complexity, variety, accent, focus, or surprise. They may see an image in one group's work. Ask them what it felt like to do the work. They may note embarrassment, the desire to do something different, the pleasure from getting a new idea, a growing willingness to be more daring.

✳ Kinetic Sculpture

Deepening the task, the group will go on to make sculpture that moves.

Leader Dialogue

Now you are to start again. This time the task for your group is to form a sculpture in which every participant is physically in contact with at least one other person. The touch can be a hand, a foot, a hip, a head, but there must be a contact. Once you create this sculpture, your task is to turn it into a continually changing sculpture. One of you will move to another pose and position, breaking the contact to change, but reattaching to the sculpture in the new pose. As soon as that person has stopped moving, someone else must move and change position, and so on. This is the rule: only one person can move at a time, but you may not discuss it or designate the mover. You must concentrate, keep looking for your opportunity to move and change, and if two of you start at once, without discussing it, one person must wait until the other has finished. But you must keep the sculpture changing.

Start the sculpture as you did before. When the last person has joined, it is time for the moving and changing to start. Anyone can make a move in any order. Just keep the sculpture changing.

Side Coaching

This exercise requires your concentration and discipline. Keep the sculptures moving and keep the interaction silent. Keep the variety in levels and shapes. Wait until a person has finished a move before making your own move. People need to make big enough changes so there is time to see the move happen; just moving an arm or a foot is not enough.

Advice to the Leader

Let the moving sculptures go on until everyone has made at least four or five moves. After two minutes or so, start around the room and quietly stop a group to watch while the others move. Then have them start again and go to another group until everyone can see how the dynamics of the interacting forms work. Freeze and then relax the groups to finish.

Follow-up Dialogue

What did you have to do to make this work? Listen for comments about concentration, awareness of others, decision making, searching for variety, becoming aware of where the body is in space and in relation to other objects in space. Question the group about what they saw. *What did you like watching? Did you like it when people repeated shapes that others had done? Did you like the stretched-out compositions? The closed ones?* If some of the groups have gone through moves where they all did a parallel movement, or if they all imitated one person, or if a form emerged with forces in opposition, be sure they note how that affected them both as performers and as audience. Let them talk about choosing to play along with something that happened or choosing to take advantage of something to create a particular dynamic. Some may note that they deliberately refused to follow a particular line. These are all parts of the improvisational process.

Deepening the Experience

Do this exercise another day. After the groups have gotten good at their work, add 48" x 1" dowels to the process. (These can be purchased at any hardware store.) When the group is moving, hand a dowel to one of the participants who has a hand free and say, "Incorporate the stick into the work." Watch how the stick influences the moves. At the discussion, ask them to comment on it. You can add a second rod and even a third. Comment on how much the group invests in the rod, how the rod gathers its own power and meaning. Ask about the interaction of human and inanimate objects. Some may use the rod as part of an abstract design, others may turn it into a literal object. These are both viable options.

✳ Human Sculptures Become Theatre Pieces with Images and Words

The basic premise under which we are operating is that any group of people can make theatre at any time and in any place. The sculptures themselves may become performance pieces with their own mysteries and internal aesthetic. They can continue to be improvisations, even in performance, with or without the dowel rods. You can add music or sound making as well.

Another step will take them to the creation of a tiny staged performance piece.

Leader Dialogue

Now your task is to create a small theatre piece. Each group is to choose a nursery rhyme. You may choose any rhyme. Once you have settled on a rhyme, go through the nursery rhyme and assign a line to each person in the group. Everyone must have at least one line, and you must get through the whole poem. You can all say a line together if you need to, but everyone needs at least one line alone.

When you have the lines assigned, you are going to perform it by creating a positive/negative sculpture, the way we did before. The person who has the first line of the poem takes the first pose, and each person joins the sculpture in the order of the lines of the poem. Don't plan it. Just make sure you know what line you have and when it comes in. You may say the line before you get in the sculpture, while you are getting in place, or after you have taken your pose. To rehearse, just say the poem in order in the group so you know where you come in. You do not plan the sculpture, and everyone can choose their own pose.

Side Coaching

Everyone is to be the audience for each other. When it is your turn to be the audience, just sit down and watch. No planning, group. Enjoy your ability to be spontaneous, to respond to the positive and negative space. Everyone gets to make their own contribution to the finished work. Be sure to applaud, audience, when each group is finished.

Deepening the Experience

The nursery rhyme is a convenient instant script because it is familiar. If a group does not know nursery rhymes, they can use the lines of a familiar song or jump-rope verse. Once they have tried the exercise with familiar material, it is time to experiment with original sources.

Leader Dialogue

Each group is to think of a topic. It can be anything—like peanut butter, or shoes, or books. Each group chooses its topic, and then each person in your group thinks of a sentence of their own about the topic. Your sentence has to be true. Finally, use the sculpture idea to present the sentences to the audience. You may wish to control the nature of the movement: All movements will be quick. All movements will be languid. But do not dictate the poses. Allow everyone to choose their own moves and poses to suit their own sentences. Don't rehearse. These may take different forms. They can get quite silly, or melancholy and serious, or angry. Let them happen.

Side Coaching

Decide on your topic quickly. Don't agonize over it. It could be silly or serious. It just has to be a topic or category about which everyone can say something of their own. Get it quickly. Eyeglasses, peanut butter, broccoli, winter. Just get something. Then each person think about your individual sentence. One sentence per person. Tell the sentences to each other. Decide the order. You can talk about the nature of the movement and the sculpture, but let everyone do what they want within that. Don't plan the final event except for the order of the sentences. You will have three minutes total. All statements must be true for the speaker because it is the honesty of the comment coming from you that gives power to the piece. Listen to each other as you tell your sentence. Decide who goes first, who is second, and so on. Is there any particular quality you want for the movement or the poses to support the topic you have chosen? Should they all be sharp? Or languid? Or open-ended? Make your decisions. You have two more minutes and then we go.

Follow-up Dialogue

What did you especially like about what you saw and what you did? Listen for comments on appropriateness, on surprises, on connections. Someone may discover that movement motivates statements and statements motivate movement. Remind the groups that they have each created a work of theatre art.

Even roughly done, such pieces have potential for a long life. Ask the participants to comment on the most effective things that happened for them. Ask them how they might go on to create something more complex.

Deepening the Experience

A group may decide to refine a piece or extend it into a longer performance work to show a larger audience. The sculpture compositions can expand to include the whole stage. A group may want to add chairs or boxes to sit on. A topic might undergo revision. Sentences could become paragraphs or little stories. As the performances evolve, the sentences could be resequenced and become dialogue.

Groups may wish to make more demanding thematic choices or form themselves around specific topics. They can talk about favorite toys, embarrassing moments, themselves and their families, dreams, joys or failures—but each person must contribute. If people object to the idea of telling something "true," it can always be something they've thought about, something they've imagined, something they've heard. But each person needs to contribute something out of themselves if the group is building toward theatre being a product of personal commitment and investment.

Advice to the Leader

These ought to be group efforts. Individuals must have the authority to design their own material and their own movements within the group's guidelines. No single person should be telling the others how to move, what shapes to take, or what to say. Instead, everyone should listen and offer advice on what seems interesting or effective. The idea is to create a set of artistic conditions, an integrated set of aesthetic choices, within which people are creative.

One of the keys to setting up these working conditions is to keep the planning and rehearsal time short. If the group needs everyone's ideas because of the shortness of the time, there is less opportunity for little tyrannies to develop.

Issue pieces and political pieces sometimes evolve in this process. A student council of an elementary school we worked with created a presentation for their school board by using this technique to tell what they had done in language arts and math. What has been demonstrated is that the potential to make theatre exists within the participants, their thoughts, their experiences, and their ability to compose themselves in a group.

Commitment to the Moment: The Life Blood of Making Theatre

Joseph Chaikin defines "the moment" as: "Before which it is too early and after which it is too late."

One of the things that becomes obvious as people begin to work in these inventive processes is that the more seriously they take the exercise, the more likely the product is to be inventive and entertaining to watch. "The moment" in theatre is that time when we are in the grip of the conceit or device. We have to take it as real. To be serious is not to be somber. There is likely to be laughter and gaiety as the nursery rhymes are told or as the moving sculptures tangle and untangle themselves. But the participants must concentrate on the task at hand, and the laughter must be internal to the process or the result of the audience's enjoyment. *The participants cannot break out of the context of the invention.* They must speak their lines as growing out of the need to tell the story, to be a part of what is happening. They must truly belong to the sculpture as they search for a new way to explore its possibilities.

If the participants were in a play in which they had specific roles, we would speak of "staying in character." But what we are talking about here is maintaining the persona of performer, of *staying committed to the moment of the presentation.*

One evening a small boy watched as Barbara, his neighbor and friend, put on a puppet show. It was a treat they had shared a few times in the past year. He sat on the rug in front of the sofa and she crouched down behind the sofa's back, using it as the puppet stage. He knew it was her voice and that the puppets came out of the big canvas bag in her closet. After the show, thinking perhaps he might want to try the puppets for himself, she stood up and asked if he wanted to hold them. He turned away and refused to talk. She had broken the spell. She had failed to understand the depth of a four-year-old's commitment to the transformation.

There is no substitute in the art of performing for the truth of commitment. And there is nothing more fragile. It can be shattered by a self-conscious laugh, by a look at the audience suggesting the performer does not think this is worthy of him, by a raised eyebrow questioning the behavior of fellow performers, by a fluttering of eyes, by a grin or a grunt or a groan that comes not from the persona of the performer but from the actor underneath. Curiously enough, any one of these same gestures, if it seems to belong truly to the performance persona, will strengthen the illusion, not weaken it. The commitment to the moment means that all details, down to breathing and biting fingernails, must be encompassed within the new world that the performer is creating in the theatre. This person I am creating for you shuffles her feet and runs her hand through her hair. She does not look you straight in the eye, she is hesitant in her speech, she seems to be expecting someone to come, she has a nervous little laugh. . . .

Carmen Decker, an actress of thirty-five years experience at the BoarsHead Theater in Lansing, Michigan, always worked hard to get her lines learned very early in the rehearsal period because it helped her develop her role more completely. It made her furious to forget a line as she worked, but she would never drop out of the scene or the character. Even as she would curse herself, or ask for a line, or say and re-say the words until they came out right, she would keep the scene going and staying utterly within the moment. Her fellow actors were able to play these scenes right along with her because they never doubted that it was the character and not the actress who was speaking. When she was back on track, the scene had not lost a beat.

Learning to Commit and Avoiding Breaking Out of the Moment

There are two reasons inexperienced performers drop out of the moment. One is self- doubt. The performers doubt that they will be able to make what they are doing seem real, and therefore they hedge their bets by letting everyone, including themselves, know that they are only kidding up here. They are easily distracted and they let inappropriate actions interfere with their concentration. This is also described as self-consciousness, being painfully aware of the inadequacies of the self and being, therefore, unable to give over to another persona.

The second major reason for dropping out of the moment is lack of patience, unwillingness to take the necessary amount of time to let the reality of the event sink in. Performers rush on, and fail to trust truth's power to sustain interest.

Both children and adults can overcome these two conditions. But self-doubt can best be overcome by working on patience. An impatient actor always worries that the audience is losing interest. When a patient actor takes time to let the event happen, to participate in the illusion as if it were real, the audience participates as well; when an audience is involved, it is never bored. Once a performer realizes he or she can hold an audience, the power is irresistible.

Patience Exercises

The word "patient" for an actor may seem strange. Why not talented? Or gifted? Partly because talents and gifts are not ours to bestow or acquire, while *patience is a trait we can develop*. Patience has to do with behavior we can control, the art of waiting. We learn to wait for the whole picture to develop in our mind's eye so that we can honestly respond to it. If I am to create the illusion that I am eating an apple, I must be able to see the apple in my hand, and feel my teeth bite into it, and feel it dissolving as I chew and swallow it. Perhaps I get a bit of skin caught between my teeth. How long does it take to pick it out with my nail, or a playing card, or a toothpick I carry in my pocket? Any of these actions rushed will crack the belief that I ever had an apple in the first place.

✳ Mirrors

Mirroring a partner's action is a popular exercise in concentration used for beginners in creative drama, mime, creative dance, and acting. It is excellent for understanding the importance of patience. Viola Spolin uses it, and we have used it ourselves in many contexts with all ages.

Leader Dialogue

Find a partner whose height is similar to yours. Face your partner. Breathe deeply, relax, center yourself, and get your mind clear. Your task is to become a mirror for your partner's movements. Eventually you will become so effective as mirrors that you will scarcely know who is making the movement and who is becoming the mirror. If your partner starts a move, follow and reproduce it as in a mirror. Take your time and start very, very slowly. Communicate by concentrating on each other's movement. You may not talk. Keep the movement face to face. Take your time. Make very small, very slow movements. Use your peripheral vision to try to mirror everything you can see your partner doing. One of you is A. The other is B. When I call out A, A is the leader. Then I will say B. You switch without missing a beat. Do not start over. Just continue. Remember, infinitely slowly. A, begin.

Advice to the Leader

The key to this exercise is extremely slow motion. You may have to slow down individual pairs. Let A go for a while before switching to B. After a while, let the time between switching shorten. The goal is to arrive at such careful concentration and patience that each participant is willing to watch the mirror for even the tiniest gesture. Call "freeze" at some point and have half the room watch the other half work. Then switch.

Side Coaching

More slowly still. Barely notice the change in movement. Be patient in moving. Notice both hands. Notice shoulders and face. Notice the placement of feet. Notice changes in level. This is a full-length mirror. Keep the movements small and slow. Concentrate. Do not touch the mirror. You may imagine only the thickness of glass between you and the mirror. Stay in the moment. Don't look away for even a second. Keep the concentration. It isn't helpful to try to make your partner laugh. Remember the mirror cannot see what you do if you turn your head. Eventually I will stop calling for A or B, and as I go around, you will not let me see who is the leader. You and the mirror will become one and the same.

Follow-up Dialogue

What did you have to do to make the mirror effective? Listen for concentration, needing to work very slowly, needing to try to watch the whole person at once. Listen for the recognition that it is necessary to become one with a partner to make it really work.

This is an important exercise in action/reaction or impulse/ response, as well as patience. A great deal of acting has to do with being a respondent to an impulse, a reactor to an action. The performer who picks up stimuli will be the exciting actor on stage. The patient actor lets the honest reaction happen and does not force it. At the same time he is concentrating on what the other performers are doing in order to have an honest response. The mirror exercise should be done a number of times because the group gets more attuned to one another as they work. The concentration grows and so does the patience.

Deepening the Experience

Add sound to the mirror. As the partner talks, the mirror must say what the partner is saying while the partner is saying it. Although this seems difficult, there will be barely a quarter-second's delay before mirroring the speech. At first the sound mirror can work alone. Then the visual mirror and the sound mirror can be connected. If people are bashful and don't know what to say, select a group topic. If the speech is excited, it is more of a challenge to concentration. The topic may be "everything I wanted to say to my mother when she bawled me out for something" or "a defense of my point of view on gun control" or any topic that leads to animated comment. After ten seconds, switch partners. Practice alternating speakers and mirrors in the middle of a speech by calling out "switch."

✳ Tossing a Big Ball: A Group Exercise for Action/ Reaction and Patience

The group is divided into two halves, one group on each side of the room.

Leader Dialogue

Imagine you are throwing a huge air-filled rubber ball, as big as the circle you make with your group. It will float a bit once it is tossed, but it is heavier than a balloon and it takes all of you to send it up in the air. Now the group to my right has the ball. It is so big it takes all of you to hold it. Get ready to toss the ball to the other side of the room. Over on my left, you get ready to catch it. Now, prepare to toss, ready, . . . and up it goes. Get ready to catch it. Watch it come down and catch it. Now, prepare to toss it back. Don't discuss it. Just read each other's actions and join in.

Side Coaching

Feel the weight of the ball. Feel how big it is. See it go up in the air. See how long it takes to come to you. Where is it going to land? Get ready to toss it back, way up in the air. Look out, it is going to land.

Advice to the Leader

Join in the illusion from the beginning. See the ball and let your commitment to the illusion guide theirs. Watch the groups as they imagine the ball. Let them discover its size and weight. Keep the side coaching going to help the illusion. Your goal is to get them to see the ball as a group, to learn to wait for it to pass through space and to feel the weight of it as it lands. You want them to begin to take cues from each other about the reality of the illusion and to go along with that reality. If they are successful in creating the illusion for themselves, they will begin to move as a group to position themselves under the imaginary ball. They will also follow through after tossing it in the air and they will all be watching it. Keep silent when the illusion is going well. Finish the exercise by having a huge gust of wind catch the ball and everyone watch it sail away.

Follow-up Dialogue

What did it take to make the ball real? Listen for comments about going along with the group, about seeing it in the air in your imagination. Ask about when it became real for them. Perhaps someone will observe that only when they began to wait for it to come over did the illusion work. It is this patience that is the heart of theatrical illusion.

✳ *"Indicating" and What Is Wrong with It*

A rushed moment in the theatre suddenly becomes merely an "indication" of what is meant but not what is meant itself. "Indicating" is one of the forbidden sins of honest acting. "Indicating" refers to superficial gestures or expressions used to *portray* a state of mind instead of evoking the honest manifestations of it. Tapping one's foot and looking at one's watch are stagy indications of waiting. Shading your eyes and craning your neck are an indication of looking off into the distance. To make such situations real, or rather to create the illusion of their reality, the performer must have the patience to sink into the moment and, once there, to rely on the gestures that naturally come out of wishing someone would arrive, or wondering what that is way off in the distance. You want to make a group of performers their own "indicating" watchdogs.

Leader Dialogue

Imagine that you are playing a sport or any other simple physical activity that you actually do. Think of your action—playing golf or tennis, digging a hole, mopping a floor, or some physical activity that involves the whole body and that you have actually done. Try to feel yourself doing it. Mime any objects you need. Pick a moment you can re-create for us. Take the time it actually takes. Sustain the activity for at least twenty seconds. Everyone will have three minutes to choose the activity and practice it. Then we will go around the room and demonstrate.

Advice to the Leader

Check to make sure people are doing things they have actually done. Variety or originality is not important. You can have ten baseball players. The goal is to have each one believe what he is doing. Give them a sense of how long twenty seconds can be. They really have to sustain the movement and the moment.

Follow-up Dialogue

What details worked for you? As a performer? As an audience member? When did you believe the action was real? Do you understand the value of staying true to the reality of the moment? Did you see any "indicating?" If you were indicating, what did you need to do to make the moment real?

Patience in Dialogue

Patience is also a feature of speaking dialogue. Images of what is going on form in the mind, and these images help a performer say what has to be said. It takes patience to make these images happen. Memorized lines spoken without letting the thoughts and images form get wooden. Patience allows performers to use the inner workings of the mind. If the images are strong enough, the audience will share in them. Once again, the actor must be patient and let the real thing happen. We have a few exercises to get started.

✳ Truncated Dialogue

There are many times in normal speech when we start a sentence but never finish it because an idea or feeling has stepped in the way. What is going on in our mind gets conveyed by meaningless phrases because something takes over what we were going to say. One of the best patience exercises is to work with these truncated phrases. Pairs work together. The job is to let the thinking go on in the head so that it is clear why a sentence was stopped short. The partner must wait until he or she has perceived a meaning, respond to it, and cut short a response in turn.

Put this dialogue up on a blackboard or a big piece of paper:

A. Excuse me, I . . .
B. I thought that . . .
A. I don't know why . . .
B. What if I . . .

Leader Dialogue

Find a partner. Your task is to create a little honest moment with only the dialogue that is here. One of you will be character A. One will be character B. Each of you has two lines. Talk together and decide who you are and what the situation is. Keep it simple, but be clear where you are and who you are, and what this conversation is about. Decide what you started to say, and what comes into your mind that makes you stop your sentence. Decide what you are reacting to in the other person. Take the time to let your thoughts work on you before you speak. Let something come into your head to make you start talking and something that cuts off your speech. The critical ingredient is deciding who you are and what you are talking about, and then having the patience to engage with your mind before you start again. Discuss and rehearse your dialogue for five minutes. Learn your two lines. Practice several times. Then we will show each other.

Side Coaching

Decide who you are and what is the situation. Where are you? Are you an angry married couple? Is this your best friend? Are you strangers? Is this an argument? An apology? As a performer you need to know exactly what you are thinking before you speak. What cuts you off? What is going on in your head? Take the time to let it go on. Stay in the moment after you cut off your sentence. Don't talk until you have a reason to. Listen to your partner and react as if you are both truly the persons you say you are. Honesty is your goal. Don't add dialogue.

Advice to the Leader

When the pairs are showing their tiny scenes, have them do them twice. Repeating an exercise really brings the experience home. It helps people see what they truly understand and can control, and what is accidental. Eventually they will learn to take advantage of the accidental and respond to it. Repeating an exercise helps participants choose what they like and get rid of what they don't like. It also establishes the elements of the artistic process—invention, selection, arrangement, finishing.

Side Coaching

Why did you stop talking? Why did you say that? Where are you going? What do you want? Take all the time you need. Let the moment play through the silence. This is hard work.

Follow-up Dialogue

When were you most convinced that the people were really interacting? Could you tell what was going on between them? If you had to write dialogue for the silent sections, what would you say? Do you need dialogue to convey the meaning? As an actor, notice how what the other person said had an effect on you. As an actor and audience, notice how easy it is for us to tell if there was no real reason for the cutoff.

Deepening the Experience

Now we are beginning to deal with intentions. What are you there for? What are you trying to accomplish with what you say? Why do you speak? We are opening the question of the subtext. By subtext, we mean what is really going on between people as opposed to what is being said. With your partner, extend the dialogue with two more pairs of sentences, finished or unfinished. See how long you can keep this going. Try writing some truncated dialogue sequences. What are some of the ways we often start sentences? What are some of the short expressions we use to answer complicated questions? "Maybe . . .; I don't know . . .; Well, I . . .; Sure, but . . ."

Working with Contradictions and Impulses

These sequences remind us that life and drama are full of contradictions. There is an impulse to do or say one thing and suddenly it is crossed by an impulse to do something else. People can exploit this internal conflict as a device for creating interesting performances. Within a line of poetry or narration or dialogue, there are often competing impulses, two ways of thinking about something at the same time. If the performer has the patience to let these conflicts enter the performance, then what is presented has layers of possibilities. The audience can engage in the alternatives. The audience's mind will be as active as the presentation.

In the English language, possibly the most famous example of a playwright using the mind's internal conflict to make great theatre is Hamlet's

> To be, or not to be, that is the question:
> Whether 'tis nobler in the mind to suffer
> The slings and arrows of outrageous fortune,
> Or to take arms against a sea of troubles,
> And by opposing end them? To die, to sleep,—
> No more, and by a sleep to say we end
> The heart-ache and the thousand natural shocks
> That flesh is heir to,—'tis a consummation
> Devoutly to be wish'd. To die, to sleep;
> To sleep! perchance to dream: aye, there's the rub;
> For in that sleep of death what dreams may come
> When we have shuffled off this mortal coil
> Must give us pause: there's the respect
> That makes calamity of so long life. (Act III, sc. i)

Thus, Shakespeare begins Hamlet's famous soliloquy on death and suicide. The torment Hamlet feels in living, the questions he has about his own responsibilities, and the fear he has of the afterlife work through the speech. He starts in one direction, and then he realizes the potential danger and considers the alternatives. The great performances of this soliloquy allow the conflicts in the mind to be realized. Shakespeare, of course, was an actor and he worked alongside actors in creating his plays. He knew the power of a character taking time with the audience to explore the ironies in a complicated world; to let them discover why these conflicts cause pain or anger. He also worked with a stage of simple sets and props and lively interaction with the audience.

✳ Exploring Performance with Complex Language— Shakespeare, Poetry, and Stories

We can treat the full *Hamlet* "To be or not to be" soliloquy (Act III, sc. i) as a dialogue exercise. It may be more interesting to hand out different Shakespearean speeches and let performers group together according to the one they would like to explore. Gender is not an issue in this exercise. Anyone can speak these words with commitment. We have used Richard II's "Let's talk of graves, of worms, and epitaphs" (Act III, sc. ii), the Chorus's prologue to *Henry V* "O for a muse of fire," Macbeth's "To-morrow, to-morrow, and to-morrow" (Act V, sc. v), Portia's "The quality of mercy is not strain'd" in *The Merchant of Venice* (Act IV, sc. i), Marc Antony's "Friends, Romans, countrymen" from *Julius Caesar* (Act III, sc. ii), and Jaques', seven ages of man from *As You Like It* (Act II, sc. vii). They are accessible and interesting to many age groups. With a few facts from the plays, you can set up the context of each speech.

Leader Dialogue

The first job of your group is to figure out the meaning of the words. To begin, the group reads together aloud. But instead of reading in unison, individuals can join in whenever they want to. The group has to keep the reading going, but each person can read a sentence, a phrase, or a whole section. The voices can double or be in unison, or be single. You can join in on a word for emphasis. Everyone in the group should be part of the reading. Start at the top and get through the speech as best you can.

Next, you work on what you don't understand. You talk together, use the footnotes, use the punctuation, and use each other's common sense to figure out what is going on. This is not the heavy philosophical meaning, or even the deep psychological state, but just the meaning of the words. How are words used, especially when the meanings are slightly different from the way we use them today? Anybody can be a resource to this discussion. Feel free to ask questions. Try to see when words are used literally or figuratively. Check the punctuation to see where the sentences begin and end. Talk to each other.

Next, look for the images that Shakespeare uses to let us get pictures in our mind of what Hamlet, or Macbeth, or Richard is thinking. Underline images when you come to them. Talk about them. "Leash'd in like hounds, should famine, sword, and fire / Crouch for employment" from the Prologue to Henry V: *Here is a picture of the fierce qualities of war being held while they strain at the leash like howling dogs. "Out,*

out, brief candle!" and Macbeth ends life by blowing out a flame. These are examples. Spot others. They may be brief or extended.

When your group has the meanings and an idea of the images, you begin to divide the lines among the performers. The division should represent voices in the head of the character, a new voice as a new thought enters. What you cannot do is just assign four lines to one, another four to the next, and so forth. The job is to perform the contradictions, the alternatives, the doubts, the asides, the inner dialogue of the mind.

Advice to the Leader

Do not hesitate to have a room full of people reading aloud. If the group is concentrating, the buzz will not bother them. The leader can move among the groups easily. It is not a good idea in these short exercises to allow people to go off to another room to practice. The desired dynamic is that all are solving a problem simultaneously. One group may have an idea or a question that will illuminate the situation for all. We use the expression "freeze" called out in a loud voice to mean "stop, listen, I have something that may help, or a direction I need to give you." People get used to listening for "freeze" and becoming silent when they hear it.

It may be helpful to point out the rhythm scheme of iambic pentameter to anyone who is not familiar with the ten-beat line. The second syllable of each pair of syllables is accented, and the "ta dum ta dum" that results is very much like a heartbeat. There are five pairs in a line, with an occasional eleventh beat added. Note that Shakespeare modifies and breaks this scheme when he wants to make a point. Sometimes reviewing the rhythm helps discover meaning. Ask people to read aloud lines where they can identify the iambic pentameter for others to hear. "Let's talk' of graves', of worms', and ep'itaphs'." "Creeps in' this pet'ty pace' from day' to day'." While it is not a good idea to let the strong rhythm dominate the speaking, it can inform the emphasis and the phrasing.

Leader Dialogue

Your group will perform the speech as if it were a conversation among you, one person starting, and when a conflicting or alternative thought enters, another reads, as if parts of the mind are talking among them-selves. Some lines might be voices in unison. Others might be pairs. Once you have worked through the speech and know well what is going on, you will present the speeches to the whole group. You may incorporate movement, stage pictures, or even moving sculptures. Get on your feet and try it. Movement will help you with your analysis. When you per-form for all of us, it will be helpful if you set up the context of the speech so the audience knows when and why it is happening.

Deepening the Experience

Invite people to use this strategy with other material. Poems. Stories. You could take a group of short works and perform them as a whole piece. Remember, whenever you see a new idea or a contradiction or a modification happening, another voice steps in. The division in voices should be connected to the flow of thoughts. Whenever a group of people encounters a difficult text—in poetry, prose, lyrics, or dialogue—that they would like to perform, the group analysis process is a helpful tool in working out the inner tensions of the material. Differences of opinion about the real meaning are healthy because they reveal complexities within a piece of writing. Remem-ber, it is the exposure of these internal tensions that makes a per-formance engaging. Encourage performers to ask about the meaning of words. Use dictionaries. Use yourself.

You cannot perform a word for an audience if you do not know what it means. Whether the writer is Shakespeare, poet Rita Dove, play-wright Tennessee Williams, or novelist Toni Morrison, the words have shades, nuances, and intention. An actor cannot speak truth he or she does not understand. This is where we start with text.

Once everyone has participated in a dialogue break-up of one of Shakespeare's monologues, or a poem from another source, indi-viduals can perform them alone, remembering the double or mul-tiple voices and the conflicts sustained by the images, drawing on the contrasts and contradictions to layer the performance with the internal drama. If several people perform the same speech, they will learn from each other, and the listeners discover many new roads to travel.

✳ Understanding the Importance of Detail

Commitment to the moment often depends on sustaining the illusion through its details. Patience exercises have at their center details in the mind. Physical and external details are equally important and often contribute to internal images and sensations. Stanislavsky advocated practice in the techniques of sensory and emotional recall, letting people recover details from their personal history. Many teachers following in his footsteps have developed their own versions of his technique. All of them are founded in the Freudian notion that experiences of the past are all encoded in our subconscious memory, and that they can be revealed to us through relaxed concentration. Once past experiences are uncoded, they can be understood and relived, and, for the actor, made use of in presenting a personality or a state of mind on the stage.

> In 1982, a director looking for music for the play *Vanities* was listening to a group of recordings from the mid-1960s. Suddenly, during one song, a deep sense of sorrow took her over. She began to sob, and it was long after the song was finished that she recovered her equilibrium. As deep as the pain went, she was completely at a loss to identify what had been the cause of her despair. Nothing specific would come to mind, even though the deaths of the Kennedys and Martin Luther King, Jr., and personal family losses had been part of her life at the time. However, it was clear that some place in her past that song and a deeply troubled state of mind coincided. She had only to think of it and the feelings returned.

Some performers will find the sensory and emotional recall exercises fascinating and will want to work with a teacher who explores them in depth. All performers will benefit from discovering what the technique has to offer.

Leader Dialogue

Find a comfortable place in the room where you can relax thoroughly. Lie flat on the floor. Close your eyes. Relax your whole body—feet, legs, hands, shoulders, neck. Let all the tension go out of them. Check each part of your body. Remove the tension. Let your mind be free so it can focus. Now think of a place where, as a child, you spent time—a room, the seat of a car, a hiding place, whatever it may be. Try to see it in your mind. Let your mind's eye look all around it. What is there? What is beneath your feet? Dirt? A carpet? Linoleum? What is to the right, to the left, over your head? Is it hot? Warm? What does it smell like? How much light is there? What is the color of the light? What is the air like around you? Damp? Breezy? What objects do you have when you are there? Now remember a particular moment in that space. Be very specific. Think of the reason you went there. Did something happen to you there or just before you went there? Can you remember what was said? How it felt? What state of mind do you have when you are in this space at this particular moment?

When you have all of this firmly in mind and in your sense memory, I am going to ask you to move to a spot in this room where you can be in that place. You are to go there silently and not interact with anyone else. Do not have any eye contact with anyone or in any way disturb your or their concentration. Now you may get up and put yourself in that place—standing or sitting, whatever you need to do. Just be there as completely as you can. Sustain it until I ask you to break.

Advice to the Leader

While they are working, take time between each of the directions to let people work through the images. Speak softly and soothingly. Be patient. Let people find their places and gradually build a repertoire of details. When they go to the place in the room, let them stay there for a while, concentrating on the reality of the moment. Then ask them quietly to speak.

Leader Dialogue

Try to condense the experience into two or three sentences, no more, and from where you are, speak those sentences out loud to tell us where you are.

Advice to the Leader

Some people will think of something too personal to share with the group. Respect this. The purpose of the exercise is the memory recall. Let them stay in their "places" for two or three minutes. Watch them for concentration, for being "in the moment."

Follow-up Dialogue

Is there someone who is willing to share more of their place and situation with the group? Tell us as much detail as you can think of. Let people talk. The sharing allows others to see what others have thought. Call attention to specific details. Note the difference between telling about an *event* and *trying to re-create the specific context of a place.* Work for the latter. That latter is something we can call "condition" and can use as a technique for creating a moment on stage. It is the whole experience—the sights, sounds, atmosphere, feelings, and thoughts. Thank people for sharing very personal experiences. That willingness to open oneself to the public is part of acting. Being able to amass a plethora of detail for a situation helps the performer sustain the illusion. Remembering a cobweb, for example, and brushing it off your face, or seeing a discarded Frito's wrapper and deciding not to pick it up, or hanging over the bed and blowing a dust ball to the other side are actions that can give credibility to a performance. They are true moments that sustain illusions.

How long did it take for the details to begin to appear? What details were the most vivid? What details that people told about caught your imagination? Did any of you begin to have the same feelings you remembered having? What use can you make of this process?

Listen for the recognition that specific details play an important part in making the situation real. They act as fingerholds for the mind to grab the original condition. Ask performers to select the details that help them re-create the whole moment.

✳ Detail Observation

Leader Dialogue

Take the person next to you as a partner. You have fifteen seconds to observe everything you can about the way your partner is dressed. Go.

Freeze. Turn away from your partner. One at a time, describe your part-
ner's dress to each other. The partner is to check for accuracy and ask
questions like: Is my shirt buttoned at the collar or not? Am I wearing a
belt? Press for more and more detail and more and more accuracy. Switch
partners. Repeat. See if you get better at your observations.

Deepening the Experience

Everyone is to return for the next meeting with a detailed observation of a stranger, noted on a bus, at a sporting event, a street corner, a restaurant, wherever it is possible to observe a person for a
long period without intruding. The observation should include
gestures, physical stance, clothing, way of speaking, mannerisms,
facial expressions, way of walking, objects they have with them,
and their state of mind as best you can imagine it. The participants
can write internal monologues for these people, trying to capture
their thoughts. They might create dialogues between them as well.
The focus, however, is on the details of the observation.

✳ Detail Reenactment

Leader Dialogue

Think carefully about your morning rising ritual. Take some small epi-
sode from it, and think it through in every aspect. It may be tooth-
brushing, shaving, bathing, putting on clothes, putting on your shoes,
fixing your hair. Don't try for too much. Take one activity that you
repeat regularly. Whatever it is, concentrate on reproducing every single
moment of it. Go find a space by yourself, and re-create it in pantomime,
as if you had the objects. Take the actual time that it takes to do what-
ever you do. Be patient. Don't rush any part of it. Try to get your mus-
cles to remember what it is like to go through these actions. Use a chair
or a table or a substitute prop if necessary—a pencil or a jacket—
whatever you need to recall all the details of the activity. When you have
gone through it all, pick out about one minute of it to show us.

Side Coaching

Do not try to make a drama out of it. Be completely truthful to the actual morning ritual. Feel yourself going through the movements. If you pick something up, know that it is in your hand. Put it down the way you would have to. Feel the sensations. If you drink a glass of milk, feel it going down your throat to your empty stomach. If you put a hot cloth on your face, feel the steam on your skin. If you get toothpaste out of the tube, what happened to the lid?

Advice to the Leader

Monitor the rehearsals and ask specific questions: *Are you barefoot? Is the bathroom steamy? Are you in a hurry? Are you still sleepy? Did you shut the door? Can you see yourself in the mirror?*

Follow-up Dialogue

The issue here is: What contribution does detail make to our belief in the illusion? What held your interest? Talk, please, about the process of remembering the detail. What is the role of concentration? Did the detail help you sustain your commitment to the moment? Did you have to commit to the moment to remember the detail? What is the difference between sensory detail and emotional detail? How are they connected? Did you have any emotional memory in the rehearsal of the morning ritual? How do you feel about morning in general? Could you reproduce a specific morning? Or is it every morning?

Leader Dialogue

One more detail. As you sit there, imagine that you have something caught between your teeth and you are not in a place where you can pick it out with your finger. Work at it for a moment. Eventually you give in. Now imagine that your hands are full and you have a hair in your face. Finally, set something down and take care of it. Realize that you can imagine these things because you know what they feel like.

Advice to the Leader

A character in a play talking about something could use details like these to give reality to a moment—not because they are talking about teeth or hair, but because people have these things happen to them. Actors can use the frustrations of such actions to give substance to what they are saying. Encourage actors to find their own actions to try—opening a knife blade, cleaning embarrassing dirt from under your fingernails, discovering lint on your sweater, brushing dandruff off your shoulders, buttoning a blouse cuff, tying a tie, brushing crumbs off a table—real things that people do that give life to a moment.

Detail exercises help people use their imagination to create physical realities. As performers work in presenting moments on stage, the creation of specific details will bring new realities to them. They have to choose the details with care to find the honest ones that make a difference.

Emotional memory and sensory memory seem to be linked. Which comes first is a chicken-or-egg question that may be interesting but not definitive. The performer benefits from the way the two help present and sustain a persona and a situation for an audience. The more a performer can invest a situation with detail, the more likely it is to become palpable, something he can live in and invite an audience to perceive. When the illusion has breath and flesh, self-consciousness vanishes, patience prevails, and theatre begins.

All the exercises we have presented can and should be practiced more than once. People can get better at interacting, at responding to impulses, at remembering emotional conditions, at investing a moment with the reality of physical details. Acting texts, such as Charles McGaw's *Acting is Believing*, Robert Cohen's *Acting One*, or Robert Benedetti's *The Actor at Work*, provide dozens of exercises for focusing on acting a specific character. All these exercises benefit the actor and should be mined for their potential in a lifetime of acting development.

Since our goal is to step beyond acting a character already created by a playwright into creating the actor's own theatre, we move now to tasks that make the performer responsible for the whole of the theatre moment. We move to taking responsibility for the stage space, for creating the words and text, and for producing the work.

Theatrical Space

The Transformation of Space

In the Palazzo del Te, a garden palace at the edge of Mantua, there is a series of rooms decorated for Federigo II Gonzaga, Duke of the once powerful city state. Federigo brought in the successful Roman artist, Giulio Romano, to create the wall decorations that would entertain his guests in this grand pavilion. Federigo had learned from his mother, Isabella d'Este, that one of the comforts of life was the employment of the finest artists in the creation of elegant living quarters. In her day she had commissioned works from Leonardo da Vinci, Raphael, Perugino, Correggio, Andrea Mantegna, and the local court painter, Lorenzo Costa. But what concerns us is not Federigo's place as a patron in the history of Italian painting. We are interested in what Federigo wanted Giulio Romano to paint in his summer palace.

These were to be rooms for entertaining. To fulfill this purpose, Federigo commissioned murals that transformed the principal dining hall into the Island of Venus. On each of the four walls were paintings of the gods at the wedding of Amor and Psyche, posed in such a fashion that the actual dining table in the center of the room would complete the picture. It would not take a Renaissance courtier long to know that he was being invited to play out the conceit that the guests, too, were attending the celebration with the gods and that the host was Jove himself, king of Olympus, and founder of the feast. The room had been transformed so that everybody in it would enjoy a dusting of divinity.

We all know about the transformation of spaces—churches for weddings, homes for holidays. With the arrangement of furniture and the placement of ribbons and flowers, we define the behavior and attitude the space now requires. These forms of theatre, rituals enacted by a cluster of people within transformed spaces, reveal how easily we adapt ourselves to a new context of behavior, taking cues from surroundings that have been altered.

In Federigo's day it would not be unusual for the entire court to arrive for a wedding or anniversary dressed in costumes suited to a theme, the host having commissioned scenic pieces, dances, verses, and musical performances for the event. When we look back upon these lavish festivities as historians, we are obliged to call them theatre. We often ignore the fact that the same thing happens today.

By walking down an aisle on the arm of her father, a bride ascends a stage, and makes an audience of the participants. When a child stands up to recite, when a singer steps to the microphone, a stage is born. As soon as someone hangs a drapery or sets up a folding screen to hide the performer, an atmosphere of suspense prevails. There is now a new space, charged in a different way from the room that preceded it.

Sometimes we call this acting space. It is also stage space, theatre space. Whatever its name, it is electric, powerful, and malleable. The more one comes to understand theatre space, the more easily one can use it to advantage.

✳ The Chair Dance

Space and shapes are basic to staged performance. This exercise explores the dramatic and emotional content of the arrangement of the stage. Select six or seven chairs. Identical chairs work the best. Set them in a line on a defined stage space, all facing forward. Ask the participants to sit in the audience and study the arrangement of the chairs.

Leader Dialogue

As you look at the chairs from the audience, think about what may be going on with the arrangement. If you walked into a theatre and a group of chairs was arranged this way, what would you say is going on? How do you expect to react to this?

Advice to the Leader

You can expect to hear that there is going to be a lecture or graduation. People may comment that they expect to be bored. After a few minutes of discussion, set one chair off to the side a distance from the rest and angle it slightly away from the others.

Leader Dialogue

Now, what do you see happening? What has happened? What is about to happen? What emotional dynamic operates in you? What are your expectations?

Advice to the Leader

The participants will have all sorts of ideas. "One person is in control of the group. One person doesn't belong in the group." As soon as you get a few answers, change the arrangement of the chairs in some way . . . such as pairs facing each other, or chairs in a circle, or a random scattering of chairs. Then ask the same question.

Leader Dialogue

What is going on now? What does this arrangement say to you? What is the emotional content of the situation on stage now?

　　When you get some answers, ask the members of the group to come up and change the chairs into any arrangement they would like. Let each person who wishes to do so develop a chair arrangement. Ask the group each time: "What is going on? What is the emotional impact of this arrangement? How would you change it?"

Deepening the Experience

After a few tries of placement without a specific intention imposed, ask members of the group to volunteer to create a chair arrangement that expresses the idea of "conflict." When one person has experimented with a schema, ask someone else to come up with another arrangement for the same concept. Push the group to explore a number of ways of creating an impression of conflict through the arrangement of the chairs. Try the same process with other concepts like *antagonism, isolation, division, unity, authority, power, domination, continuity,* and so forth.

The chair dance helps participants recognize the impact of stage composition. It helps performers realize that the placement of objects and people on the stage contributes to an overall statement. It also helps people manipulate the stage composition to achieve a desired emotional or conceptual effect.

Deepening the Understanding

Here is an opportunity to discuss the difference between the literal reality of film and television and the abstracted or suggested reality that the theatre can offer. In many ways, all we need are a few chairs. Because this abstraction is something the theatre can do better than film or television, it is something to celebrate. It has power to be exploited. That power is at the heart of Hi Concept - Lo Tech thinking.

Focus Exercises: Controlling the Audience's Perception

Once people have looked at the chair dance, they will be aware that physical relationships have a direct effect on the way an audience interprets a stage situation. The next step is to learn to control and affect those audience perceptions.

The single most important element in designing a stage performance is establishing focus. If the performers understand that, their work will gain clarity. Simply stated, focus is the tool by which the audience is led to pay attention to the element of the performance that is most important at any given moment. This may be a speech, an action, or a reaction. Because the stage does not have the camera's ability to zoom in or cut away, to frame or isolate, it is the task of the director and performers to force the audience to listen to and look at the key actions throughout the performance. One of the most powerful tools in establishing focus is the use of stage space. The elements in manipulating stage space are composition—background, foreground, and positive and negative spaces on the stage—movement, gaze, and pace.

Performers can improve their ability to guide the audience's attention. They can learn to assess the stage situation, to move at the right moment, with the right energy, and to use their bodies to contribute both variety and continuity to the whole picture.

Learning and Practicing with Stage Space

To set up these exercises, divide the room into two halves. These will be stages. Put some chairs and tables or boxes on each stage. The group will work in halves.

✳ *Dressing the Stage*

Leader Dialogue

You remember when we did the moving sculptures exercise. Your job then was to fill in the negative spaces, to stay in contact with the group, to move when no one else was moving, and to keep the composition developing. In the chair dance, you learned something about the way compositions affect the way we perceived the situation. This exercise in dressing the stage expands on both those experiences. Divide yourselves into two even groups. Each group imagine a stage in your half of the room. Group A will be the audience to begin. Group B: It is the job of each of you to take a body position on the stage that is completely your own. As a group you are responsible to use the entire stage. Your pose cannot be like anyone else's. Each of you is responsible for contributing to the whole composition. You also must be able to be seen by the audience. In the whole group there must be low, medium, and high figures in the composition. Go ahead and take your poses.

Side Coaching

Do not discuss the arrangement with anyone. Just take responsibility for yourself. Remember, use the whole stage, vary the body positions, be sure you can be seen. When you have decided on your body position, freeze.

Leader Dialogue

Audience, can you see everyone? If not, advise the person who cannot be seen, but let them choose to make their own changes. Now, when I clap my hands, move to a new place and take a different pose. All the same conditions apply. Variety, levels, being seen, whole stage. Go.

Follow-up Dialogue

Audience, tell us what are the most interesting and effective aspects of the composition you see? Look for varied levels and varied body positions. Help the group notice that variety is important. The group may observe that certain body positions convey certain attitudes. The goal is to get people to become conscious of their ability to contribute interestingly to a stage composition.

Advice to the Leader

After two or three compositions with one group, switch groups and repeat the discussion. If you use both halves of the room, you can have two different setups of chairs, tables, and platforms; each group will solve slightly different problems.

Deepening the Experience

Go back to one group and ask everyone to take a position to suggest boredom, anxiety, waiting, or being frightened. Everyone must still take a different position, but they must contribute to the meaning of the whole. Switch groups and ask the audience to suggest an attitude.

Advice to the Leader

As soon as both groups get on to the idea and begin to do some varied and interesting things, go on to the next exercises in focus.

✳ Focus

Freeze the last group in a pose and address the audience group.

Leader Dialogue

In that freeze, who has the focus? Where do we want to look? If there is disagreement, or more than one answer, identify one person who is upstage, and ask all the participants on the stage to look at that person and to adjust themselves slightly as necessary to do so. Choose a downstage person and ask the onstage group to give them focus. *Have they succeeded? What is it that helps give focus? Note that* the gaze *is the direction in which someone is looking.* Gaze is a major feature in giving focus.

Switch groups and have them take a pose. Have the group move the focus around by picking people in different spots on the stage. Begin to note how a person can take themselves out of the picture by making simple adjustments—dropping the head down, closing off slightly upstage, dropping a hand. Likewise a gesture in a direction helps give focus—pointing is the most obvious.

Ask someone to stand on a chair if there is no one at a high level in the composition. Note the effect of level in focus. Ask another one to lie on the floor. Each time, require the other performers to adjust themselves so they can give focus to the person indicated. Ask the watching group how to correct any composition so that the designated person has the focus. Try asking someone to start with their back to the audience and then slowly turn around while the others are watching.

Follow-up Dialogue

What does it takes to get the audience to watch a particular person? People will quickly discover that a person facing the audience, or fully open, will generally take focus away from a person closed even partially. They will also note that lines created on the stage by height or by people's bodies contribute to giving a person focus. They may notice that to give focus to a person requires not only adjusting the gaze but also body adjustments from the other performers. Note that a tiny shift in the shoulders is a strong focus-changing element, as is dropping the head.

✳ Focus and Movement

Leader Dialogue

Group A on stage. Now, your task is similar to the moving sculptures. One person must move to another part of the stage and take a new position. As soon as that person has finished moving, another person moves, and so on. Only one person moves at a time, but the composition must keep moving. Go.

Side Coaching

You may take a position that complements someone else—facing them, looking over their shoulder. But you cannot completely cover someone. You may touch someone. You do not need to create a character or a scene. This exercise is about making yourself a contributing part of the composition. You may move at different paces. You may run. You may crawl. You may fall. Make your change big enough that we know it is happening. Switch to Group B, same exercise.

✳ *Giving and Taking Focus*

Leader Dialogue

Group A will be the watchers first. Group B, once you have established your beginning pose, your task is to continue your movement exercise— but this time, your job is to give the moving person focus until they have taken another pose and stopped. If you have to adjust your body position to give focus, do so. One person moves. All others give focus to the moving person until that person has stopped completely. Another person moves, and so on. Go.

Side Coaching

Give us enough movement so the group can follow the focus. Don't forget after you move that you now must give focus to the next person. Remember you can vary your pace in the moving. You can use your gaze and your body position to give focus. If you are open and the person who needs the focus is partially closed, you may have to do something more dramatic with your body to direct the audience's attention to that person. Ask the audience group if the focus is clear. Let the audience group identify split focus, or persons inappropriately taking focus. Let that person adjust as necessary.

When everyone in the group has moved at least once, freeze them and switch to the other group.

Follow-up Dialogue

Evaluate your experience in getting focus on stage and then giving it away. Talk about what ideas you had, what things they saw that worked effectively. They may observe that in using any of these focus tools, variety, accent, and rhythm are important. They may note that what comes after what, how long we wait, how sudden or how slow a movement is all affect our desire to pay attention to certain things on stage. The next step will be how to translate what they have learned in large compositions to small groups.

Deepening the Experience

Ask the group to divide into twos and threes and create a composition where two or three people share the focus because they are in a continuing conversation. Ask the duos to create a situation where one person is talking continuously. Switch the focus from the speaker to the listener. Ask the trios to create a situation in which two people are siding against one in a disagreement. Through the composition let us know who is speaking by the focus, either shared or not. Then have one person switch sides in the argument. Show this change by moving and changing the composition. The group may come up with other scenarios to help generate thinking about dramatic compositional focus.

There are essentially three elements we can use to give focus to the person who needs to have it. Our *gaze*—the other actors looking at that person; *the composition* itself—location in the stage space, levels, and open and closed body positions, as well as lines on the stage we make with legs, arms, heads; and *movement*—if all others on stage are still, the moving person is likely to have the focus. That is even more true if the moving person moves suddenly or decisively. When we combine these elements—movement, directed gaze, and compositional features—the focus is strong and clear. The audience will see and hear exactly what we wish them to.

Space from the Performer's Perspective

Space and Time Variations

We began our explorations of space when we began explorations of acting, with exercises in simple movement, with studying levels, and with group sculptures. When performers introduced themselves and made entrances and exits, they began to understand what it means to be "on stage." Often people working "on stage" have a distinct sense of discomfort—alienation, self-consciousness. When the body must be the focus of the audience's attention, it suddenly becomes awkward. The hands loom large, the throat goes dry, or as one drama teacher put it, "the fog rolls in." Things that you thought you knew vanish and normal clues no longer signal normal behavior. Everything that creates the "fog" can be put to advantage—if understood. Understanding comes from exploring stage space as a performer and as an audience member, consciously analyzing its features and learning to manipulate it. Gradually you learn to have a third eye, to stand outside, to see the effect of every move and gesture, making it possible to choose where and how to invest your stage energy. As the outside eye matures, internal order grows as well.

✳ Discovering Space and Time

To prepare for this exercise, place a chair or a box on your stage space so that it is about one-third the distance between the limits of the space. It should be off center in the performance area, in a spot where a person could sit or stand on it and speak to the audience. Since pace is an important feature of movement, you may have to remind the participants that in previous exercises they have changed pace according to the drumbeat. Now they must create a sense of pace in their own head.

Leader Dialogue

This is an exercise that requires you to be aware of your body in space, both where it is and how fast it is moving. First you must make up two sentences. The first one tells us your state of mind; *the second tells us* something you are going to do because of it. *For example: "I am totally disgusted with my insurance company. I'm going to cancel my policy." Or: "I am exhausted from staying up all night. I'm going home to take a nap." Your job is to come on stage, stop, give us one sentence, move to another space, give us the second sentence, and exit. In the course of your performance you must accomplish two things: (1) take at least two different body positions, and (2) move with at least two distinctly different speeds. You have two minutes to decide on your sentences. Your change of pace can be fast to slow, or slow to fast, or moderate to fast. You can run, skip, saunter, crawl, or use any locomotor movement.*

Side Coaching

As always, your sentences should come from true experience, even if they are not true right at this moment. Be specific. Not just "I'm mad," but "I'm mad at my book bag." The truth of the statements will help you perform them. Be patient. Let the state of mind come into you before you enter. Go to a place on stage. Take a pose. Remember there are three levels from which to choose. Remember that your body can make many different shapes, natural or contrived. Let us see distinctly different paces as you enter and exit. Don't cut yourself short in any of your moves. Begin and end completely off stage. You may use any entrance or exit you choose.

Advice to the Leader

It is difficult to have several tasks at once, but these are common to the job of making theatre. See if the participants realize that they can motivate the choice of pace and the pose by the frame of mind, and vice versa. They can express the frame of mind by the choice of pace. Let them discover this on their own, rather than making it an explicit part of the instructions. They may also discover the comedy of disassociation (i.e., the pace is unexpected or in direct opposition to what is said). They may discover that getting into the frame of mind is dependent on taking the right body position to begin with.

Follow-up Dialogue

What happens to the stage space when a person enters it? What is the relationship between body position, movement pace, and frame of mind? How do they interact with each other? How do you perceive them as a performer? As an audience member?

Deepening the Experience

Repeat the exercise, using the same sentences. People may make changes in the movement if they like. Experiment with moving the chair to the center. What happens when both the entrance and the exit are the same distance? What is the audience's perception of the relationship between stage and performer? What is the performer's experience of the space? Note the differences between short fast entrances and exits and long slow ones; or short slow ones and long fast ones. Try other experiments with moving the furniture and let people repeat their sentences at will with different spatial opportunities. Look for realizations that an actor can manipulate the space to her advantage.

Follow-up Dialogue

What effect does stage composition have on the performance? Think of the positive and negative space exercises. What are the relationships between positive and negative space with regard to the performer and the stage space? The performer and other objects? How do you react to the performer in the center? The performer at one side? Where did you as a performer like to be? At what moments did you feel most in control? Did you begin to have patience with being in the stage space?

There are no rights or wrongs to these questions. The purpose is to become aware as both audience and performer of the dynamics of the body in space and one's ability to manipulate that space with the elements of pace and movement.

Deepening the Experience

Have everyone take a partner. Use the same sentences, and make the pairs interactive. The first person comes on and makes a statement to the audience. The second person must enter and interact with the first person making her statement to the first person. The first person makes her second statement to the other actor. They continue to interact until they are both off stage. This should not be planned. Have them try this a second time, trading partners, and encourage adventuresome interactions. Encourage them to react physically and emotionally to the other person's statement. Allow the participants to touch, but discourage the use of force. Watch how the expressions of states of mind interact and influence each other.

Watch how the poses affect each other's state of mind. Discuss these changes with the group.

✳ Making the Stage Space Assist the Performer

Leader Dialogue

We are going to examine the stage space as we have set it up. Identify any elements in the room that contribute to defining the stage space. What elements distract from observing the performers? What can we do to modify the space so it contributes to our watching the performer and not the background? Are there elements that assist in framing or otherwise supporting the performers?

Advice to the Leader

Posts, windows, posters on a wall, or lamps behind the performers become features of the stage space. Some items that are otherwise interesting can pollute the visual field when you want to focus on the performers. Other things can have dual functions, helping in one instance, hindering in another. Note serendipitous moments such as a head perfectly framed in a window or a doorway that balances a figure in space. Be aware of light—how dark a face becomes when it has sunlight behind it. Notice how a clean blackboard or a plain wall frames figures.

✳ The Actor and the Object

Leader Dialogue

Go back to your two sentences—state of mind and an action. Now elaborate on the state of mind. Add another sentence or two, or a phrase, explaining or describing more about your experience. "I got a bill yesterday from MasterCard. And they had double charged me for two items. Two items, can you believe it . . . I'm going to tear it up." Pick an entrance, one of the spaces between the chairs. Enter and talk to us. At some time within your performance, pick up and move the chair to a second location. You can sit on it, or use it any way you want. The next person deals with the chair where the last person has left it and moves it during his or her performance. You can change the pace if you like. Your job is to deal with the chair and to move it as part of your performance. Do not hesitate to talk while moving the chair. *Exit when you are finished and the next person comes on. Keep this going.*

Deepening the Experience

Another variation will be to ask each performer to carry a large object on stage during the exercise, such as a book carton, a carpet roll, or a stack of newspapers, and deal with it during the sentences as they choose. The next person must then get the object off stage. Discuss the way the presence of the object alters the space. Discuss the way dealing with the object affects the performance.

Advice to the Leader

The purpose of the task is to explore self and objects in space, and to solve physical problems within the context of communicating something to an audience. People will discover that they can emphasize a point, even motivate an action with objects in space.

Follow-up Dialogue

What uses could you make of the object? As an audience member, what did you look for? Try to help the group discover the way that performers "work" a space through movement and the way they invest an object with power when they are no longer able to concentrate only on what they say and how they move.

Discovering the Arena

So far, we have been dealing with stage space as a proscenium: the performer up front, the audience facing them. We have always given the performer a backing. There is an important alternative to this process: *the arena, the stage space in which the audience surrounds the performer.* To people who have always imagined a stage as a proscenium, this kind of space is alarming. There seems to be no safe haven, no way to turn your back and get away, no clear sense of where to focus. But what is alarming can become liberating and powerful.

With audience on all sides, the performers are free to focus all their attention on the other performers, on the interactions of the stage space itself. No longer having to be concerned about facing the audience or turning their backs, the actors can concentrate on each other.

✳ Arena Exercise

Set up a circle of chairs with openings at three or four places for entrances and exits. Or set up a square, with openings at the corners. Ask the group to become the audience and be sure that there are people on all sides. Put a stool within the newly created arena stage space, preferably not at the very center. Repeat all the phases of the sentence and object exercises. Let the performers discover the need to interact with an audience that is in front of and behind them. Note the physical relationships of center, outside edge. Ask each other questions about what made it possible to see, what needs the audience felt. Did they want to see faces? How is it to see backs?

Leader Dialogue

Try these variations with your movement choices. Go from one corner to the other. Stand close to one side and address the people across the arena. Sit on the stool and let your body rotate as you talk. Walk in a circle or half-circle. Walk across the space and turn sharply to the other side.

The arena will radically alter the performer's relationship to an audience. You can expect people to be disconcerted at first. Eventually they will discover a centering that happens when the performer is free to act with the whole self—the back as well as the front. The presence of the chair or object helps the performer discover a new way of focusing on an interaction, investing it with power while communicating to an audience.

Deepening the Experience

Go back to the truncated-sentence exercises and play them in the arena. Help the performers identify their ability to concentrate on each other when the audience's placement is no longer an issue. Here the performer begins to refocus on the power of the action/reaction dynamic of acting.

Try playing the moving sculptures in the arena. Help the audience discover the pleasure of multisided compositions on the stage. Let them become aware of the whole body, the whole composition, the mixture of faces and backs of heads, the dynamics of changing physical points of view.

✳ Discovering Focus in the Arena

Leader Dialogue

We are going back to the focus exercises. We need a small group—four or five. First you dress the stage in the arena. Use the whole space, as before, and everyone has a different body position and varied levels. You must be seen by some of the audience—as many as you can. Freeze the pose. Now give focus to [pick a person.] *Audience members, tell us what you see. Now play the moving/changing focus game. One person moves, and the others give that person focus until he or she stops and takes a pose. Then another person moves, and the group shifts focus to that person until he or she settles.*

Advice to the Leader

Let this go on for four or five changes. Then ask for another volunteer group. You will be letting the performers discover that gaze still works, that levels are important, and that groups and isolation have an effect. Together the group may discover that movement is a critical tool for creating focus in the arena. People can discover different movement patterns for both the object of focus and for those giving focus.

Deepening the Experience

Put pairs of people in the arena and let them both share and exchange focus. Let the audience comment on its experience. See what can be discovered about opening and closing oneself in this spatial structure. Discover the effects of different amounts of distance between performers.

✳ Movement and Dialogue in the Arena

Leader Dialogue

Go back to your Shakespeare monologue. As a performer, you have a responsibility to let the audience in on what you are saying. Take your monologue and rehearse it on your feet, knowing that the audience will be all around you. Within your speech, discover when you want to be moving and when you want to stand still, and when you want to turn around or change direction. Think of the different voices, the changes of internal thought that you discovered before. Plan to mix stillness and movement. Think about changing direction. You may use a chair or an object.

Advice to the Leader

Let the group work independently for about five minutes, and then have them perform individually in the arena. You can freeze different moments and discuss them.

Follow-up Dialogue

There is a lot to discover about arena space. What is the effect of seeing other audience members? What places in the arena seem to have power?

What is it like to be close to one side and far from another? How close together can actors get before they close each other off?

It will become clear that if the audience can see one face in a conversation they will be satisfied, but if they cannot see anyone they will lose interest. Notice that in a long speech the audience can accept an actor's back more readily if the actor is very near to them. The audience sees what she sees, almost speaks with her voice. Traveling the perimeter works well because it creates the expectation that the performer will soon arrive at your own feet. You are free to be still at aisles because by simply turning your head you can take in everyone. Note that the center has its own force but, because it is unnatural to pivot in place as you talk, you can't stay there very long. Sharp diagonal crosses are strong because they allow everyone to participate—the actor is seen in profile, approaching, or receding. In the arena you can lie or sit on the floor and talk straight up to the ceiling because everyone can see you. The floor, in fact, plays a strong role in arena staging since it becomes the primary background for the action.

Taking Control of Stage Space

These exercises are the performer's primer of visual form. Through them they become aware of their own and others' appearance within the stage space. They discover how powerful space can be around and between actors. They see how symmetrical and asymmetrical balance work within stage space. They learn how an object can become an active participant in defining space. They learn how movement and pace change the dramatic effectiveness of space. A performer's ability to command and use stage space will be one of his most effective tools.

A roller-skating street performer in Milan performed in the square outside the cathedral. He defined his stage by simply skating around in an oval from time to time, doing mime tricks and engaging the crowd in byplay. Although three and four rows of people jostled each other to see the clown, the audience never closed in on his imaginary stage. Even when he skated up to tease a child at one end of his arena, the audience at the other end respected the imaginary line. To keep the audience in his power he alternated slow gestures—pulling himself along on an imaginary rope—with swift crosses that ended with sharp stops, startling or embarrassing a spectator. He was in absolute control of his arena.

Transforming the Space with the Body

As performers become familiar with themselves in stage space, they become more active at transforming the space to their own purposes. That transformation can begin with the most intimate space of the hands, arms, and body. One way to approach space is to play, like the mime, with imaginary objects in imaginary space. These exercises may precede or follow the previous movement exercises. Both attempt to ignite the imagination, to fill the void with the energy of the performer's body. If you imagine a baseball in your hand, then you also imagine the space it occupies when you hold it or toss it in the air. When you imagine wind across your face, you imagine where it comes from, and you create distance. The stage space may be so small it exists only around the performer. Or it may grow, to encompass a large arena or an entire theatre. Stage space is brought to life through the performer's insistence on its magic reality. The transformation of "ordinary space" to "stage space" can be delicate or expansive.

If you see me light an imaginary torch in my hand, I can make you duck out of its way. If you toss me an imaginary ball, I will hold up my hands to catch it. Children love to create an imaginary tug of war with an imaginary rope, and if you pretend to cut the rope between them with a knife, they will all fall down. In the end we can create theatre with or without real properties, but we learn from the next exercises to make our bodies serve the imagination of both the actor and the audience.

A simple beginning exercise starts with the participants in a circle.

Leader Dialogue

I will start with an imaginary object I have in my hands. I will create this imaginary object by holding and using it. I will hand the object to the person next to me in the circle. If she knows what it is, she will take it, use it, and then transform it into an object of her own. If she does not know what it is, I must take it back and continue to define it by what I do with it, until it is clear. If she takes it and uses it in a way that I know she thinks it's something different than what I intended, I will take it back, and work with it until she knows what it is. In this way each of us will take an object, use it, change it into something else, use it, and pass it on to the next person.

Side Coaching

Remember to take the time necessary to use the object as it would be used. Don't rush. Feel the actual space that it occupies. Think of the specific details of the object. Think of its texture and size. Take the object and use it. Do more with it, if you can, rather than just repeat exactly what the first person did. Remember to consider the object in space, its weight, how it feels in your hands.

Follow-up Dialogue

Which details were most helpful to expressing the object to the audience? What problems did you see? They may note the difference between clear and bold gestures and small, imprecise gestures. They may place a high value on unusual objects, or objects that were a surprise, or objects used in a surprising way.

Deepening the Experience

At the end of a day, send each person to prepare a scenario using a four-foot, half-inch dowel as the substitute for an object. Each individual is to devise sixty seconds of continuous activity with the object, represented by the dowel. Each person should imagine the space in which he is operating. These should be rehearsed. There should be a beginning, middle, and end to the sixty-second scenario. If every person in the audience makes written notes for ten seconds after each other's presentation, the critiques offered will be very detailed and helpful. Emphasis should be placed on making both the object and the environment clear by the way the person moves and the way the dowel is handled and used. Once again, patience is critical to the success of the illusion.

✳ Transforming the Body

Leader Dialogue

Take a partner. Remember playing "wheelbarrow" when you were little? Someone held your legs and you moved along on your hands? Well, this is an extension of that game. One of you is to become an object—a tool, a machine, a piece of household or office equipment—and your partner is to use the object that you have become. Use your whole body. Don't be afraid to be upside down or roll on the floor. One of you is the "thing." The other uses it.

Side Coaching

Don't worry about scale. What you have become can be in fact very small—like a pair of scissors—but you are it. Try to find the key ingredient that makes the object what it is. Don't be too elaborate in your use. Find the important gestures that indicate using the object. As soon as you have an object and user, hold up your hand and we will stop to watch you. Then you can switch users and create another object. Think simply to get yourself started: a pencil, a pair of scissors, a bottle opener—anything you might use.

Advice to the Leader

This sometimes takes a little work to get going. You are trying to get people out of conventional ways of thinking about their bodies. As they try ideas and see other people try ideas, they will get more and more inventive. Make sure everyone comes up with at least two choices. You are trying to help people imagine with their bodies and create new realities.

✳ Machines

Leader Dialogue

Divide yourselves into groups of three or four. Together your group is to make a machine with moving parts, using your bodies to create the illusion. These can be ordinary household machines like a can opener or a typewriter, or more elaborate machines like a merry-go-round or a drill press. Every person must be actively involved in the machine. You have three minutes to come up with your machine. Think of offices, automobiles, stores, kitchens, factories. Machines, or any kind of mechanical equipment, are everywhere. As soon as your group has created a machine, hold up your hands, and we will freeze and watch your machine working. Then go on and make another one.

Advice to the Leader

In all of these exercises it is important to go beyond the first solution to the problem. It is not unusual for people simply to do something they have seen done elsewhere on the first try. To stimulate the imagination and creative thinking, everyone must be challenged to go beyond the first idea. This is also a way to pass leadership around in the group. At first one person will have an idea. After several tries, everybody will participate. If a group is stuck, suggest where machines exist—weight room, laundromat, library checkout. If one group realizes another has duplicated their machine, both should go ahead with what they started. They will, no doubt, find a different slant on what the others did. It doesn't matter whether or not people guess the machine, so long as it appears to be doing something real. The group can tell us what it is if we fail to guess.

Deepening the Experience

Viola Spolin suggests starting a machine with one person who does not tell what it is. Then other persons must join in as soon as they figure out what is going on. Nothing is spoken. It may be that in the end people are actually participating in different machines in their minds. The important thing is that they are using their imagination to manipulate the mind of the audience.

In the machine exercises, people are drawing on gesture and rhythm and they are creating theatre space. They use their memory of details to guide their imagination. They are also making tiny scenarios, because they will soon discover that if the machine does a full action, with a beginning, middle, and end, it is more engaging. The participants may want to add sounds to these machines. The machine may have different sounds made by different parts. The audience could be asked to contribute the sounds. Groups may wish to select sets of machines that could work together, simultaneously or in sequence. A person might be selected to operate a series of machines, or a set of machines might become an environment for a group of monologues or dialogues.

Bodies can be animals, or elements in the environment—trees, clouds, wind, smoke, a waterfall, lampposts, buildings, or bridges. Human bodies can convert a space into any setting they desire. When a specific movement or gesture captures the precise nature of the thing, making unnecessary any further explanation of the situation, the theatre is at work. A person playing a parking meter rolls his eyes to indicate that the meter is turned on. A person playing a stamp machine sticks out her tongue to deliver the stamp. Theatricality depends on that communicative gesture, selected from other possibilities, timed, delivered, and recognized at the necessary moment. With extension, the gesture becomes the environment for an entire theatrical moment—a street, a kitchen, a post office.

The exercises can evolve into abstractions. Search for the essence of the particular machine. Extend it to the whole body. Repeat it. Take it into one part of the body. Make it part of a human character. People do machinelike things without actually trying to create a specific machine. Bodies do droplets, bodies flutter, pound, fly, cut, trace, knock, grind, rotate, repeat.

We are trying to help each of us reimagine the body and its power to communicate both the concrete and the abstract, to establish a specific setting or to create a mood. This is the body in space, transformed and transforming, bearing a new and heightened reality for itself and us.

Words at the Center

Selecting and Using Literature in Performance

Language, words, speech, talk, chat, chatter, conversation, dialogue, lingo, slang, rap, discussion—there are words, words, words to express the human ability to communicate through subtle variations of mouthed sounds. It is phenomenal, this ability to speak, and we humans like to think it sets us apart from other animals, although we know that languages do exist among other species. No matter, we human beings have worked hard enough at making use of our language faculty to deserve some of the credit we give ourselves for its uniqueness. We have learned to express our enthusiasms, our doubts, our confusions, and our certainties through shades of spoken language. Language and action, speech and gesture are sister wellsprings of drama. We can make theatre with one or the other alone. We can make theatre with either one or the other at the center, or we can make theatre with both in active play. If we wish to take the gift of speech to the center of the ring, then we must harness its power.

Words have power. It is not true that "sticks and stones can break my bones but names can never hurt me." Words can hurt, and they do. They can sting, surprise, delight, caress, engage, alienate, persuade, entreat, entice, seduce, destroy, humiliate, enlighten, inform, amaze, bewilder, captivate, betray, beguile. In short, words are human actions. When we use words in the theatre, we take responsibility for these actions, and we arm ourselves with mighty weapons. Words are loaded guns, a stream at the edge of a cliff, ice breaking up at the water's edge. Words have the potential to shatter the stillness and change the character of the future. They redefine the past. They shape the present.

What to Put on Stage

What words do we choose? Knowing the power of language, we must put onto the stage words that are worthy of being spoken there. The only significant criterion for putting a piece on stage should be: It has merit to be spoken aloud before an audience. This stands for work spoken by children or adults, to children or adults. The work should be worthy of the attention paid it.

We have to put the merit of the work ahead of such considerations as "It has to be short, it has to have one set, it has to have a lot of people in it, or it has to have only two people in it."

What has merit? *De gustibus non disputandum.* There is no disputing taste. One man's meat is another man's poison. What is good for one is not good for all. All things being equal—which they never are—it is fair to say that each individual or group has a right to choose what pleases them. But the theatre has some rights of its own. It is a place that honors whatever happens there. Put something on stage and no matter if it is trivial, profane, commonplace, or banal, our attention is drawn to it. The mere performance lends credence, whether the work is fine or shoddy. And so we must ask ourselves, literally, what are we doing? Are we choosing to stage things for the public, whatever public we call our own, that are worth their time and ours? Or are we giving voice to sentiments and expressions that have little substance or style; that are thin on character, thought, dialogue, and story; that are mere soap operas in disguise or uninspired retellings of tiresomely familiar tales?

A great deal of literature has been written and published to exploit the market for children and adults wanting to put on plays. There are responsible publishers and there are others. There are some good writers and there are hacks. It takes a huge amount of energy and time to discover the strong work, especially when cat-alogue entries are so limited. We propose that it is better to spend time developing performances with original material, favorite sto-ries, letters, magazine articles on current issues, diaries, poetry, and interesting essays than to rehearse and perform a weak piece of drama.

The Selection Process

So far we have said it is important to do good work. But we have offered nothing useful for determining quality. If we are to select material for the theatre that will justify itself once put there, how will we know it?

In the forest of unfamiliar written material, there are some tests that can be applied to finding something that excites your theatrical imagination. It is fair to assume that a piece of literature that is generally regarded as a classic, shows up in anthologies, has survived the ages or won major prizes, is taught in school, is quoted often, or is referred to as a model of its genre is a good work of literature and deserves our attention, at least. But there are thousands of other possibilities as well. Whether you are looking at plays or other lit-erary forms, here are some tests of quality that will help you choose.

The Language Test

Regarding the quality of the language itself, can you answer "yes" to these questions?

> Is there a flair to the words that makes one want to listen to them?
>
> Are the words chosen to create distinct voices with their own unique qualities?
>
> Do the words create strong images?
>
> Can you follow the thoughts and feelings of the speakers without being told what to think?
>
> Does the language reveal relationships through interactions, images, or colorful expressions?

Do the words ring true?

Do the words bounce off each other in a stimulating sequence?

Does the language flow naturally and yet avoid clichés?

Are there rhythms established that carry the energy of the language?

If more than one person is speaking, are the characters given their own voices?

Does the language invite you inside the head of someone or something?

Are there pleasing surprises in the choices of words?

Can you answer "no" to the following or, if you say "yes," has the writer used language in such a way that there is satire or irony intended?

Are the words trite, ordinary, and predictable?

Have you heard all these phrases in these sequences over and over?

Are the speakers recognizable types with no individuality or subtlety?

Are the images predictable?

Are the situations predictable and formulaic? Are they far-fetched for no purpose?

Are we told what the characters are feeling rather than shown?

Do the sentences go on and on without creating any interesting tension?

Does the language feel forced as if trying to be clever or unique without succeeding?

Does it all sound the same regardless of the speaker?

The Subject Test

With regard to the topics and content of the writing, can you say "yes" to the following?

Are the topics addressed with new points of view?

Are ideas revealed through interaction and observation rather than declared?

Are thoughts juxtaposed so as to give new meaning to familiar things?

Are feelings expressed with nuances attached?

Is the listener stimulated to come along with the thoughts?

Are commonplace things charming? Or put into a new framework?

Is something old brought into new relief?

Are myths, rituals, legends, or traditions used for the depth of meaning they carry?

Are listeners taken on a journey, starting at one point and arriving somewhere different?

Are thoughts engaging, enticing, even when they are controversial or unpleasant?

Can you say "no" to the following (always recognizing the possibility that the writer is using a stereotype or a cliché to be ironic or satirical)?

Are demeaning stereotypes reinforced?

Are complex problems given simple answers?

Are commonplace solutions accepted without exploration?

Are classes or groups of people insulted or exploited?

We know that both clichés and stereotypes have their functions in certain kinds of comedy, satire, and political work. What we are challenging are the gratuitous stereotypes that serve only to make fun of a group of people who are often the subject of ridicule. We also encourage you to avoid simple-minded formulas that offer no thoughtful consideration to the material. Soap operas and situation comedies give us all we could ever want of these.

The Interest Test

In the end there is only one central question.

Do I care about what is going on—am I caught up in this in some fundamental way? If the answer is yes, then the piece has a chance to work in the theatre.

Action and Response: What Good Theatre Does

When you are looking at a play, you ask first, "What happens?" But then, and more important, you ask, "What does this play want me to feel or think about what happens?"

Suppose the main character sets himself against a king and is eventually killed for it. That is a basic action in a plot. If the man was trying to revenge his father's death and lost his life in the process, that is very different from a man who is beheaded for standing up for his religious beliefs. One play is *Hamlet,* the other is *A Man for All Seasons.* Our summary is an oversimplification, of course. But the point is that in neither play is the action of the plot sufficient. We learn how to think about these people by what they say and what is said about them. We are given certain circumstances and points of view that we are allowed to consider. They are presented in a certain order, and certain people say certain things. The words let us know how we are to respond, and *how we are to respond* is what counts.

A good piece of theatre makes us see an action or an idea in a fresh way. It gives new significance to human behavior. The gesture need not be grand and the understanding can be fragile. But something must spark a new awareness. Even a reminder that certain images give pleasure or that a story always ends a certain way can have theatrical value. Good theatre is not accidental. The new understandings are intentional. They are the reasons to choose a work.

Determining the Stage Worthiness of Poetry, Essays, Letters, and Other Nondramatic Material

You can always choose to perform a play that already has a reputation and eliminate the risk that the piece may not have theatrical value. But we would like to encourage you to look at untested material, works that have not been constructed originally with the idea of being performed, or works that the group will assemble themselves out of their own writings or a variety of sources. Some of these will have all the characteristics of conventional drama, but many will not.

> In the 1950s and early 1960s, various forms of Readers Theatre emerged on the American stage. The Second Drama Quartet toured with *John Brown's Body,* Stephen Vincent Benet's long narrative poem about the Civil War. Charles Laughton and Cornelia Otis Skinner traveled the country reading aloud, like their cousins on the Chautauqua circuits, making theatre of poetry, essays, stories, letters, and diaries, anything that told a story or painted a word picture. In the late sixties, Paul Sills and his Story Theatre Company used music, dialogue, and narration to stage fairy tales, keeping faith by speaking the original texts. In 1975 The Royal Shakespeare Company created a story theatre version of Dickens' *Nicholas Nickleby,* using long passages of third-person narrative along with Dickens' own dialogue. In each case, someone knew that a particular piece of writing had theatrical value and used the stage to reveal its undiscovered power.

What Will Work in Performance?

How do we decide if a nondramatic work will make a good performance piece? The fact that we like reading it doesn't mean it will necessarily make good theatre. When something works in the theatre, it satisfies the audience's demand for involvement—in action, character, discovery, or point of view, or any combination of these. It engages. It makes the audience want to listen, watch, and come along. A theatre piece takes people on a journey together—a journey in thought, image, place, story, idea—but a journey nonetheless.

> Will the piece (or pieces) engage an audience? Does it catch you up and take you somewhere? Does it invite a listener in?
> A theatre piece is alive. It exists in the present, even when it tells a story from the past. Does the material you are con-

sidering do that? Does it gain something by being said out loud to an audience?

Does the work have a natural build to it? Does it start somewhere and end somewhere?

A piece must satisfy a rhythmic need for changes in movement and thought. Does the work have variety? Does it have any surprises?

The experience must have a sense of wholeness, something having begun and ended. Does the piece let you know it has started? Does it come to a close?

Not everything meant to be read by the eye, in silence, can be translated to the stage. Sometimes that is because there are long intricate passages of speculation or commentary that do not invite the reader/listener to engage in the mental debate. Some long descriptive passages set a scene in elaborate details that lose the listener's attention. Sometimes the comment is so abstract that it requires explanation. Sometimes the text itself is primarily a visual experience or an internal experience of thought.

The Mystery Test

Remember that "suspense" was the first thing on our list when we looked for the qualities of good theatre. We said that every good theatre piece was in some way a mystery. For some reason the audience wants to know what is going to happen. How much can the audience be invited to be involved with the work? To want to know? To care? Theatre is a two-way experience. Something is sent to the audience. The audience must do something with it—absorb it, go along with it, get it, wonder at it, care about it. They send back their concern and the theatre answers them with more to consider. Ask yourself whether your material can make the audience wonder, "How is this all going to come out? What will it add up to in the end?"

This does not have to do with plot. It has to do with engaging the audience in the theatrical journey. The journey can be through an emerging idea or the evolving images of a poem or essay. It can be increasingly ironic observations on modern life through a string of advertisements for a product. It can be combative selections from controversial newspaper articles on a current topic. It can be a glimpse of a life through a diary. It can be a mosaic of comments or stories from a group of individuals on a common subject. Any of these can make us want to know how it will all come out. What will I think when it is over?

Making the Mystery Happen

The mystery lies in the theatrical presentation. If we dramatize *The Three Little Pigs,* the question for the audience is: What are they going to do with this familiar story? No telling of it will be exactly like another. As an audience member, I am engaged because I want to know if their version will be like the one I carry in my head. Whether the answer is yes or no doesn't matter. I carry the question with me and it gradually gets answered.

If we create a stage presentation of something very familiar, like "The Midnight Ride of Paul Revere" or "The Raven," it will be what we do with it that counts. What is our point of view as we present it? We can caress it lovingly. We can make it breathless. We can find it heroic. We can mock it or betray it as well. The action of the theatre requires that we do something. If a literary work inspires no point of view, no desire to say something about it, then it is not a candidate for the theatre.

The Essential Theatrical Reality: Real Time

The theatre happens in real time—while we are all there together. In a sense, that real time is the only reality of the theatre. Everything else about what we do—how we treat past, present, distance, place, characters—can be manipulated, reversed, interwoven, reinvented, fantasized. But we cannot change the fact that we come together at some moment and pass through time together and then separate. What we choose to do together in that real time is the materiality of the theatre. That is what we have to work with. That is what is exciting.

Theatre is relentless. It keeps going. You can't go away and come back and pick it up where you left off. You can't go back to read something you forgot. An idea must be expressed in a way that can be grasped on hearing it. The audience has to be able to get what is going on. They must know what you need them to know when the next thing comes along. Works that are going to be presented in the theatre must be able to be absorbed in the seeing and hearing of them.

As you are considering a piece, read it out loud and find out if you can keep up with all the ideas. Are you hearing much more than you need? Are you getting lost? Do you get bored or tired of reading? If so, the audience will abandon you.

Who Are the Performers and Who Is Their Audience?

If theatre is essentially an encounter of the performer and the audience, who are the audiences? In a way it is a silly question, because each audience is different. Audiences have personalities. They come together for hundreds of different reasons in hundreds of configurations, but we have a few thoughts to offer.

Children, Aged Five to Fifteen

Look at literature and subjects that children enjoy for themselves. It does not have to be from a familiar canon, nor does it have to be about children. Children watch hours of television that is intended for adults. They see the news and commercials. They watch reruns of old movies. Their capacity to work within different genres is quite broad. They like everything from nursery rhymes to mystery stories, to adventure classics, comic books, newspaper ads, television commercials, and street jargon.

They are not, however, particularly interested in long descriptions, lengthy speculation, or highly abstract logical questions. Very few theatre audiences are, in fact. Children aged five to fifteen are a good test for the theatricality of material. They demand variety. They demand involvement. They demand changes in tempo and focus. After lives of television watching in which the image changes every three seconds or less, they are likely to become bored or distracted easily, and they have learned to expect new elements to challenge them. A magician can keep their attention all by himself for an hour because there are constant mysteries. But songs, dances, and uninterrupted dialogue wear thin after three to four minutes unless they advance the story or contain funny action. Children appreciate action and emotion. They like to feel deeply, whether it is fear, pain, ridicule, sympathy, or suspense. They are happy to have familiar stories if the dialogue and action are engaging and/or amusing. Young children are not very interested in love stories unless they are also adventure stories. They like to see themselves as heroes, but they identify easily with all kinds of protagonists.

Children as well as adults will ascribe human characteristics to animals and machines—even to abstract shapes. They are quick to identify character traits through dialogue and behavior, and do not require explanations.

Children like conflict. And as conflict is the essence of drama, they are again good tests of the theatricality of material. But young people like their conflict served up in strong characters and clearly defined situations. They like danger and the potential for great rewards. They like vigorous dialogue that pits virtues and vices. They like to see enterprises succeed after being thwarted and they love to see villains defied. So do we all. Children do not require happy endings, but they do require justice and fair play. They understand that things die, that punishment is sometimes deserved, and that pain is sometimes inevitable. Children recognize cruelty and cleverness. They do not take either lightly, and they can see that sometimes the two are combined and have to be sorted out.

Children are even susceptible to tragedy. However, subtle machinations in which good people are destroyed for abstract reasons escape them. In most tragedy, destruction results from the obvious violation of basic laws, made mistakenly, or for compelling reasons, perhaps on the horns of a dilemma or the overwhelming cataclysm of circumstances beyond the protagonist's control. Willful or accidental, tragic consequences are often as clear to children as they are to adults.

Adults, Aged Sixteen and On

Nearly all of the same criteria apply—well-defined characters, conflict, comedy, and melodrama, as well as tragedy. But adults are much more tolerant of speculation, of conversation that explores relationships and ideas. They are willing to take their conflict in longer sequences and in more drawn-out perambulations. They like the pleasures of word play, of satire and irony—the more pregnant the language, the more effective the theatre. That is one reason that Dickens is so good on stage.

Adults and children both like comedy, but adults are able to pick up social humor and language humor that is out of the range of children. A play like *Harvey*, in which a man has a seven-foot invisible rabbit as a friend, is funny to both children and adults because it is essentially a situation comedy with well-drawn characters and improbable action. A play like *Private Lives*, Noel Coward's witty tale of a divorced couple meeting again with new spouses, is not funny to children, because it is essentially a comedy of manners and social satire. Jane Austen would make very good theatre for adults, because the characters are strong, the romance is compelling, and the social satire is pointed. One suspects children would get bored with it very soon.

Action-Packed Adventure

A piece of literature that demands escapes from prison, chases through forests, battles of armies, or falling off buildings has limitations, especially when these exploits are the center of the action. Such sequences are not impossible for the theatre, but we have to think in suggestion and convention. It takes ingenuity to create stage events that build up the energy and tension that these actions imply. It has been done—and even with minimal technical expertise. The danger lies in attempting to stage literal re-creations of such events. Successful *spectacle* requires considerable technical sophistication; successful theatre does not. Successful theatre counts on the imagination of both the performer and the audience.

Appearances and disappearances, internal images like dreams and daydreams, fanciful journeys that change habitat or encounter exotic species require ingenious solutions. Never say never, but consider the device you will use and its complications before making a decision. A giant or monster or elf, for example, is a nice challenge, perhaps to be imagined through the use of several individuals or a set of gestures. Body language can easily make humans into animals. Masks add other possibilities. Narrative can supply what cannot be shown. Never underestimate the audience's capacity to make believe.

Suppose you are looking at a story full of action. If the narrative is strong and the characters well drawn; if there are plenty of dialogue or monologue sequences—or sequences that slightly modified could become dialogue or monologue; if you can solve the spectacle with simple conventions; if you can engage the audience and take them with you—then you have a candidate.

Does the Piece Have a Punch?

A theatre piece has to start somewhere identifiable. It has to have its own momentum. The listener/viewer cannot go back to reread something missed. And it has to have an end. We need to know that it is over. Stories or poems that drift off into speculation and have no "punch" are difficult to pull off. Of the classic poetic material, Kipling is good. Longfellow is good. Coleridge's narrative poetry is very theatrical. Keats and Shelley are less so because they tend to work in abstract images. Contemporary poetry that is witty, creates characters, gives them a point of view, and makes a clear comment about them is effective. If there is a narrative strand, that is also helpful. John Stone, Rita Dove, Nikki Giovanni, Shel Silverstein, and Diane Wakowski are contemporary writers whose work has strong theatrical potential. David Budbill's poems about a town in Vermont, *Judevine*, have been successfully translated to performance.

Fairy tales from all cultures and from all periods are good for all ages. If you keep an eye out in libraries and the children's sections of bookstores, it is possible to build a collection of American, English, Irish, Italian, Japanese, and African folktales, among others. Those that have a hero or heroine who encounters and surmounts difficulties and defeats villainy, especially through cleverness and cunning rather than sheer force, work well. A single battle, chase, or fight in a piece is more effective than a string of battles or chases.

Length

There is no perfect length. There is only that fundamental reality of time. If we are involved, the amount of time is irrelevant. But there are considerations of how we use the time. There needs to be some buildup. The middle is as important as the beginning and the end. It takes a little time to create suspense, to create the identity of a character, to establish the problem to be solved, to establish sympathy with a protagonist, to reveal the outlines of the picture that is unfolding. There is no formula for the length of the development portion of a work. But the piece can't be over before we've caught on to what is happening, nor should it drag on after.

Theatrical Presence

Theatre makes its own demands. Recognizing the nature of the theatre—its palpable and relentless presence, its constant wholeness, its demand that we attend to all of it—requires our thoughtful consideration. Just as we cannot turn back pages, we cannot close in on an actor's face or switch viewpoints down a hallway or through a door as we can in the movies. We see all of it all the time, and our perspective can only be changed by actions and words of people present before us. Theatre engages our imagination and we contribute mightily to its illusion. But it is a great critic of that same illusion.

Gayley's *Classic Myths* lists the labors of Hercules. "For his sixth labor, Hercules had to clean out the Augean stables that had not been cleansed for thirty years. Hercules ran the rivers Alpheus and Peneus through them, and purified them thoroughly in one day." Neither the labors as such nor the listing of them is inherently theatrical. There is no setup, no dialogue, and the action—running rivers through the stables—is not meant for the stage. However, if we establish Hercules as a character and the labors as his test, we have a theatrical moment. The action itself is more suited for an animated cartoon. Because children have seen a great many animated cartoons, they might see no reason why such an action could not be translated to the stage. They focus on the action and not the telling of it.

Many legends and myths involve sweeping actions or grand explanations of natural phenomena. In the theatre we have to have a reason to want to hear these stories. They may not be essentially dramatic in themselves. They work when the audience has a need to know, when you have a device to create the theatrical presence. Anansi stories from West Africa and Coyote stories from the American West, or Kipling's "Just So" stories play well because they have compelling central characters who draw us to them. These characters respond to challenges. They defeat villains. Their stories have built-in suspense.

Adapting Nontheatre Literature for the Stage

Should a story be rewritten to be translated into dialogue and characters? This is not really the point. A good piece of literature should not be extracted from its bed of fine language and turned into a thin, mediocre play. Rather than convert a piece of narrative or poetry into a conventional play, you can take literature as it exists into performance. We call it "theatricalizing."

The Process of Theatricalizing

There are many works of literature that are delightful when spoken aloud, "theatricalized" so to speak, presented by performers to an audience. Their essence is their language; their means of expression is their words. The words must be kept intact in order for us to engage in what happened and what is said about it. Here are three elements in the process:

1. Whenever the material allows for voices to speak, whether in literal dialogue or in passages that have alternative views expressed, turn the passages into dialogue among performers. Assign voices and create dialogue and monologue as appropriate.

2. Trim and select within the text to keep essential elements and to eliminate confusing passages. Remember the law of real time and the need for the listener to keep everything in his or her head. Material will have to be short and direct. Editing, shortening, and tightening will be necessary.

3. When there is a long narrative passage, it may have within it some currents that change. Several speakers can be used to express these different currents. Moving different voices through the narrative gives the text a personality on stage.

✳ *An Exercise for Discovery: Spontaneous Group Reading*

One way for a group to discover the theatre within a written piece is to read it out loud in an impromptu oral interpretation. We have used it in our Shakespeare exercise. It works here for many of the same reasons. Pass out copies of the work to the entire group. Then the group reads it aloud, *not in unison,* but creating a vocal ensemble on the spot, listening for changes in the tension, discovering the pauses and accents, and spontaneously creating a point of view.

Leader Dialogue

We are going to create a group performance of this poem/story. Your task is to keep this piece going. There are only two rules. The group must keep the work going, and everyone must read something, but no one is to read throughout the entire thing. If you and another person start to read the same passage together, you may go ahead and read it as two voices. If one person starts reading a line, then that person may go ahead and read it as a solo. You can join in at any time, especially when you see a need for a change or a new emphasis. You can lie back and listen, and join in on words or lines that you feel you would like to read. You should read with as much understanding and clarity as you can. It is all right for the whole group to be reading together, especially on parts that are empha-sized. It is all right for single or double or triple voices to be reading. You may join in on an important word or phrase. But remember, you must keep it going.

Side Coaching

Keep the rhythms together. Don't get sing-songy, but listen to the pace of readings of your neighbors and join them. If you start out alone, don't be shy. Take over. Remember, everyone must read something, but no one reads everything. Let others have their say. It is the entire group's job to keep the piece going.

Advice to the Leader

Start reading with the group to get them going. Then listen your-self. You may want to participate as a reader throughout. This device is a great way to get a group to read a poem out loud and to understand its meaning. Because all are reading, no one can just stop listening or following. As a person testing the theatricality of the work, notice the reactions of the readers and listeners. Are they interested throughout? Do they seem to notice good places to put emphasis? Do they bring closure at the end? Is there a group reaction to the piece?

Follow-up Dialogue

What is this poem/story about? Did you think it was funny/sad/witty/ true to life? What parts seemed to work best during the reading? If we read it again, what physical arrangement would you like to add?

✳ Instant Staging: Making the Work Theatrical

If your group has done some of the acting exercises, they will be familiar with the focus and stage composition tasks and with the moving sculpture and poems. Divide up the large group into groups of four or five. Give each group the poem, or separate sections of the poem or story, if it is a long piece. You may wish to move on to a new set of poems and give each group a different one. Then give them this task.

Leader Dialogue

Your task is to go through the piece again (or the new piece you have in your hands) and to divide up the reading among yourselves. You may have some solo voices and some pairs of voices and you may have some voices in unison. You should change voices when there is a natural change in the piece. It is not enough just to have one person read the first part, another the second part, etc. The division needs to make theatrical and dramatic sense. Think of contrast and emphasis. If a new idea comes in, change the voice. If there is a feeling of question and answer, change the voice. At the same time, begin to think of the stage composition and movement you would like to use to stage the piece. Think of levels, shapes, focus. You may have some movement as you go. Use the readers to give a clear idea of the work to the audience.

Side Coaching

If it is a new piece, you may want to try doing a group reading like what we just did to get started. As you are reading through your piece, discuss what is being said. Imagine how it will sound and look. Remember all the acting tasks. Be truthful to the meaning. Stay in the moment. Divide up so that everyone has a good chance to read. Plan the action and composition so it helps the focus, but also trust the spontaneity of your group. Someone may have a good idea as you work. You can use chairs, tables, stools, or just stand, sit, lie, or walk. Get on your feet soon. Try doing some reading and let people move spontaneously. Take advantage of the creative energy of everyone. Don't overplan.

If you don't understand something you have to say, clear it up. You cannot be expected to speak something you don't understand. Avoid getting too literal. You don't have to "act out" the poem. It is better to express its basic tone or ideas. Or if you want to act out something, then be very selective. And remember, no indicating. Be honest to the underlying sense of the material.

Advice to the Leader

Allow about ten to fifteen minutes for this activity, especially if it is the first time. Avoid losing spontaneity in the staging. The longer the group has to plan, the more likely they are to be too literal or too full of clichés, especially if they are inexperienced. As they get experienced at staging material, they will be careful to avoid clichés or indicating gestures and will work instead for ingenious and unusual ideas that bring out the inner values of the material.

Leader Dialogue

You have two more minutes, and then we will present these to each other. When you are ready, indicate who wants to go first, second, etc. When your group is ready, tell us where you want the audience to be. Audience, listen, and do what they say. Be a good audience. Remember, spontaneity is good. Just stay in the moment and everyone make your contribution.

Follow-up Dialogue

Audience, what really worked for you in the different pieces? What features stood out? Were there any movement or composition ideas that seemed to be especially effective? It is the leader's job to try to find effective features in everyone's presentation. Then ask for performers' comments on their own experience. *What part did you especially like doing? How did the ideas get generated? If you had time to work on it some more, what would you do?*

Deepening the Experience

The groups can decide to make a complete work of the pieces they have created, or put them together if they are parts of a long work. They may decide to take individual ideas from each other and create a single piece that uses everyone. Each participant can bring in a poem or story he or she would like to add to be worked on. The small groups can each do four or five pieces and create a complete ten- or fifteen-minute performance, devising movement or sound transitions between the pieces. Then the entire collection can become a full performance. Music, sound accompaniments, or some form of consistent simple staging device, prop, or costume embellishment might be considered, especially if these seem to create a point of view for the whole.

✳ The Five Frames Exercise

Mapopa Mtonga, of Zambia, and director of the Grass Roots Theatre and the Centre for Performing Arts at the University of Zambia, gave us this exercise. Once you know a story or a poem, or you have established a scenario, create five *tableau vivants,* or still-frame pictures of events or scenes within the story. This is a way to express the basic outline of the story and to discover essential images.

Leader Dialogue

Think through your story or poem, and find four or five key moments that you can express with a frozen scene. Everyone in your group should be in the scene. Let each member of the group determine how he or she wants to contribute to show the action in each scene. Set up the order of the scenes, and practice going from one to the other. When you are ready, we will show the freeze frames to each other.

Side Coaching

To begin, just think of a scene. If you have an idea, go ahead and take a pose and tell the others what you are doing. Let them join in as they figure out how they can contribute to it. Then go on to another scene. Don't try to plan everything. Each individual can think of how he or she can contribute to a scene. You can be a person or a part of the scenery. When you have five still frames, put them in order and practice them once in sequence. Remember, still frames—no movement.

Advice to the Leader

This should happen in five or six minutes. The idea is to summarize or redramatize the work and find its key moments. Give the group a one-minute warning and then bring them together for showing.

Leader Dialogue

Now, audience, when I say "Eyes closed," you close your eyes. The group will get into position. When they are in position, I will say "Open." Look for a few seconds, and I will say "Close." The group will change to the second freeze frame. Then I will say "Eyes open," and so forth until we have seen all the freezes.

Follow-up Dialogue

How can you use this exercise to stage your pieces? What if you added some simple embellishment, such as a drum, or hats, or dowel rods, or bells, to each of the frames? What if you added the change movement so that we saw both the changes and the freeze frames?

Variety and Consistency

Presentations for an audience can be spontaneous, like these exercises, or they can be rehearsed and developed at length. In all cases, variety and consistency are both important. Changes in voice, changes in composition, variety in a still composition, changes in mood of text, changes in rhythm, dynamics, vocal tension, location of voices—there are endless sources of variety. The principal source of variety may be in the works chosen. It may be in the various ways voices evolve. A person can speak her own narrative as well as her own dialogue. Variety creates surprise and surprise creates suspense. And suspense is part of the theatre mystery. What will they do next?

Consistency tells us that these works are part of a theatrical whole. Consistency can come through themes, staging devices, the visual look of the work, the use of clothing or properties. We will say a lot more about that.

The group will find that it has endless ideas about what to do with a given work. Part of the fun will be deciding on the ones that are most interesting and that fit together to make a whole.

Life and Art

Yes, we are going to make art. In art, one makes choices. In life, one may not be able to exclude or include things at will. One has to make do. But our goal is to discover how to make art out of life. In our case, it is the art of the theatre. *So we make choices, we don't make do.* We decide what belongs in our work and what does not. The criterion for deciding is our aesthetic point of view.

Establishing an aesthetic point of view is one of the principal differences between an artful performance and a disjointed or meandering one. The artistic point of view is the glue that holds a work together. We are putting a frame around things. We are deciding what fits within the frame and what stays outside it. We are doing what artists do—creating out of what exists, according to a set of guiding principles that we have established.

We have talked some about theatrical conventions. The next exercises and discussions elaborate on the use of theatrical conventions in creating work out of material other than play scripts. These comments also apply to any production. These are decisions about how we look at the work and how we want the audience to see it.

Bert O. States, in his difficult but illuminating work, *Great Reckonings in Little Rooms: The Phenomenology of the Theatre,* is very helpful in making us understand the way that theatre works in the mind of both performer and audience. He helps us see that theatre puts aside everyday reality and organizes a reality in and for itself. Audiences accept what is created as the theatre's reality, and they participate in its assumptions. One illustration he uses is the difference between the audience's response to an actor on stage and to a live dog. The audience knows the actor is acting—making art—and that the dog cannot do this. The dog can only be itself, trained, or not, even if it is a bona fide character in a play. Consequently, there is a break in the theatricality of the moment when the dog comes on stage. The audience hopes the dog will do what it is supposed to do. In fact, anything the dog does will attract attention to itself. The dog cannot entertain the duality of the theatre. The dog cannot make art, but the human being can.

Creating an Aesthetic Point of View

Whatever form the work eventually takes, it is critical that there be a guiding aesthetic. Each small group must have a guiding concept that includes what belongs inside the art and what does not. If props are used, they must have some consistency in their quality. If some costume device is used, it must be there to consolidate as well as differentiate. Hats, for example, might be all that are needed, but in that case, there must be hats used on everyone or a hat used within every piece. Or everyone might wear a distinctive pair of gloves or dress in black. But whatever device is used as part of the theatrical moment, it must hold together as a consistent element, fitting with other choices, even as it may be varied or deliberately omitted to make a point.

Transitions need to be worked out so that they tie one element to the next. Transitions should also have an internal logic. They fit with the transitions that have preceded them. They carry the audience along the journey we prescribe.

The aesthetic choices will come from some point of view about the material. Are we helping you discover something about each poem? Does each poem have some tie to the one that preceded it? Are we strangers? Are we your friends? Are we inviting you in or keeping you at a distance? Are you to take this part seriously and then feel free to laugh at this other part? The point of view will guide the audience's response and let them in on the artistic reality of the theatre moment. Since engagement is our goal, letting the audience in on our point of view is essential.

Exercises to Establish Conventions and Understand Aesthetic Point of View

Assemble a set of items that might be used as generic props or embellishments: a collection of percussion instruments, simple black Halloween half-masks, large pieces of sailcloth in plain colors, large bags sewn at one end made out of tubular jersey (to crawl inside and make abstract shapes), large-scale household tools like plumber's helpers, brooms, brushes (to be converted into whatever objects are needed), or a set of one-inch dowels, three-feet long.

✳ Making Objects

Using one of these prop items, invite the group to experiment with their imaginations creating everything they can using the prop. Lay out the household tools.

Leader Dialogue

If these mops, brooms, plungers, and brushes were all you had to play a scene, how would you use them? Think of a situation. A police scene? A shipboard scene? A farm scene? When you have an idea, don't tell us, just take the prop and use it to establish who you are and what you are holding. For now, let's keep these ideas silent. If another person gets the idea, pick up a second item and join in. Try to make different things that belong in the same scene.

Advice to the Leader

Let each one go as long as it is generating new ideas. Call freeze and ask for another one. Give people time to think. Encourage all to try ideas.

Follow-up Dialogue

What choices worked for you? Why? Listen for the elements of surprise, appropriateness, originality.

Leader Dialogue for Deepening the Experience

Let's return to the five frames. Here are the dowel rods. Use at least one but no more than three dowel rods and integrate them into your five frames. Use the dowel within the context of the story. You can use it as a literal object or as a design element. It can be just an abstract line or a symbol. You can choose not to use it in some scene, but it must be left out for a reason. You may wish to add movement. Find out what the dowel rod can do for your five frames.

Side Coaching

Try different possibilities. Discover how you can unify your five frames with the dowel rods. Consider focus. Consider variety. Resist the temptation to illustrate everything. Remember that the dowel rod is also a simple straight line all by itself.

What did you have to do to make decisions about the dowel rods? Listen for thoughts about consistent use, the important elements of the scene, how they looked, what different uses they could make. Note that the group is using the convention of the dowel rods to provide unity and consistency—a guiding aesthetic—for their work.

✳ More Generic Props

Lay out a cloth on the floor. Use a piece of sailcloth that is about four feet by eight feet and in a solid color. Blue works well because it inspires ideas about water and sky.

Leader Dialogue

This is just what you think. A big piece of blue cloth laid out flat on the floor. But what else could it be? When one person has started to use the cloth in a way that you recognize the situation, you may join in to indicate that you know what is going on and join in the use of it. You can talk or not, as you choose.

Advice to the Leader

When a group has used up an idea, call "freeze" and have them put the cloth back as it was. Let people take plenty of time to set up a situation. It may be that a person is not clear enough about what they have chosen. Ask them to keep at it, working differently until others know what they are doing. Start with the cloth laid out on the floor. Then, if the group does not do it themselves, give the cloth to two people to create a wall, and then see what others do. Then try giving it to four people to hold up as a roof or sky. Stop when the group seems to be running out of ideas.

Follow-up Dialogue

Notice the difference between very abstract ideas and concrete ones. That is, when the cloth was used as something made out of cloth—a blanket, a sail, or a robe—and when the cloth became something else–sky, a wall, or water. The point of view changes toward the prop when it goes beyond itself. We are beginning to get clearer about the idea of establishing a convention.

Think of how you can convert the cloth to something theatrical— as a backdrop to action without being anything in particular, or desig- nated stage space on the floor. A cloth does not have to represent some- thing made out of cloth. It can be a concrete object or an abstract idea. It can be wind or sky. It can represent a division of space or a concept. Think about the chair dance and consider the cloth the same way you considered the chairs.

✳ Adding Sounds

Lay out a box of noisemakers and musicmakers, such as drums, wood blocks, Lemme sticks, bells, tambourines, whistles, tin whis- tles, folk flutes, Chinese noisemakers, ratchets, and any other items that create varied sounds. Let the group experiment with the sounds that can be made with these.

Leader Dialogue

Gather in groups of four or five. Your group will create either an animal or a machine with some of the group. The others in your group will use sound to express the action of the machines or the animal. Experiment with sounds that accompany action or sounds that express dialogue. Coordinate the movement of the animal or machine with the sounds. When you have an idea, show it to the group. Then create another one.

Follow-up Dialogue

How did a prop or a sound idea used in different ways make a comment on what you created? Imagine making a whole theatre piece with just one generic prop, using it in as many ways as you can imagine. What do we mean by the notion of consistency of the attitude toward the work and the embellishments?

Advice to the Leader

The literal thinking reinforced by movies and television is tough to overcome. Sometimes you will want it. But the theatre has the great possibility of going beyond the literal. You may have to try many times to get people to understand that they can extend an idea, embellish it, underscore it, and reflect on it, as well as illustrate it.

In the beginning, most people, adults and children, will see generic props and embellishments simply as substitutes for the real thing. That is great, especially when you use a category of objects for all the props, as we did with the brooms and brushes.

But sometimes people just look around for something that could work. A tambourine gets put on a head to become a crown. This is what we mean by "making do." Its value as a music-making instrument is gone. It can no longer be true to its nature or embellish as music. It is simply a literal substitute for a hat.

In the same way a group may look at the whole array and take dowel rods for swords, the big piece of cloth for a cape, and drums for the sound of explosions. None of these elements has the chance to perform a variety of tasks or to be used as a convention. A theatrical convention contributes its own value to the art. It extends as well as facilitates the meaning of the work. It ties things together. It makes its own comment.

Follow-up Dialogue

What happens if you mix different points of view in the same piece? For example, you use the cloth literally as a blanket and then abstractly as the sky. What is the difference between using a lot of elements and using one element all the way through? When does it get muddy?

How far can you stretch the use of a thing? When have you converted it beyond its nature? This is a subtle notion, but you can figure it out. A cloth does not have to represent something made out of cloth. It can be a concrete object or an abstract idea. But if you ball it up and use it to be a rock, does that work? It is a difficult idea. You have to work it out case by case.

Consistency

If you establish the convention that in a fight scene no one is ever touched when struck, then you cannot have someone get touched. If you establish the convention that all characters speak with funny voices, then they all have to speak so. A set of conventions becomes an aesthetic point of view for the piece.

Exceptions

Exceptions can reinforce the convention. If everyone except one character wears a half-mask, then we know that the one character is special. If everyone is in black, but one is wearing a red bow tie, the exception makes a point. A clearly identified exception is a means for defining focus. An exception might be for a whole section, or for a particular moment in a work.

✳ *Finding a Point of View for a Simple Piece*

Select a familiar story. We have used both *Little Red Riding Hood* and *The Three Little Pigs*.

Leader Dialogue

Going back to small groups of four to six, each group is to create its own version of the story. You can use sound equipment or generic props or just your bodies and voices to create what you need. You can use chairs, tables, or nothing. You will have twenty minutes to come up with your ideas. Whatever you use, however, stay consistent with its use; if you make exceptions to your devices, make them with care. If you work silently, then keep it silent. If you use props literally, keep them literal. If you establish the convention that speaking is eliminated and music or nonhuman sounds are substituted, then that cannot be violated—or if it is, the purpose of the violation must be clear. You may use anything from the sound box or the prop box, but be selective. Take a point of view toward your piece, and stay within that point of view. You may use narrative, dialogue, or both. Have fun. Experiment. Then make your choices.

Side Coaching

Get on your feet to try ideas. Check out if everyone knows the story. Everyone is a contributor. Select what you want to work with. Remember your own bodies can be houses, tables, chairs, whatever you need. Simplicity is a virtue. Leave room for spontaneity and improvisation as you work. Remember your machine exercises and your ability to create theatrical space from simple elements. If you decide to use an element, use it all the way through. Avoid the trap of simply substituting a generic prop for a literal object. Consider the quality of the object itself and what it has to say.

Advice to the Leader

Go around to see if the groups are having trouble getting started. Let them know that they can move the narration around from person to person, or have each character speak his or her own narration. Invite them to remember the nursery rhyme and composition exercises to get started. As they are developing their work, you can shorten or lengthen the rehearsal time, but don't let them overplan or stand around too long. Give the groups a five-minute warning and then one minute to finish. Then ask who wants to go first and where they want the audience to be. Let each group instruct the audience. Encourage them to enjoy and to stay in the moment. There is likely to be some improvisation in the final performance. That is fine.

Follow-up Dialogue

What ideas worked well. What you would like to do to polish these into a final performance? Ask the group to notice aesthetic choices and points of view toward the piece. Ask the performers to comment on their decision-making process.

From Workshop to Main Stage

The processes described with poetry and familiar stories can stop at any spot in their development. They can be class or group exercises intended only for the illumination of the literary work for the participants themselves. They can go on to be small-scale presentations at meetings or for workshops, or they can move to a fully produced and realized stage event for a general public.

If the performers want to create a full-length piece of theatre, they have only to identify what it is they want to present to an audience. We stress from the beginning that a work of theatre ought to be worthy of the time people are going to spend on it. It should be something the group genuinely wants to do, something they feel strongly about, something they believe has something to say to an audience.

> In the 1990–91 Broadway season, theatregoers were taken by the power of a work created from John Steinbeck's *The Grapes of Wrath,* developed by the Steppenwolf Company of Chicago under the direction and literary guidance of adapter Frank Galati. Galati is a working member of Steppenwolf and was a longtime colleague of Chicago improvisational artists Paul Sills and Viola Spolin. He and the company understand the value of literary language and the capacity of the theatre to tell stories. As a group they were moved by the great drama of the Joad family's trek to California in the worst years of the dust bowl and the depression. Thus, the piece grew out of passion and commitment, and the result was a stunning evening of theatre that told a story people wanted to hear, using dialogue from the novel, songs, and the Joad's car as the basic set piece and prop.

Over time a group will make hundreds of decisions: selecting material, cutting and arranging, establishing sequence, choosing the voices. They will create compositions and movement. They will decide how to extend meaning with embellishments. They will establish their own theatrical conventions. They will decide how it is to look and how to add focus and make the ideas clear.

There is no strict formula for this work, but there will be a gradual process of refinement as movement ideas are clarified, as compositions are corrected, as actions are simplified or elaborated, as timing is sharpened. One set of changes may affect others. The process is organic: pieces may come and go, parts may get longer or shorter, sections may get combined, roles may shift.

If a group takes on a long story as a whole, there will need to be a lot of discussion about how the individual parts are to be worked out and then connected, and what will be the thread that ties them together.

Much of the finished work will come out of group exercises, sent back to the groups for more development. A few leaders may emerge who seem to have a strong sense of the way a piece is heading. If the group is doing a collection of pieces, it may be that different people will take the lead on different sections. Side coaching will be required to keep a sense of the whole as individual parts are created.

You are making difficult decisions. You are doing high conceptual thinking. You are developing a guiding aesthetic as you work. You are making art!

As you adapt material, a few guiding principles may help.

1. Be true to the character of the original piece or pieces. If it is whimsical, keep it whimsical. If it is gloomy, find its gloom. If it is melancholy, present it as such. Be true to its language and make cuts with loving care. You may simply be eliminating some "and he saids" or you may choose to eliminate an entire subplot because it is too hard to keep the audience clear about what is going on.

2. Include all the performers in the performance and give them interesting things to do. Avoid having a couple of people narrate and a couple of people "act out." That gets boring quickly, though it might be appropriate for a short passage. Pass responsibility around. Let people perform things they really want to do.

3. Remember that variety helps everything. Repeat only when repetition is called for to make a point.

4. Be conscious of the physical composition. Any composition will work if chosen well: a straight line, people moving rapidly through space, people artificially posed, people naturally posed. Just be sure your composition and movement contributes to our understanding of the piece and your point of view. And over the length of the performance, vary everything.

5. Have your beginnings and endings tidy so the audience knows what is going on.

6. Experiment with ideas before settling too quickly on one.

7. Remember the audience and treat it with respect. Be sure it can see and hear what you want it to see and hear. Remember the focus exercises.

The chapters on guiding performers, choosing stage space, creating simple stage furnishings, and costume and sound embellishments will provide specific details on ways to rehearse a piece of theatre to make it a public event.

Length of Material

If people are going to leave their homes to come see a theatre event, it probably should last at least fifty minutes or so. If a theatre event is part of a series of events, then ten minutes, twenty minutes, half an hour—whatever seems to work is fine. There is really no requirement. If the audience is intended to include children, an hour's time limit should be considered. A sit of more than sixty minutes can be very trying for children under twelve. Adults like short works, too. On the other hand, if children are having a wonderful time, they will sit for hours. Wouldn't you?

If there is continued interest and action, continuing mystery, continuing intrigue with what is going on, the time will pass quickly. The length of the work will be of no consequence. A sharp, short piece of five minutes, especially if it is a work by children, will be just as satisfying as a long one. "Suit the action to the words, the words to the action," as Mr. Hamlet has said. There is no magic in the formulas of Broadway or the West End. You are your own producer. You will gather your own audience. There is nothing to require one act, two acts, or three, and if the work is powerful, no reason to limit its length.

It is the work and the suitability of the performers and their audience that will guide you. If children are engaged in the excitement of presenting something they care about, you can help them sharpen it for the audience. If adults have found a work they care about, they can develop a process to make it theatrical and meaningful. Once the match of performer and material is made, the rest will be satisfying hard work. The time is best spent making that set of choices.

Rights and Copyrights

A piece of writing is the product of a creative mind and labor. The author, at least while living and for fifty years afterward, has a right to receive income based on his or her work. Hence, the limitations on making free photocopies of books. The author has a right to have the book sold and to receive income from the sale. Likewise, the publisher, who has invested money in creating the book, has a right to have the book sold and not copied. The law argues, however, that the right does not go on endlessly, and that at some point, works become public domain. But by renewing a copyright, an author or an author's estate can continue that right for a number of years. Similarly, the law argues that there is a "fair use" notion for copying material for use in classrooms and one-time workshops and meetings, and for use in part rather than as a whole.

The great majority of contemporary material (written and published within the last hundred years) will be under copyright. If you are doing a piece as part of a class or workshop, *with no public exposure intended beyond the working group*, then you can feel free to use anything in print. Authors, after all, write so that people will read them, and familiarizing people with their work is what they hope for.

However, if you wish to do any public performances of copyrighted work, you must obtain permission. That means poems, stories, articles, essays—everything. Write to the publisher. Permission will usually be granted. You may be asked to pay royalties. That is, after all, how writers earn their living. If you are an educational institution making no profit, you should identify the scale of your budget, the size of your audience, the number of performances planned, the approximate dates, and the limitations on your ability to pay. If any of you are earning money by your stage work, royalties will become a way of life.

If you wish to do an adaptation for public performance that significantly alters a living or copyrighted author's work but uses its ideas and language, you will need permission from the author or whoever owns the copyright.

If the material you use is folk literature—no one person's adaptation of it—or classics that are in public domain (not specific translations of them and published and not renewed for copyright for at least fifty years), you are free to do whatever you like with the material; there will be no copyright or permission issues involved. The fact that an author is dead does not guarantee public domain. Spouses, children, and estates often exercise strong control over the use of an author's work. This must be investigated. Look at the copyright information on the inside cover of the book.

It is the obligation of the artists, teachers, and theatrical performers to be responsible for the rightful use of someone else's material. It is not the author's responsibility to police the world to find violations of the copyright. Gross violations of copyright have been perpetrated through copy machines, and the publishing industry has used its legal avenues to establish their claims. Authors have naturally been supportive of these legal actions that help guarantee them income from the sale of their work or the use of their material.

The whole copyright issue makes the use of classics (not specific translations under copyright), folk material, and original writing very attractive. However, one should not hesitate to contact authors, especially poets and short-story writers, about using their works in performance. They are often flattered and may even try to come to see what you are doing. Authors vary in their reactions. Some consider that once a work has left their hands, it is up for grabs, to be read and interpreted however it will. Some are very protective and would, if they could, control the reading of every word. The best way is to write to the author, in care of the publisher, and explain your intentions.

Writing for Performance

*W*ill it surprise anyone if we report that the repertoire of plays done across the country in high schools and community theatres is tired? It includes a cluster of scripts written between 1935 and 1965, a sprinkling of more contemporary work from the New York theatre, and a list of well-worn musicals. Most of them have conventional set, property, and costume plots. Few address the needs of either young people or ambitious amateur performers. In spite of the efforts of a small group of responsible publishers, too many collections of scripts for children are there only to exploit the school market. They are dominated by material that is unimaginative, trite, or dull.

We have both been part of this history. For years we accepted the scripts anointed by London and New York—both on and off Broadway. We produced them, along with a canon of Western European classics, in regional and community theatres, and we taught them in the textbooks and anthologies in our courses in dramatic literature. We watched through the sixties, seventies, and eighties as theatres who produced an occasional new play relegated them to single slots and rarely sought work from within their own communities. We believed that what theatre has been was all that it could be.

Encouraging Alternatives

However, we are living proof that people can learn. In the same sixties and seventies, a rift began to form in the theatre world as politics generated street theatre and free theatre. We saw a desire to escape conventions turn inventive people to performance art, happenings, and improvisational play making. Mabou Mines, The Performance Garage, the Hysterical Ontological Theatre, Jerzy Grotowski, Joseph Chaikin, and Richard Schechner are famous examples. They clustered together with companies. They wrote their own material or rewrote traditional material. They built an audience of interested friends. Eventually they wrote books. They spun off and involved new people. We paid attention.

What we discovered in our work with teachers and community theatre was that theatre of this sort didn't get translated into alternatives for working at the school and community level. There the legitimacy of Broadway and academia retained its controlling interest. Alternative theatre did not lend itself to the creation of large institutions. It did not often penetrate the productions at universities where people got their basic theatre education. Even the wonderful writers of work for young people—people like Susan Zeder and Max Busch—are known only inside a small fraternity of children's-theatre producers.

Then, in the eighties and nineties, Broadway theatre took its audience to the most lavish spectacles since the Romans flooded the arena and staged sea battles. Extravagant musicals became plays about scenery and effects. People jumped off bridges, chandeliers fell, buildings pivoted and exploded, actors roller-skated over dizzying heights, and people came away humming the set. This is what you were most likely to see if you went to New York. This is what toured to major cities. This is what sells CDs and T-shirts. These big spectacles have colored many people's imaginations and confused all of us about what theatre is and can be.

In the meantime, as if to prove the fundamental pliability of the art, small independent companies and individuals—Theatre Grottesco in Detroit; Theatre de la Jeune Lune in Minneapolis; The

Road Company in Johnson City, Tennessee; Lime Kiln in Lexington, Virginia—and their kindred spirits in dozens of unexpected places have insisted on creating their own magical theatre, small in scale, committed to the basic inventions of the stage. Whenever we have seen them, they have reminded us that theatre still needs only imagination—"four boards and a passion."

During these same two decades, the eighties and nineties, art in America has moved from being driven by a generalized canon and aesthetic to a multiplicity of sources and communities. Another regenerating force for theatre has come from African-American companies, Asian-American companies, women's companies, Hispanic companies, gay and lesbian companies—making theatre within their own communities, out of their own stories and their own agenda, creating their own scripts, and working with minimal production conditions.

Some of this highly individual work has received wide audience acceptance in spite of its audacious simplicity. Spalding Gray's *Swimming to Cambodia* required only the actor, a chair, and a table. Jane Wagner's solo piece for Lily Tomlin, *The Search for Signs of Intelligent Life in the Universe*, had a complex light and sound plot in production, but its essence was Tomlin on stage alone. Whoopi Goldberg introduced us to a new family of characters through her own flexibility as a single performer. From Chicago, Steppenwolf's spare production of *The Grapes of Wrath* depended only on the elegance and truth of Steinbeck's writing. Adapted by Frank Galati with simple theatrical devices, it had a successful New York run.

However, the general public, including parents, teachers, amateur theatre groups, and children in school, are much more aware of the big sensations: *Cats, Phantom of the Opera, Les Miserables, Starlight Express*. These precedents throw down a daunting challenge. How can a modest group of students, amateurs, or other serious beginners satisfy an audience titillated by all this wonder? We have to restore the fundamental nature of theatre. We have to write and produce our own work.

Writing for the Theatre

There is enormous satisfaction in performing your own writing. Writing for performance begins with the exercises we described earlier: telling each other's stories, moving in the stage space with sentences of dialogue, personal statements added to body sculptures, taking other literary forms and performing them. Singly or combined, these exercises lead to work that can be polished for an audience.

The next step is to write dialogue and monologue and structure a script that has its own internal drive. Here are a few simple exercises that help children and adults develop those skills. If they find themselves eager to write more, the lessons they learn in these exercises will continue to assist them.

Dialogue Writing

The first thing to remember is that theatre is made up of dialogue and action: the things people do and what they say about them. Plots in themselves are not theatre. They are just plots. Unfortunately, new writers believe they have to come up with a plot first, and when nothing clever comes to mind, they become discouraged from writing. Remember, Shakespeare rarely, if ever, made up a plot. He borrowed them from other stories, historical materials, and other plays. He modified and changed them, but his genius is not in plot. It is in commentary, play of character, juxtaposition of ideas, exploration of images—brought to us through what the players say as much as what they do. Therefore, the first exercises are directed at discovering how to make characters speak on stage.

✳ The A-B Dialogue Trick

This strategy is credited to screenwriter Jim Cash, whose movies *Legal Eagles, Dick Tracy,* and *Top Gun* were big hits in the 1980s. Jim, whose partner Jim Epps lives in Hollywood while Jim writes in

East Lansing, Michigan, taught a screenwriting course at Michigan State University, and he started his students with this technique. Since learning the trick from Jim back in the late seventies, we have played with it, modified it, and used it again and again with writers of all ages.

Leader Dialogue

You are going to write a dialogue. Your characters are just A and B, for the time being. You start with a sentence, any sentence. Eliminate any "Hello, how are yous" or other introductory trivia. Look around you and let something that strikes your eye or mind start you off with the first sentence. It might be "I wonder how they got the holes in the ceiling board," or "I just hate it when my right sock is bent one way and my left sock is straight up." The sentence might come from something that happened in your day or something you heard someone say. Whatever it is, that becomes A's first line. Then let B respond to the first sentence. Then A goes on in response to what B says. Remember two things:

1. The essential ingredient of drama is conflict. *Let A and B have conflict. One reason love scenes are so hard to write is that two people telling each other how terrific they are is boring. Two people in basic agreement are boring. If they agree, you don't need both characters. Let conflict emerge.*

2. Let the dialogue tell you who these people are. Don't force it. *They will be just A and B when you start. As they talk, they will become distinct characters with personalities. They may become specific people. Go ahead and start writing.*

Side Coaching

Don't worry about where to start. Just make an observation and assign it to A. "I'm out of toothpaste." "This room is stuffy." "I saw that blue dress on a sale table. Now I'm glad I didn't buy it." "I hate the smell of the lunch line." "If I have to sit next to Donald, I'm not going to walk into that room." "The windows in this room are exactly square." Once A makes a statement, it is up to B to respond. Then A has to say something back. Let it go on as long as it keeps going. You may find that it has a natural close. Conflicts don't need to be resolved. Let ideas leap across gaps through what people say and how they respond to what someone else says. Feel free to have nonsequiturs and misunderstandings. Feel free to have single words and interruptions. Listen in your head for how people really talk. Tensions can build. Good drama is based on the building of tensions, and on wondering how the conflict will end.

Advice to the Leader

That's all it takes to get started. You may wish to write along with them. It lends credibility to their own work. Keep your eye open for when the writing is beginning to die down and people are looking around or waiting. It may go on for fifteen to twenty minutes, depending on the age and concentration powers of the group. Call a minute for finishing. Then invite participants to read their dialogues to the group. They can just read the lines. They don't need to introduce A and B. Encourage everyone to read, but respect someone who really does not want to read aloud. People sometimes write quite revealing or intimate material, even in this simple exercise. They should not be forced to subject themselves to public scrutiny. Acknowledge that, but encourage people not to censor their work because it is not "good" enough. Since people will be writing in longhand, it is better to have them read their own work. Others will have too much trouble reading handwriting to be convincing. You may have to solicit reading to get started. You could read your own writing at some point.

Follow-up Dialogue

What elements really caught your attention in the dialogues? Did you get to know the people? Did the dialogue seem honest? Honesty in dialogue means it sounds spontaneous, unforced. The characters may be fantasy figures, but they still must speak honestly. *Can you hear two distinct voices? Finding the voice of a character is part of bringing a person to life on stage. What kind of words do they use? How do you know they are two different people?*

Note details that made things especially real or true. Discuss the element of specific detail as part of writing, as you made it part of acting. Little details anchor characters in our minds.

Talk about the nature of the conflicts within the dialogues. *Ask, Did you hear tensions? What moments had the most validity? What had the most compelling interest? Try to analyze why. As writers, can you tell us how the dialogues evolved. What led you in particular directions?* See if they have discovered the spontaneity of a character writing itself, of surprising the writer with what they wanted to say.

Let writers discover the principle that it is better to reveal feelings and relationships than to tell them. Discovering indirectly, or in passing reference, is more interesting than being told what to think. Do not tell us a character is unhappy. Make her unhappy by what she says and does. Do not tell us a person is kind, make him kind by what he says and does. This is even true of events and relationships. Exposition is necessary in the sense that we need information to carry us through the action. However, it is more efficient and interesting if characters slip the exposition into dialogue that is also exploring character and relationships.

A: I hate your Aunt Flora.
B: How did you know I just talked to Aunt Flora?
A: You have that "aren't I cute" look.
B: I do not.
A: And you start denying everything I say.
B: I do not.

If we need to know that Aunt Flora raised A as a child, we can find out without A's saying, "You know my Aunt Flora raised me since I was three, and I love her as if she were my mother." As the writers gain more and more experience, they will become skillful at revealing rather than telling. It is a fundamental axiom of good writing.

✳ Monologue Writing Out of Dialogue

Think of a monologue as simply a long speech by a single person. A monologue can be an internal dialogue spoken out loud. It can be a dialogue with the audience. It can be a long solo speech made in the presence of another person or persons on stage who listen but do not say anything. Any good long speech will have its own inner tensions, its own questions that are asked and both answered and not answered. It will have its own conflicts. To practice monologue writing, use this exercise:

Leader Dialogue

Pick one of your two characters, A or B, and explore their thinking with a monologue. It can be an inner dialogue with the character speaking out loud, or it can be a speech meant to be heard by someone else present on stage. The monologue may start from something within the scene that you wrote or it may come from somewhere else in that person's life. A monologue may come from inner tension and conflict. It may come from memory or fantasy. It may come from wonder or dismay, but it will be articulated in words that reveal feelings and attitudes. Write a monologue for one of your characters. "To be or not to be" is one of the English language theatre's most famous monologues. Think what it does—how it goes from thought to thought. Let your character's mind do the same sort of questioning and commenting.

Advice to the Leader

Allow fifteen to twenty minutes, and then invite the participants to read their monologues aloud to the group. What you will discover is that everyone can do this. Everyone can write dialogue. Everyone can write monologues. Some are better than others, but all can do it. Once people discover that they can write for the theatre, they are unstoppable. It is not necessary that these initial monologues and dialogues have the capacity to go on to bigger and better things. These are beginning exercises. However, someone may discover a person, a character, a situation that inspires her to go on writing. Here is the start of something bigger.

Deepening the Experience

The next task will be to expand on the dialogues and monologues, to begin to ask the question, "What if?" What if another person enters the scene? What if these two people talk under different circumstances, before this dialogue? After this dialogue? What if a monologue precedes this dialogue? What if one of them does something drastic—unexpected in the previous dialogue—becomes ill, quits her job, invites an ex-boyfriend to the house, decides to relive his life and wants to start all the conversations over again, decides to come to live with the other character, gets thrown in prison, or just does something simple that somehow makes a difference to these people—forgets to buy groceries, loses her car keys, brings in the mail, runs a stocking, spills spaghetti sauce on his tie.

The whole group may take one of the scenes and play "What if?" Or each individual may play "What if?" with his or her own scene. Or you may divide the group into several small groups who play "what if?" with each of the participant's scenes. *The writer does not need to accept any of it.* Writing is very personal. People need to own it. Brainstorming for another writer has to be done with the recognition that these are just ideas thrown into the pot. One of them may catch on or spawn a new direction a writer wants to explore.

Side Coaching

At any point in writing, your characters may write themselves into a corner, with nothing more to say, no further conflicts, nowhere to go. You have several options. You can quit there and decide to keep the dialogue for later use, or abandon it and start something new. You can have one character make a jump with a totally new thought and start fresh. You can go back and see where the conversation took the turn that led to the dead end and change it. Have them say something different. Or you can introduce a totally new person into the scene in order to see what will happen.

Advice to the Leader

A-B dialogue writing never wears out. It is a way to start over and over again, letting characters work out things they have to say to each other. It is a way to discover new facets of a character. It is a way to discover new characters. In the process of collecting dialogues, writers may start altogether different scenes and then realize they belong in the same play.

Making a Whole Play

If a scene and some characters begin to have potential for the writer, this is where the real play begins. It can take any form suitable for the content of the work. It might end up being one long monologue. It may be a series of dialogues strung together. It might be a string of monologues. It might get hung onto a simple plot that is made up out of the characters' experience or borrowed from somewhere else. Eventually the playwright will have to consider how the people get on and off stage. And eventually the playwright will have to figure out how to begin and end the whole thing. These things are rarely thought about completely before writing. It is the writing process that reveals them to the writer.

Plays actually develop in this haphazard way. Many writers have spoken about plays and characters writing themselves. They seem to take on a life of their own and dictate what they must do or say. What happens in this process is that characters and situations develop. Relationships are revealed. Gradually they become more complex, and events occur or are invented that alter the relationships or reveal answers to hidden questions.

We don't claim that there is no work involved! Writers must learn to structure their writing. We have to edit, arrange, make connections and alterations in our work. We learn that what A said in this scene really belongs in the mouth of B in the next one. We realize we have written the same scene twice and have to get rid of one of them. But for now, the job is to get writers writing, to get dialogue going, to get characters to come to life.

What About Plot?

It is very difficult for people to "think up" a story. That makes it seem very hard to write for the theatre, since so much has been said in conventional literature about the importance of plot—exposition, inciting incident, rising action, climax, reversal, resolution, and denouement. These are valuable concepts, and understanding them can help with fixing a theatrical piece once it begins to take shape. However, it can be paralyzing to start with an attempt to construct a conventional plot.

We say, never mind the plot to begin with. Start with what comes much more readily to mind—people talking; then a set of situations can form around them. A point of view about them begins to take shape, and we realize how we want to reveal their conflicting wants and needs to the audience. We begin to see what we have to keep secret, what we want to hint about, and what we want, finally, to reveal.

Sometimes a situation cries out to be a play. It may be a conflict among people you know. It may be an item in the newspaper around which you can construct a set of people and conversations; it may be a relationship you know about or an event you've heard of.

The play becomes what the audience knows, what they become desirous of knowing, and how it is revealed to them. These, of course, are the essential ingredients of a plot. But we don't necessarily start with trying to come up with a set of events. We discover it by writing dialogues and monologues, by listening to what our characters have to say and how they say it. We find their distinctive voices. We begin to take a certain attitude toward them. We begin to want our audience to think about them in a certain way. We take a point of view. As we let our people talk, they tell us who they are and why the audience should care. Gradually we discover what they do in order to reveal themselves and their stories to the audience.

Writing Exercises and Prompts

Writers need stimulation the way painters need subjects. It is not necessary to drive through a piece of writing like a car speeding down a freeway. Digressions and side trips enrich the view of the landscape. Here are some of our favorite tricks.

✳ *Place Memory*

Leader Dialogue

Remember the exercise of going to a place from your childhood. Close your eyes and see if you can take yourself there now. Remember the details—the smell, the temperature, the objects, the surroundings. Take your time to see it clearly. Put yourself there. Now put someone there with you. When that person is clear, write a dialogue with that person in that space.

Advice to the Leader

Allow five to ten minutes for people to recall vivid memories. Some may wish to write monologues. Let them. The purpose is to find the stimulus for writing in the memory experience. They can put anyone in the dialogue.

✳ *Diatribe*

Leader Dialogue

In the next two minutes, make a list of things that need fixing. These could be small things like a switch in the bedroom or big things like world hunger. Think fast. Don't censor. Write them down.

Side Coaching

Offer starting points if people seem stuck. "My haircut," "political cam-
paigns," "those little plastic tags you have to cut off new clothes, but you
never have a pair of scissors when you're trying to get dressed in a
hurry"—things to stimulate the thinking of the group. Warn people
when they have only a few seconds to go.

Leader Dialogue

Let's go around the room and read down the lists, quickly. No comments.
Just the lists. Now, once you have heard all these things, you are going
to pick one—from your list or someone else's—and write a monologue for
some character who is going on and on about that topic, something
wrong, something that annoys him or her a lot. This character could be
you, or it could be a character you create. This speech might be addressed
to a particular person or to a general audience. Let your character say
anything you've always wanted to say about the subject. What do you
feel strongly about sometimes and just want to get off your chest? Write
that monologue. Let it meander. Let it lead to anything it wants to lead
to. Just fire up and go.

Advice to the Leader

Once the group has written their diatribes, invite them to read
them aloud. As with the A-B dialogue, not all will want to share
publicly. You may invite them to read to a single partner. It is
valuable for the author to hear aloud what is written.

These little speeches can help define a character, help create
vitality in a voice. It is important to have strong feelings on the
stage, and it is important that not all characters are completely
reasonable or rational. We enjoy the committed, the slightly nuts,
the extreme. These monologues will help define characters and
help the audience move along the journey. Also, remember, people may go on and on about some trivial annoyance when they are
really trying to say "I hate my life" or "I don't believe you" or "I
am lost" or any other fundamental human affliction. The diatribe

can serve the purpose of revealing fundamental truths about a character or relationships even if the topic is hangnails.

✳ Wishes and Desires

Leader Dialogue

Do you wish something particular would happen to you? Or that you could do something you've never done? Large or small? Trivial or of great import? Let A tell B about it and have B call it into question. Write that dialogue.

✳ The Darker Side

The next exercise belongs several sessions into your work as a group. Not everyone will be able or willing to do this. You will have to develop a sense of the readiness of a group of writers to use this strategy.

Leader Dialogue

Think of something about yourself that you don't like. Attribute that quality or feature to character A. Have character B needle character A about it, or otherwise call it into question. Or write an inner dialogue about it. This can be a personality feature, something you've done, something physical—anything you truly find unfortunate in yourself. Let your discomfort be a driving force in the writing.

Side Coaching

Writing will be good only if it comes from truth. Truth is not the same as accuracy. Don't confuse accuracy and truth. *What you write may not be accurate. You may have given one person's qualities to another person, or put two events together, or changed what really happened to what might have happened. That is the writer's job. Write what you know to be honest. You often have to sacrifice accuracy to get to the truth.*

Truth means real feelings, real conflicts, real struggles. The events may not have happened but they are what you know would really happen if things went together in a certain way. Don't hide from the truth in your writing. Don't cover up or protect your characters from their own truth. You have to write from tough places, from mean places, from hurtful places. You have to recognize when you are hiding something. If your character is hiding something, that is different. Characters do that. But writers have to know it.

Writers have to betray people and themselves. *If you are not prepared to do this, you are not prepared to take the consequences of being a writer. Only those things we would* rather not reveal *are interesting. We are not talking about confessionals of personal history or psychodrama, but rather revealing the real nature of feelings and experience. Good theatre comes from seeing the deeper levels of human experience. Funny or serious, minute details or huge events, we want to feel the honesty of it. Deeper levels can be revealed by little things—tiny details, halfhearted jokes, offhand remarks. Being embarrassed by two different colored socks reveals a sensitive shyness; laughing at a girl's discomfort over her first bra reveals a desire to hurt. A desire to hurt may reveal an injured person.* If you cannot betray a person, you may not be able to write about them. You may have to stick to writing about those things that you can betray.

Advice to the Leader

All of this side coaching will come at an appropriate time. You will not be able to guide people through all the stages of their writing development at once. Not everyone in the theatre will want or need to write at this deeper level. But the group will want to have good writing. These exercises are some ways to get to it.

✳ Being a Good Listener

Try to teach your group to be helpful critics of each other's writing.

Leader Dialogue

Could you hear the characters' voices? Tell the writer what you heard. What did you want to know more about? Were there any special details that made the moment work for you? What were they? Does this writing connect to any other writing that this writer has done?

Advice to the Leader

Try to keep people from rewriting other people's work. If they start with "you should" then ask them to simply tell what you, the listener, missed or wanted. Let the writer decide how to respond. "I wanted to hear more from Aunt Clara." "I couldn't follow why David did what he did." "I loved the fight between Clara and David but it was over too quickly for me." Then the writer can decide whether or not the scene needs changing and what to do with it.

Group Writing

A great deal of wonderful theatre develops from group writing. People of similar ages often have similar themes. Or people of different ages may choose to look at something from many points of view. Childhood memories, favorite places, parents and children, understanding a new place, discovering pain, being betrayed— these are just a start at possible topics. Getting a group to write a piece for the theatre can begin with monologues or dialogues. If the pieces seem to go together in some way, then they can be turned into a theatre piece using the same techniques we have offered for other people's poems and stories. *What you are searching for are the stories people have to tell.* It may surprise you that *not everyone recognizes their own stories.* Discussion about the topic will lead to people telling stories. It may be necessary for a leader to point out when people say something that is their story. It is not something they need to make up. It is their story, the thing they have to tell others.

Finding the Structure

In the case of a group work, and often in the development of individual pieces, the conventional notion of plot is irrelevant. What we are talking about is a dramatic structure, a structure that creates a sequence, that has contrasts and development, and that arrives at some concluding element. When you are putting a work together, consider what pieces make good endings, good beginnings, good development. What pieces contrast with others to keep the dynamics varied?

The Reality of Actual Time: A Useful Premise for Thinking About Structure

We need to go back to the idea that theatre is an event of a specific length of time for an audience and performers. That actual time is the only reality. It starts when the audience enters the room and it ends after the curtain call. In that time together, the audience goes on a journey constructed by the performance. Every minute of that time is an exchange between audience and performer. It is created through mutual understandings that build upon one another. Information is given and taken. There are setups so that people can laugh at jokes; there are introductions so we can know what to expect; actions and dialogue that reveal who people are and what they think.

We can jump forward and backward through imagined time or we can have action that takes up the exact two hours. We can be mystified and find out later the truth of the matter. We can discover that we made wrong assumptions and find ourselves corrected. We can share insights with some of the performers, and watch others who are out of this special knowledge. All we need are cues to where we are.

The playwright and performers must make that real time count. At the end of the journey, the audience knows something it didn't know before. When the audience and the performers leave the room, they have something they made together. The play, the theatre piece, is the vehicle for them to do that.

Form and Structure

To make theatre time work, it has to be structured. Form and structure are always an issue in making art. Art is built on premises and assumptions. It is not random or haphazard—even when it uses randomness or accident as one of its premises. When we put a piece of theatre together, we connect things for a purpose. We have to answer a number of questions.

> How do I engage the audience in the action? Do we have hooks to bring them in? What are we revealing and what are we leaving unanswered?
>
> What are we doing to their feelings? Whom do they like? With whom do they identify?
>
> Does every life on stage have its own validity, its own legitimacy? Even the antagonists must have real things to say!
>
> What is the mystery? What does the audience want to find out?
>
> How do we keep the tensions going? Are we adding to the information in a way that makes the audience want to stay with us?
>
> What are we writing about? Does anyone care?
>
> Who has to talk about these things? What people have to be in this piece?
>
> What other perspectives do I need? What scenes have to be here so we know what is going on?
>
> What has to happen to make our ideas clear? What stage or story events are needed?
>
> Why is this person saying this now? Is this the best spot for this revelation?

Each moment in the theatre is driven by what the writer/performer wants the audience to know or feel at a particular time in the journey. It is the journey that counts. Our job is to keep them wanting to go the next step.

Here are twelve considerations to help construct a theatre piece that moves along with real momentum:

1. Make each scene or element take us to a new place in a relationship, or reveal a relationship that augments or complicates what has happened before. Avoid writing the same element over and over in simple variations, with the same issues and the same problems unresolved. Or, if that is what the piece is about—that people keep repeating the same issues and the same problems—then each scene needs to have its own particular twist on that problem. Variety is as important in writing as it is in production.

2. Don't end the piece before it is over. A lot of thin writing has many endings in which there are no reasons to go on to another complication, other than the desire to write longer. Leave each section with some element of question or suspense, some element of tension that compels the audience to want to go on. Leave knots untied, questions unanswered. At the same time, avoid answering one whole set of questions and then raising entirely new ones just to keep the piece going. That is, of course, how soap operas sustain themselves. And, just as any rule can be broken to good effect, remember that a lot of good farce is based on the apparent resolution of a problem with a last-minute complication undoing the resolution and starting the plot going again. The key? Know what you are doing to your audience as you make your choices.

3. Vary the length of elements. Move around short dialogues, long dialogues, monologues, quick exchanges, long exchanges. Consider that major changes in the dynamics— the energy levels, revelations, or complications—can happen at any pace, but it is better if they happen at a pace that is in contrast to what has just happened.

4. Work on endings—of scenes and of whole works. What interaction needs to happen to make the point? What

does the audience need to let itself down properly? What tension needs to be resolved or maintained? What new question or mystery needs to be begun? A-B dialogue exercises can help write endings. Sometimes you will write an ending long before you have written the entire piece. It just happens in a dialogue experiment, and you know that is where you want to be when it is over. Then you have to work on the complications that arise before they can get to that spot.

5. Remember that the audience has to keep the whole piece in mind as it watches. Be aware that things need to refer back, or to reflect back or to be somehow consistent with what has gone before. Wholly new elements need to be introduced with care, with some logic and preparation, even if they are surprise elements.

6. Don't hesitate to play with embellishments, with flights of fancy, interruptions, or diversions. Things do not need to be pursued relentlessly. Apparent tangents can shed new light on the whole.

7. Let individual characters or poems or narratives have their own peculiarities that contribute to the complications and subtleties of the relationships. Let them have their own stories and subplots. You can always cut if you have too much.

8. Decide what you are writing about somewhere in the writing. Are you writing about children's dreams? About men and their work? About growing up? About being a mother? About having an adventure? About being afraid? About being honest? At first you may not know exactly what you are writing about, but somewhere it will be clear. Let that decision guide you as you develop. Discover what you think about what you are writing about. That will guide your conclusions and your complications. Don't be afraid to have conflicting ideas. That will make your piece interesting. You can also be writing about

more than one thing. But you must know what you are writing about.

9. Mix arguments and fights with speculation, memories, humor, songs, tricks, or whatever comes to mind. Don't hesitate to laugh or cry as you write.

10. Use yourself—your most intimate thoughts, doubts, and fears—and those things you have seen in others to bring truth to your writing. Writers cannot be afraid to reveal themselves and others to the world. Only the deepest truths will finally be interesting. Don't be afraid of being confused. The revelation of your confusion and working out its possibilities will be the core of your theatre.

11. Avoid the one-joke, one-issue piece. You may have a funny idea, a pet peeve, or a burning passion, but then you realize that this single idea is the only thing you have going. You may not need to write a whole evening's work about it. Perhaps it wants to be a piece of dialogue for one character, a story that someone tells, or a moment in another scene.

12. Avoid beating dead horses. Some points can be made glancingly, obliquely, from references or inferences. It gets boring if characters lay in too heavily on a point that is obvious or that has already been made. And sometimes people use other topics to get at real issues. This is what Chekhov and Harold Pinter's writing has taught us. People may talk about chrysanthemums, but they are really accusing each other of neglect, or indifference, or cruelty. Audiences are smart. They get things. They don't need to be beaten over the head with points of view. Of course being oblique for its own sake can be annoying. Pay attention to what you are doing to your audience.

There is no formula as to what must be in a piece of theatre. We offer as proof this short list of very successful theatre works with very different structures.

Christopher Durang: *The Marriage of Bette and Boo*

A son delivers a series of monologues about himself and his family, which he compares to characters in Thomas Hardy as if he were doing a school paper. Scenes from the life of that family are played out, not necessarily in chronological order, and largely as he remembers them, often distorted and bizarre, sometimes repeated.

David Mamet: *Glengarry, Glen Ross*

A set of short scenes among a group of real estate salesmen, in which we learn about their lives and relationships, are centered around a scam they are pulling. The short dialogues carry all the action of the play.

Lily Tomlin and Jane Wagner: *The Search for Signs of Intelligent Life in the Universe*

A one-person show with a set of characters, some of whom return and have a continuing story and some of whom make single appearances. A particular character, the bag lady, reappears often and acts as a sort of guide. Some of the appearances are very short. Some scenes are as long as twenty minutes.

A. R. Gurney: *The Dining Room*

A dining room is the witness to generations of family scenes that are connected by the fact that they take place in the dining room. These scenes reveal a lot about the class and attitudes of the family that owns the house. They are not in chronological order.

Thornton Wilder: *Our Town*

A stage manager introduces a play about a town in which there are many short scenes of town life, centering on two families. Chronology makes leaps. One character dies and asks to replay a scene of her childhood that was seen earlier. Dead people talk in the cemetery. There are no props and everything is created in mime by the characters. The stage manager freely stops and starts scenes to make a point.

Arthur Miller: *Death of a Salesman*

Some scenes work back and forth in time, showing themselves to us as we need to know them to understand what
has happened to Willy. Others are happening in a theatrical present. Willy's mind is wandering, and we wander with
him as we see the family confront his decline.

Tennessee Williams: *The Glass Menagerie*

The narrator, Tom, is telling us why he left home. He reen-
ters the scene back in time where it is played out in chronological sequence. He talks to us about his present life
between moments in the story with his sister and mother,
and then he brings back the present at the end.

Emily Mann: *The Execution of Justice*

We hear actual testimony from a court trial juxtaposed
so that we are forced to consider the events and their
reality.

Neil Simon: *Brighton Beach Memoirs*

A pubescent boy talks to the audience about the gross injus-
tices he suffers at the hands of his family and interacts with
them in scenes that reveal their trials. His asides to the
audience give us his ironic perspective and are the source of
the audience's enjoyment of the story.

In these pieces you will find direct address to the audience, dialogues and monologues both short and long; many characters; few
characters; multiple performers, single performers; multiple settings, minimal settings; overlapping time sequences; linear time
sequences; fantasy; realism, plot, and plotlessness; single action;
absence of action; attempt to understand past action; daily life;
exotic life. There is simply no rule. Each thrives on the inner tensions of the theatrical moment.

Each writer has set a conceit, or a device, and then used it. Each
work sets its own limitations and expectations. The writers made
their own rules and then stuck to them. They found their guiding
aesthetic.

One way of thinking about structure is to recognize that there are a few basic plot structures that people have used over and over with a thousand variations. You can use any of these without hesitation and make your own variations. All you need is something to hang things on, some framework that allows you to talk about what you wish to talk about, to explore the characters and relationships that fascinate you.

Here are twelve classic plots and an essential technique to try:

1. "I've Got a Secret." There are many variations as to who has the secret and who knows it. The character may have a secret and people find it out as the play goes on. One group may have a secret and keep it from another group. The secret may be known by the audience and not by the character. In that case, the audience watches the character find out. *Oedipus Tyrannous* is our most famous example.

2. "The Trial." A trial is inherently dramatic. There are two sides and there is combat, and someone wins and someone loses. *St. Joan, The Andersonville Trial, The Caine Mutiny Court Martial, Twelve Angry Men*—not to mention an abundance of television series—suggest that actual as well as conceptual trials are always good meat for theatre. Some scenes within other pieces are trials—positions weighed, arguments presented, judgments made. The trial is a metaphor that serves theatre well.

3. "The Wager." In a sense, the wager is a version of the trial. Someone bets someone that he or she can do something. The conflict is built in.

4. "The Contest." Not the same as a wager, but with the same ingredients, a person or a set of people compete for stakes that may be cosmic or trivial. They may be life and death. The audience is hooked wanting to know who will win.

5. "Boy Meets Girl, Boys Loses Girl, Boy Gets Girl." Love stories are the stuff of musical theatre, Shakespeare, even

Chekhov and Strindberg. They have tragic, romantic, comic, and ironic potential.

6. "Mistaken Identities." From Plautus to Shakespeare to Feydeau, mistaken identity can be the source of comedy or tragedy.

7. "The Misunderstanding." Likewise, a misunderstanding can lead to comic or tragic complications. The misunderstanding can be intentional or accidental. It may promote the telling of many stories. Misunderstandings are basic to farce.

8. "Why the Leopard Has Spots." Plays are often hung around explanations, or discoveries of reasons for something that exists. One version reveals that the obvious reasons are false. An important variation: "How I came to be the way I am."

9. "Tell Me a Story." Another cousin of the "why" series, theatre work sometimes is based on a group of stories of people who happen to be in a particular place at a particular time. *Roshomon* is a play about four versions of the same event told from the point of view of each participant. *Chorus Line* began with dancers telling stories about dancing. Once the stories were collected, they were hung on a plot of "the contest"—who will get cast? A "boy-meets-girl" subplot was intertwined with the stories and the contest. Together they made one of the longest running Broadway musicals in New York history.

10. "Whodunit." From Hamlet to Agatha Christie, audiences are intrigued by questions of murder and thievery, crime and punishment. But the questions do not need to be about crime. The variations include "Did he do it or not?", "Will she be found out?", "Who is telling the truth?", "Will the evildoer be punished?"

11. "Robin Hood." A lot of plays are about righting wrongs. Some happen by magic, some by ingenuity, some by

charisma and character. Sometimes "Robin Hood" is a variation on the trial and the contest.

12. "Peeling the Onion" or "The Archeological Dig." Each moment uncovers still more layers of something until it is quite different from what it appeared to be. Each layer compels us to know more. In *Top Girls* by Caryl Churchill and in *Betrayal* by Harold Pinter, we start out with one set of assumptions and work backward through time until we discover a different set of realities. "Peeling the onion" is often combined with "I've got a secret."

We don't mean to make light of major dramatic works. They are great because of the depth of their characters, the strength of their dilemmas, the wit and poetry of their language, the revelations they offer us of human nature. But they are often hung on very basic structures or combinations of structures.

The Setup and Payoff

An old saw of the theatre is the proposition that if there is a gun on the set or a gun mentioned, it has to go off, or pointedly not go off, because once its presence is known, the audience expects a response. Facts stated, events mentioned, topics raised, attitudes identified, characters introduced should be there for a purpose and should have some payoff, however subtle. Theatre makes demands that each piece be part of the whole, connected by some thread to other elements. Certainly tangents and embellishments are possible, variations and excursions are desirable, but in the end, things must seem to be a part of the same performance. Jokes, revenge, punishment, justice, revelation are all possible as payoff only if they are set up. References of all kinds are more enjoyable, more meaty to the audience, if they have been let in. If we know a character doesn't like bananas, then banana jokes have more impact. The setup and payoff are part of the craft that make story or plot devices work, that make a whole of many parts.

✳ Mapping a Final Piece

Advice to the Leader

Once an individual or a group has created a collection of dialogues and monologues that seem to be leading to a single work, once characters are developing and a basic sense of what the piece is about is becoming apparent, it is necessary to map the likely nature of the whole event. One way to do this is to make a visual map.

Leader Dialogue

Collect all you have written or thought about writing that seems to go into one piece. Assign each scene, written or not, a title and assess its weight. By "weight" we mean how important each is and how much time it takes. Using different colors of construction paper, cut out shapes that represent the nature of each piece that is either imagined or written: big shapes for weighty items and smaller ones for single moments or connecting tissue. Use the same color for similar pieces—either for scenes of a certain quality or scenes or monologues of certain characters. Let the shape reflect what it is—small and gentle and round, big and explosive, a long string that runs through other things. Write the title on the paper and place these on the floor, on a table, or on a big piece of brown paper—some place where you can see them and move them around.

The idea is to figure out what goes next to what; what comes early, what comes late; what makes a good beginning or ending. At first, just place things where you think they might fit. We will take time to arrange them as we get a look at what we have.

Side Coaching

Remember, theatre is sequential in actual time, but it can do anything with imagined time. The map is where you begin to see the audience's journey. What should they know first? One thing will come after another. Perhaps a spoken and a silent piece will go on simultaneously. Our job is to construct a visual map of what will take place. You can move things around. What will the audience experience moment to moment?

Advice to the Leader

This process can happen quickly or it can take several weeks, with new work being introduced and changes being made until you feel you know what you are creating. If you are working on a big sheet of brown paper, you can use removable stick-on dots to hold things in place temporarily.

Try performing segments. People may feel a section needs to have weight added—made bigger. One story may need to be broken up and told in pieces throughout the work. Another story may become the framework on which everything else is hung. Other elements may overlap or be excerpted or combined. People will discover where they need transitions. They will discover repetition and see ways of cutting.

When a map seems to make sense, it is time for the writer(s) to script the whole work in the order they have mapped out. They can then perform it and see it happening. Changes will inevitably occur as the work evolves in production.

To prepare for this exercise, a group may wish to take a theatre work that already exists and make a visual map of it. If you really want to get better at writing for performance, read every piece of theatre you can get your hands on and go see work everywhere. *Don't hesitate to borrow.* You can pick up devices, conventions, and structures. The theatre of every age and every nation has something to teach you.

Remember that in this age when most of us get 80 to 90 percent of our information from film or video, it is important to be clear about what can be done on the stage and what the film medium can do. Theatrical performance must account for the whole stage, for the entire picture at all times. People have to come on and off. Entrances and exits must be written. Once a person is on stage, he or she has to be accounted for. People cannot appear and disappear. Dead bodies on stage have to be removed in the course of the action. Young writers are tempted to use blackouts and lighting effects to get around the need to understand the physical, fixed reality of the perpetual stage space.

Advice to the Leader

At the beginning we say, "no blackouts" and "no stage directions" unless it is a basic action of the plot. ("He kills her. He runs off.") No directions like, "she smiles knowingly." The job is to write dialogue that allows the actress to know how to play the line and to get on or off stage. Action should always be possible on the simplest bare stage. "He disappears in a crowd of children that seem to come from nowhere," or "She looks down the hall and sees a door open" are both actions for a movie rather than the stage. The best way to test the playability of something is to perform it as soon as it is written. We think writing for performance should be integrated with acting and performing—in exercises, in small bits, as part of the whole task of learning to make theatre. The immediacy of the theatre is its great virtue and its own discipline. Learning to manipulate that immediacy is what writing for the theatre is about.

Finding Personal Source Material

Family histories, town histories, individual histories are rich source materials for theatrical writing. Even sketchy material can provide the backbone for interactions that become dialogues and monologues. When there are letters or diaries or other first-person records, they can be used verbatim as monologues. Most things will need to be cut and edited. But it is important to use the actual language of the original text. Some rearranging may be necessary. Try to choose sentences that tell the experience most colorfully or succinctly and reveal the kind of person who wrote them.

Unless you are doing a documentary for its precise historical accuracy, you should feel free to invent, rearrange, and reassign material. It may not matter that there were two maiden aunts, not one, or that it was really a cousin who said this. What is important is to get the words into a dialogue. One character may need to have a particular personality in order to reveal the real nature of an event, even though that neighbor or judge wasn't like that at all. Remember, accuracy and the truth are not the same thing. You are striving for a theatrical truth that reveals a situation to an audience. So you give grandmother's characteristics to mother, and make a scene that really works. Remember, only you will know—and after a while you, too, will forget. The characters will live their own lives.

Newspaper articles are begging to become theatre—everything from the tabloid murders to little one-column, human-interest stories. You can decide to research the details or you can make them up. Sometimes these newspaper stories have plots built in. Your job is to create the middle parts, the complications, and to ask the question, "What am I writing about?" Does it matter what precisely did happen? You write what must have happened, given these characters and the situations as you imagine them.

The Living Newspaper is a theatre idea from the thirties that is still valid. Have the group look for print media, either a topic they choose or one provided. Then they search for actual written sentences, phrases, or paragraphs. They may be trying to expose the way people are lured into buying things by the promise of being beautiful to the opposite sex. They may want to look at AIDS or homelessness. They may want just to be silly and try to find all the words used to describe dental care or all the statistics of baseball. When they have collected their material, they assemble them using all the tests of variety and rhythm. They can perform them adding music or sound. The news people have done the writing work for you. It will be the editing and the structure that makes the piece.

A drama teacher in Arlington, Virginia, worked with her class on a piece they called, "Two, Twenty-three, Ninety-three." On that February day, each student was to get something from a newspaper, journal, magazine, or memo that had the date 2/23/93 on it. It was to be an item that caught their attention for whatever reason. They assembled the work and made a piece of theatre from it. It included obituaries, ads, sales, weddings, political news, school memoranda, personal and business letters, and international events. The thread that tied them together was the date. There were one-sentence pieces, collages of phrases, and longer monologues. They created a living time capsule of that day. The work made a statement about contemporary life in Arlington, Virginia, much the way Thornton Wilder's *Our Town* made a statement about life in New Hampshire at the beginning of the century.

Group Personal Writing

In the summer of 1991, a group of twelve junior and senior high school teachers were part of a theatre workshop at Virginia Tech. They tried the A-B dialogue exercise, and the results were a startlingly effective group of writings. To illustrate how this technique works, we reprint three of them. They are purely spontaneous responses to the exercise, without further development or editing. It will be immediately apparent that a theme evolved in this writing, and that it would not take long for that group of twelve women to build their own theatre piece. Here is Jean's:

A.   Just wanted to call and see how you're doing, Mom.

B.   I'm all right, I guess. Feeling my aches, though. Went to the doctor this week. But you know, they don't tell you anything. I'm so tired all the time and my toe is all swollen up I can hardly walk and I have this rash on my body. I told him I thought my arteries were closing up again, and I think I have gout—but he didn't do anything.

A.   But what did he *say*, Mom?

B.   Oh, I don't know. He just said these things happen with age and to take my vitamins. But they're so expensive.

A.   Why don't you go to another doctor, Mom?

B.   This one is close—they're all alike.

A.   Do you want me to come home and help you find another one?

B.   No, no. I'll get along.

A.   Well, let me know what you want. Let me tell you our news. We're so excited. Bill and Mary are going to have a baby.

B. Oh my goodness! I hope they know what they are doing. Babies cost a lot of money. They're not settled yet . . . They should wait until they are settled.

A. Look, Mom. What would you have them do now? . . .

Here is Joyce's:

A. Well, your daddy's feeling a little better today, but he still has that cold.

B. Is he taking the allergy medicine the doctor gave him?

A. No, it makes him feel so woozy and it doesn't help too much anyway.

B. You should call the doctor back and get him to send you something else.

A. Well, maybe we will if he's not better in a few days.

B. Mother, he's been feeling lousy for three weeks. It won't hurt to just call the doctor.

A. Well, maybe I will, but I hate waiting around for him to call back. I've got to run out to Kroger after lunch. They've got a good special on chicken breasts. You know, if you just pick up a few things when you see them on sale and freeze them, it can make a big difference. I got all that corn last summer on a real good special. Dottie Hancock paid 39 cents an ear last week and I didn't do a thing but just take a little out of the freezer and put it in the microwave. I had some roast beef left over from Sunday and some of those good biscuits that your daddy likes. And I opened a can of green beans and cut up a tomato. We had a right good little supper. 'Course I guess it would be easier just to buy corn fresh when you need it. You wouldn't have to go to all that trouble to freeze it, but I tell you I just hate to pay those prices. I guess growing up in the depression—we just didn't have money to throw away. We made do with what we had. Your daddy says I'm being fool-ish. We have more money now that he's retired than we ever had, but I still don't see any sense in spending if we don't need to. We've got everything we need. We don't really go anywhere that I need a lot of fancy clothes. I almost never wear that mink jacket he bought me for Christmas. I guess I ought to try to wear it more often. He really shouldn't have bought me that. Why do you think he did that?

And here is Meredith's:

A. We are surrounded by blackness.

B. I hadn't noticed.

A. How could you *not* notice? The ceiling is black, the walls are hung with black, and . . .

B. And . . . ?

A. And . . . nothing

B. And I'm wearing black. Is that what you mean?

A. No—let's talk about something else.

B. No, let's talk about what you said.

A. What did I say? I've forgotten.

B. You always do this—say something that will provoke a reaction from me—something that implies a judgment, and then you walk away emotionally, leaving me to deal with my feelings alone. . . . Not this time, Mother.

A. Why are you so upset—all I said was—we are surrounded by black.

B. It's not what you said, Mother, it's the way you said it.

A. I just said it.

B. No—you said it with disapproval. I know it was my choice to come here. Disapproval. That's what I heard. That's what I felt.

A. You are too sensitive. I was just making conversation, after all . . . and I still don't understand why we had to come here? Wouldn't we have been happier at home?

B. You would have been happier. But I chose to come here. You could have stayed home.

A. Alone—

B. Being alone is not so bad.

A. Being alone is death.

It was an accident of the moment that each woman wrote about her mother. But when that happened, we saw we could refine these pieces and work them into a performance about mothers and daughters growing older. There are real personalities in them already, real conflict and real feeling. This is the essence of good theatre.

Producing the Writing—The Essential Last Step

If you look at the canon of plays that are usually identified as the great classics, you will see they were written by and for the players who first presented them. In America in the second half of the twentieth century, playwrights have gotten separated from production. For the most part, they send scripts to literary managers, artistic directors, and new plays competitions. They are often isolated from the production itself. Few modern plays have been written for a group of performers known to the playwrights. In the large regional companies, there are only a handful of writers in residence or writers who are full-time members of companies. Theatre managers have tended to believe they have to produce known works with established reputations, and writers have tended to believe that without the validation of a director choosing to produce a work, they are failed writers. We think this process is upside down.

We argue that every script that gets developed, whether it is by children or adults, should lead to a production that is guided by the writer or writers themselves and their collaborators. We propose that a script is only a script once it is realized in some staged form. However, a realization can be modest. Theatre is, after all, a thing of the moment.

Some works will be created with group interaction and through improvisation and rehearsal techniques. Others will be written more privately by individuals and brought to the group. Once a theatre piece gets into any form that the writer or writers are ready to share, it is time to produce it. *That is a must!* This can be done for short pieces, long pieces, parts of pieces, early drafts, or polished material. The production can be simple or it can go through natural stages of development, stopping at any point that seems appropriate:

The group does a cold reading when a section or a piece is ready for a hearing.

The group rehearses one or more times and reads the piece aloud with no staging and with or without an audience.

The group stages the work, either with scripts in hand or memorized, using minimal sets and scenery, and performs it in a classroom or studio for any interested persons.

The work is rehearsed and presented as a piece to a group of outside listeners who might already be gathered—a church group or a women's club, classmates, or another school. They come as a ready-made audience. They might be encouraged to discuss the work.

The piece has a more public showing. It is rehearsed and presented during an open house, a conference, or at a meeting for a more general audience.

The work is rehearsed, fully produced, advertised, and presented for the general public in a formal theatrical setting.

Good theatre happens when writers and actors are committed to producing their own work! At every level of sophistication, the script is essentially valid. It does not need to be justified by a long production history to make it good theatre. One must always remember that the unique experience of an audience with a performance can never be duplicated. Our goal is to make theatre that connects in the moment.

If the writers and performers take charge of their own artistic lives, they will present their work with a greater sense of ownership. If a theatre maintains a high-concept and low-tech profile, there will be many opportunities to create and perform. Cost or equipment will not stand in the way.

If the work has merit, it will attract its own audience. No one can say what theatre will have a continuing production life. Some theatre is meant to speak to a particular situation and a particular group at a particular time. Some theatre is developed and turns out to have implications for a great many people. In the larger theatre world, many pieces that have received a great deal of hype and were big expensive productions have disappeared. We just cannot know about the future, so posterity will have to take care of itself. Our job is to use the art of theatre to speak what we have to say and to help others find their own voices.

Sustainable Theatre: The Stuff of Public Performance

We have been trying to help people rethink the art of theatre. Even with our emphasis on the basic encounter, there is no denying that theatre has its technical side. For some people it is the most fascinating aspect. Children and adults can be consumed with lighting, sound, sets, costumes, makeup, and props—all the machinery of stage illusions. Every month the catalogues are full of new, exciting inventions. Colleagues tell you hundreds of neat ideas. We understand the attraction. But we would like to help you think about something we are calling "sustainable theatre." We borrowed the term from agriculture. Experts in agriculture warn us that a great deal of agricultural land has been exploited beyond its capacity to renew itself. Mass production requiring expensive equipment has driven small farmers off family land. Overuse has rendered the soil barren. In agriculture, there is a move to find sustainable means to continue, means that renew the land, that do not deplete the natural systems, and provide us the food we need to live.

Sustainable Theatre

We see the same need in theatre. Larger and larger productions thrive only in very rich environments. They create expectations that only a few can fulfill. They consume all the resources and leave little for young projects to feed on. They push the family farmers off the land. We would like to think of *sustainable theatre*— theatre that lives within a modest range of resources of people, time, and effort. We search for theatre that can continue to re-create itself because it does not harvest all of its energy in a single season, theatre that sustains its own life and keeps nourishing the people who feed on it. To think about sustainable theatre, we have to rethink all our assumptions about what is necessary and valid on the stage.

Looking at Public Performance

So far we have been making theatre in the classroom or rehearsal studio. What about the performance for a larger public? We have said that all we need are the performer, an audience, and a space in which they might engage with each other. What about all this other stuff? What about sets, lights, costumes, properties? What about the theatre itself?

The Auditorium

For many of us, years of going to public performances have led to the false assumption that theatre can only be performed in an auditorium. We conclude, without really questioning it, that if we want to produce theatre, the auditorium is the logical place to do it. In some cases, it might be true. Often, however, the typical school, church, or community auditorium imposes theatrical deci-sions that are not in the best interests of the performance. It demands huge investments of scenery. It forces performers into awkward postures and strains young or undeveloped voices. It is difficult if not impossible to get much intimacy when one hundred people sit in the first ten or twelve rows of a nine-hundred-seat auditorium. The audience will be twenty, thirty, or even fifty feet away from the performers. Even if all members of the audience are convinced to sit close together in the first rows, the fixed architecture undercuts any attempt to engage. Seats facing the stage may be more formal than you want. There is no sense of unity in an audience when only a few people occupy a space designed to hold many more. The emotional/psychological bonding that makes an audience feel free to laugh, sigh, moan, or cry without embarrassment is gone. An audience must feel comfortable in their communication with the performers in order to believe in the truth of the moment and respond unself-consciously. The auditorium hinders far more than it helps.

Audience First, Then Space

Rather than accept the traditional space as a given, we suggest you begin by determining the nature of the audience/performer interaction that you want. Then locate a space that permits that level of engagement. There is no reason to conclude that any one space is appropriate for every production. Each production should demand a space that best suits it. How do you want to communicate with your audience? Who and how many are they? Then consider the spaces that might be appropriate for each piece of theatre you create. Ask "To whom are we attempting to talk?"

> A specific age group?
> Mostly female? Mostly male?
> A specific ethnic group?
> A specific class or classes?
> Whole families?
> A group with specific social issues?
> A group with specific emotional issues?
> The parents of a specific group?
> A specific profession?
> Singles?
> Couples?
> Our friends?
> Fans of a particular author or style of work?
> Anyone who will come to see us?

A lot of what we have studied about uniting performers and audience teaches us that there is no such thing as the "general public." Different theatre experiences attract different groups of people. The work we do will be meant for people with particular interests. We need to understand this and to imagine who our audience is, where it is, and how we want to reach them.

"How many people can we reasonably expect to come?" Look to your past experience and examine realistically what you will do to gather an audience. Look at why you are doing the work in the first place and ask what it means about your audience. If you are performing for an existing group or for a targeted audience, you need to do research about how many of them show up for certain activities. We cannot let ourselves be caught up with the pleasure our work gives us and assume that there are hundreds of people waiting to leave their homes and interrupt their busy lives to come see us perform. More questions:

> How many came to our past four productions?
> How many people from the group we have contacted can reasonably be expected to attend?
> Is a whole class of children or a whole group of seniors being brought here?
> Do we need to go where the audience is already?
> Is any space we choose accessible to handicapped members of our community?

"What level of interaction do we desire with this audience?" In the process of creating the work, we are constantly aware of the effect we want to have on the audience. What have you decided? Some possibilities:

> We want the audience to be moved to a specific action.
> We want to entertain the audience with our stories and songs in a friendly manner.
> We want to share a deep emotional experience.
> We want to remind the audience of an ancient tradition.
> We want to provoke hearty laughter.
> We want to evoke a change of attitude.

We want to share how far we have come with developing this
piece.
We want to provoke discussion about a topic.
We want the audience to learn a lesson or moral.
We want to expose a particular audience to a new theatrical
experience.

Whatever journey we want the audience to take must be nurtured
by the shape and size of the space where we perform.

✳ The Needs of the Production

So far this has all been about audience. You can't forget the size
and scope of the production and the number and needs of the performers. If there is not enough space to accommodate the number
in the cast and allow them to move around, then you jeopardize
the effect. If there is too much space around an intimate work, it is
also in danger.

In some cases you may start knowing the performance space.
In other cases, you discover what you need only after a piece has
been developed to a certain point. In either situation you have to
think through some obvious and some not-so-obvious questions.

Leader Dialogue

Before we choose where we perform, think about these questions:

*How many people are in the cast? What is the maximum number on
the stage at one time, for how long, and what will they be doing?*

*If there is dancing, or procession, or musicians, or other formal
activity, how much room is needed to execute the movement patterns?*

*How clearly defined should the audience area be from the perfor-
mance area? Is it important that boundaries exist or is there a
desire to create a sense that both audience members and performers are equal participants in an event? Does the entire space
become simultaneously an audience and a performer area?*

*Is width and depth of floor space as important as height? If verti-
cal variety is important, requiring platforms or tall scenic units,
is height of the room more important than floor space?*

*Are certain technical considerations, such as lighting, sound, and
rigging of special effects, essential to what we are doing?*

*Are there important differences in floor surfaces that will affect the
production?*

*Should the floor be wood, linoleum, concrete, sand, grass, carpet, or
plastic, or should it not be any of these?*

*What differences will it make if the audience is on one side, two
sides, three, or four? What choices of these movement dynamics
do we want to make for this presentation?*

*What are the needs for entering and exiting the stage? For people?
For props and scenic objects?*

Advice to the Leader

Once you have determined answers to the questions about your
relationship to an audience and the needs of the performance as you
imagine it, you can begin exploring spaces and seating arrangements. Although you may not always be able to establish the configuration that is ideal, some options may work better than others.

✳ Rethinking the Auditorium

Suppose for a variety of good reasons you choose to perform in a
big auditorium with a large stage. Often productions suffer because
people feel they have to fill up a space because it is there. A space
can always be redefined downward. Remember that the distance
between performers has a strong impact on how well they are able
to relate to each other.

Leader Dialogue

*We are going to create a smaller area within the large one. How wide do
we really need to open the act curtain? We don't have to fill the huge*

void with scenery or action. Prepare yourself for radical thinking. Try out different spaces on the stage. Reduce the stage by opening the curtain part way. Look at the auditorium. Where do we want people to sit? Can we rope off the seats we don't want used? Our job is to figure out how to get better control over the experience.

✳ Any Room as a Theatre

Any room large enough to provide adequate space for the performance and an audience can be a viable theatre.

Leader Dialogue

How can different room arrangements influence the interaction between the audience and the performer? Pick a room and consider its potential for performance. Sketch out possibilities for seating and for performance space. Consider the issues we have talked about: floor surface, height of ceiling, floor space. Do whatever you can to improve sightlines: elevate the performers or the audience, curve rows to surround more of the action, use stools instead of chairs in a back row. Good sight lines make the experience more satisfying for everyone.

Advice to the Leader

If your group is stuck, look at the diagrams in Figure 6–1. See if your group has variations on the diagrams.

Side Coaching

Watch the location of doors for the flow of audience traffic as well as access of the performers. Think about the doors that already exist when you plan your arrangement. If there are windows, you may have to use curtains, shades, or blinds to cover them. If you are performing in daylight and you can't cover the windows, consider whether it is better to have a window located behind the audience or behind the performer. See how light from behind silhouettes the performers and makes it hard to look at them. What does light do if it comes from behind the audience?

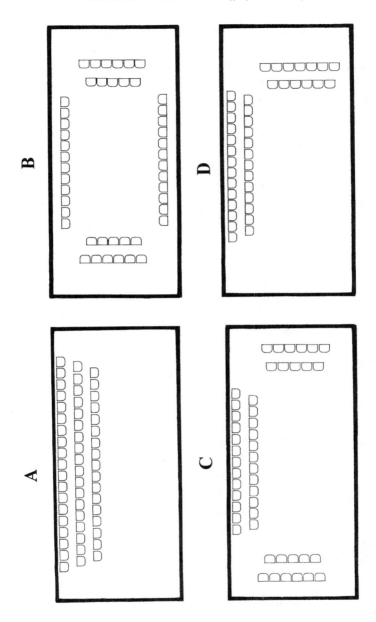

Figure 6–1   Alternate Seating Arrangements

Advice to the Leader

If there is the possibility of using risers or platforms in the room, do it. In Arrangement A, for example, if all of the chairs for the audience and the performance area are on the same level, the third row will have difficulty seeing. Except for the front row, audience members will not be able to see any action that occurs on the floor. One solution is to raise the stage area. You need at least twelve to eighteen inches elevation to improve the sight lines. Twenty-four to thirty inches is better. Another option is to elevate portions of the audience area. The most desirable arrangement would be to raise each row of seats at least six to eight inches higher than the row in front of it. In any situation, two rows on the same level with the stage is the maximum number before there will be sight line problems.

The Auditorium Stage as a Room

But suppose you want technical or lighting support for the performance—the very thing you have in abundance in the auditorium, even though the space is too huge for your production. Consider the stage area of the auditorium as a "room." Close the front curtain and the stage becomes the total space, accommodating both the performer and the audience. For many productions, this combination of intimate audience/performer relationship and technical support offers you the most workable, flexible, and desirable space. It can be treated with the same variations as the room. It has lighting positions, a board and instruments, cable, electrical power, a suitable floor surface, height, and often hanging curtains that can be adjusted in a variety of ways. Sometimes it has choral risers that can be used for seating and is equipped with pianos and sound equipment. If the audience is likely to be large, the performance can be continued over time to accommodate them. Performers enjoy developing their work over several performances and audiences feel welcomed and included in the intimacy of the activity.

Multi-Purpose Room or Cafetorium Theatre

Many schools built in the sixties and seventies have spaces designed to serve as gym, cafeteria, and auditorium. Such spaces exist in churches, YMCAs, and other public buildings as well. The stage is often small and has little height or flexibility. This kind of space offers the exciting asset that it is a large area that can be used by performers as well as audience. Before settling on the stage as a stage, view such rooms as rooms, with all the various configurations you can imagine. Of course, you will consider the permanent platform as a possible playing area. However, if you want to have large movement patterns, processions, and dances, you can use the existing stage as a seating area and the open floor of the room as the performance space. With the use of risers and/or platforms, it might be possible to configure the space as shown in Figure 6–2. By combining this arrangement with the one represented in Arrangement C (Figure 6–1), you can increase the number of audience members without sacrificing either intimacy or sightlines. Such an arrangement might look like this (Figure 6–3).

We need to remain creative and responsive to both our artistic needs and the needs of our audience. We must not get caught up in using an existing space as it has always been used just because it has always been used that way. The performance should drive the use of the space. One goal of Hi Concept - Lo Tech thinking is Hamlet's advice, "Suit the action to the words, the words to the action." We seek not to be tortured out of shape by invalid assumptions and inappropriate expectations, by technical capacity just because it exists, or by past practice for its own sake. Honesty to the meaning of our work extends to choosing the performance space and working within it.

✳ *Found Theatres*

Thus far, we have focused on how to convert a space to make a theatre. We should not, however, ignore existing architectural spaces that can serve our production with little or no alteration.

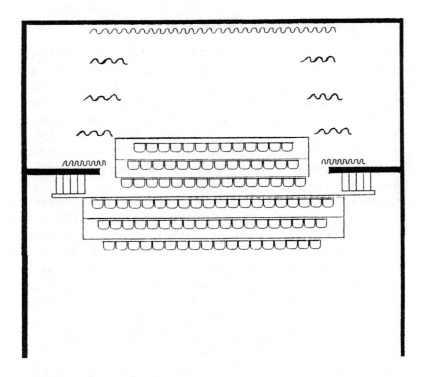

Figure 6–2   Stage as Seating Area

Leader Dialogue

We ignore the theatrical possibilities of spaces we see and use every day. You know what you want to achieve with your audience. Go on a tour of our community. Select an existing space to perform your piece. Staircases, large hallways, lobbies, and foyers are potential places. Consider the place's own charm, feeling, mood, dramatic power. Use as little effort as possible to make it work. As you rehearse, explore its theatrical possibilities. In our next session together we will look at what you have found.

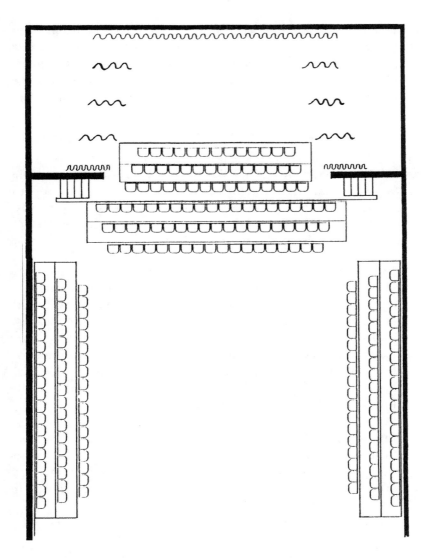

Figure 6–3   Multi-Purpose Room with Stage as Seating

Side Coaching

You can use interior or exterior spaces. There are obvious disadvantages to performing outdoors—heat, cold, bad weather, visual distractions, and extraneous noises. See if you can figure out how to control what matters. Consider the possible size of the audience and where they would be. The key is to control or manipulate the audience and performer relationship.

Advice to the Leader

If performances are scheduled during the day, lighting is not a problem. Your scenic needs may be satisfied in ways never possible indoors. The total environment of the exterior space may add to the presentation. Look at hillsides, fronts of buildings, courtyards, areas between buildings, and wooded areas. Remember Shakespeare and Sophocles had only the sun to light them.

> In 1972, Lansing Community College created a performance of *West Side Story* in a downtown parking lot behind a group of stores. In addition to a three-foot-high simple platform erected at ground level, the show used existing rooftops, fire escapes, doors, and apartment windows. Only a few connecting runways had to be built. Rented football bleachers held the two-thousand-plus audience, and at the end of the rumble real policemen riding real motorcycles arrived with sirens screaming to drag off the dead bodies. An ingenious sound man miked the performance, assisted considerably by sound bouncing off the brick wall of a laundry building opposite the performance space. The performances drew huge crowds who hung out in the streets, sitting on cars and watching from buildings nearby. Local kids watched rehearsals and did their own versions of the dances and fights during breaks. Downtown merchants stayed open late to accommodate the crowds.

It should never be assumed that the presentation of a theatrical performance is limited to just one particular place. Do yourself and your production a service by exploring as many potential spaces as possible. Any space that can serve to reinforce the desired relationship between the audience and the performer is a candidate.

Sets, Lights, and Costumes

For those new to making a piece of theatre, as well as those with some experience, the technical worlds of costumes, lighting, and setting produce a certain amount of fear. They can easily devour substantial sums of money and unexpected amounts of time.

Before any time is allocated in that direction, it is critical to consider which elements are essential. Sometimes visual components play a major role in the event and the financial and human resources required to create them are justified. Sometimes they are not. We have to be aware that our decisions are influenced by a tendency for us to think in realistic rather than theatrical terms.

Television and movies have implanted in our imagination a standard of realism that is based on reality as we experience it daily. Once we choose to have on the stage the walls, doors, windows, coffee tables, living room furniture, lamps, and all those things we associate with living spaces; or mountains, gardens, barns, and streets that we might want to create an exterior space, we are faced with needing the technical skills to design, construct, and paint this environment. When we do not have these skills, we try to locate and convince someone to assume those responsibilities or we try to figure out how to do it ourselves, however awkward or unconvincing the results. In either case, time is taken away from the element of production preparation where most attention should be placed: working with performers.

Evocation Rather than Description

Robert Edmond Jones, often considered to be the founder of American scenic design and one of Broadway's most important designers, makes the following observations in his book, *The Dramatic Imagination*:

all art in the theatre should be not descriptive, but evocative. Not a description, but an evocation. A bad actor describes a character; he explains it. He expounds it. A good actor evokes a character. He summons it up. He reveals it to us . . . Truth in the theatre, as the masters of the theatre have always known, stands above and beyond mere accuracy to fact. In the theatre the actual thing is never the exciting thing. Unless life is turned into art on the stage, it stops being alive and goes dead. So much for the realistic theatre. (81–82)

Although Jones was commenting in the early twentieth century on a nineteenth-century tradition of realism, his words and ideas continue to ring true today. The notion of scenic elements as being evocative rather than descriptive has served well the production needs of a century of designers. There is no reason why it cannot also serve you.

Eugene O'Neill developed his 1928 play, *Marco Millions,* around the travels of Marco Polo. Within the first thirty minutes of the production, Marco Polo travels through five different cultures. The scenic designer was Lee Simonson, a veteran of Broadway and author of a history of scenic design, *The Stage Is Set.* Rather than represent each civilization accurately with any sort of realistic architecture, Simonson established a scenic convention that put focus on the very careful selection of a limited number of scenic pieces. Items such as lamps, urns, and silhouettes of identifiable human and architectural shapes made clear the location of the action of each scene. This convention made for a quick and easy change of locale and immediately evoked in the mind of the audience not only place, but the mood of the encounter between the world of the traveler and the world of the inhabitants. The latter communication would not likely occur if Simonson had chosen only to offer that which was real or historically accurate. Each item or silhouette was selected to evoke a particular response from the audience and provide them with emotional as well as geographical information.

✳ Selective Realism

Leader Dialogue

Pick a time or situation that calls for a specific locale in performance. Consider what might be the single right item to provide the necessary information as well as evoke the desired emotional response. You can try to find it, or make it. If several such items are needed, take the time to explore how they come and go from the stage. Develop a consistent convention of how the transition from one scene to the next is executed. Perhaps performers move the objects. In Marco Millions, *Simonson used a large turntable on the stage. Not everyone can afford that kind of device.*

Side Coaching

Your job is to imagine a technique that can work consistently and efficiently and require little time and expense. But transitions are important. There should be as little time as possible used to complete them. Time spent on transitions is attention taken away from the performance. Transitions should become a part of the performance and not just practical activities that have no connection to the rest. Transitions must be part of imagining the piece in the first place. It becomes the company's responsibility to make these acts of function an integrated part of the whole theatrical event, rehearsed and choreographed with as much attention as any other part of the performance.

Standard Scenic Units—The Blocks and Platform System

An audience will accept virtually any scenic convention that is presented clearly and consistently. A simple method of providing a functional and effective set is to use various shaped blocks. With careful thought, it is possible to build and use simple shapes in various ways to create a whole range of things. The drawings in the Appendix will give you one possible method of constructing units that are both functional and flexible. They can be part of a rehearsal room and studio, and they can go right into performance.

In a world of diminishing resources of all kinds, it is important to invest in things that can be reused without major modification. Simplicity and durability are also considerations. The suggested design and construction of these units allow for their quick assembly as chair, sofa, or table. Further, the bases are designed to fold for easy storage. It is possible to build the same blocks in a solid and nonfolding manner with only slight modifications to the design.

 Cubes

Leader Dialogue

Take the cubes we include in this book as a basic unit. Each group make at least three different arrangements of the blocks for your pieces. Consider how you can move them as you perform. Arrange and rearrange yourselves on the blocks according to the needs of your piece.

Side Coaching

The blocks can become virtually anything and are immediately changed by their use. When stacked on each other, they can become gates, columns, walls, or decorative pieces of sculpture. They can be rearranged in countless formations with very different effects.

Advice to the Leader

A coat of paint or a covering of some sort can enhance the blocks' flexibility. The stock of blocks can be increased over time. Perhaps one of the primary advantages of using the blocks for a production is the fact that they are available from the very first day of rehearsal. They are there for experimentation during the entire rehearsal process—their use and composition can be discovered at the same time the performers are discovering their characters and intentions. Don't underestimate this advantage.

✳ *Platforms Galore*

Platforms provide variations in level on a performance area. By building units based on four-foot sections, the construction becomes uncomplicated. The four-foot module also makes for relatively light and portable units. By having several four-by-four units, some two-by-four units, and a few triangular-shaped four-by-four pieces, it is possible to configure them into a variety of shapes. Stacking them makes stairs.

Provide your group with rulers, mat knives, corrugated cardboard, and pencils.

Leader Dialogue

We are going to represent sets of four-foot-by-four-foot platforms, eight inches high with four-inch-by-four-inch pieces of cardboard. Each group should draw and cut out a set of eight four-by-four units. Then you are free to cut them in smaller but regular shapes. Arrange them in various ways as you think about staging possibilities. You can cut more units as you choose. Think about all the ways you can use them, either for performers or for audience. They can be painted as well. You can combine them with the blocks. Just draw and cut paper to represent the blocks.

Advice to the Leader

More interesting stage compositions, with better focus and variety can be achieved in a production that uses different levels. A range of textures can be achieved by painting and coverings. As with the blocks, a stock of platforms facilitates experimentation and change of relationships during the rehearsal. Platforms can also create seating levels for the audience.

The Unit or Simultaneous Set

It is possible and often very desirable to establish an arrangement of platforms and boxes that do not change during the production but serve the needs of many locales. Such an arrangement is referred to as a "unit set" or "simultaneous setting." With this approach, all locales are defined by use of the performer and by a consistent use of a convention. Perhaps lighting may define a particular part of the setting but that is not necessary. A street may be suggested by using the most open playing area on the stage, a room by the location of some blocks used as furniture, a front porch could be defined by having performers sit on steps, and a secret hiding place might be made known to the audience by the way the performer enters that area of the stage.

Establishing Scenic Conventions

The unit set idea is theatrical, offers a variety of playing levels, and provides fairly simple answers to a whole range of scenic needs. It has its own system of logic.

Once an area has been defined, it should be treated the same way consistently. The porch, for instance, should always be played on the same steps. If, for some reason, it is necessary to use the same area of the setting for more than one locale, some device needs to let the audience know that we are somewhere different. A blanket placed over blocks that were previously used to indicate a bench in a garden can now be defined as a bed. A simple change and the way performers use the units can provide the audience with all the information it needs.

A slight rearrangement of blocks may also indicate a change in place. What is important is the development of a consistent device or convention to indicate such changes clearly to the audience. It can be confusing, for example, if some locales are indicated with real furniture while others use blocks. Because the audience makes direct connection with the real furniture as being identifiable for what it is, it may also believe the blocks to be nothing more than blocks. As a result, it will not accept their becoming other things. Either all real furniture or all blocks could work within the concept of a unit set, but a mixture of the two will require a convention to give logic to the mix.

Costumes and Clothes

Costumes are visual communication. Choices we make every day about the clothes to buy or wear tell others something about us. The color, style, fabric, combinations of tops and bottoms, footwear, and accessories all reflect who we are and how we view ourselves. Whatever the choices, we make a statement. The costume on the stage provides information about the performance.

Costume Statements

In most productions, a performer is seen before he is heard. Each day, we meet new people. Our first impressions about them are built on what they are wearing and how they move. We decide if we want to engage them in conversation, we make assumptions about their status, what kind of work they do, and if we would be comfortable being alone with them. All those conclusions are quickly formed in our minds in a matter of one or two seconds. This is an involuntary reaction based on years of making such observations. Are the conclusions always valid? Perhaps when we do get to know someone better, some of those impressions become altered. However, experience tells us to trust our initial instincts.

✳ *The "Look"*

In many ways, the costumer for a production draws on stereotypes to make choices about what a character should wear in a performance. Costume choices are built on how an audience might predictably respond to a specific "look."

Leader Dialogue

We are going to create a "look" for performers in our pieces and we must also develop a "look" for the production. Each performer is an individual about whom we are attempting to communicate information. But each person is also a member of a performance ensemble. All individual costume choices must be made in the context of the overall look of the performance. Each production will demand a different look. Your job now is to think about the "look" of both individuals and the whole group. Think about using garments already in the closets of the performers. Think about only single purchased items. The important thing is to imagine an overall visual statement. Imagine your choices with no budget. Imagine them with unlimited budget.

Side Coaching

What do you want in the look? Is it very formal? Casual? Sloppy? Sophisticated? Are the characters wealthy? Poor? Well-kept? In battle? Is there a color range that makes sense? Do you want the audience to like these people? Do you want the audience to be surprised by having their assumptions reversed? Do you want to identify a time period, a place, a class? A point of view? Do you want particular pairs or groups of the company to go together visually?

Follow-up Discussion

Consider the overall production look of performers who are all wearing their favorite jeans and white T-shirts. There is a unity to the costumes, yet each individual will be slightly different in fit and condition of both items. What happens if everyone has new jeans of the same color, tight-fitting, and new, long-sleeved T-shirts? What happens when they all wear white dress shirts, or each picks a different color T-shirt? What is the effect of having everyone in black turtlenecks and black pants? What happens when a vest is added to any one of the above? Should the female performers wear something different from the males? What do hats do? Gloves? Belts? Period accessories?

Unity and Distinction

Within any of these examples, it is possible to create a sense of unity to the look and still offer individual character identity by developing a consistent costume convention. The right hat for each character can provide as much information to an audience as a very elaborate costume. Pieces of material used in a variety of ways to create head coverings, shawls, headbands, armbands, sashes, scarves, slings for broken arms, or other items can also provide a practical way to deal with a range of character statements. Whatever the choice, be consistent with the convention. The purpose is to provide information to the audience, not confuse them.

In a production of Story Theatre, all the performers wore white clothes that might have come from their own closets. Some had shorts, some skirts, others had long pants, and each had a different kind of white shirt. All of the different characters were created by changing hats and footwear. A round of applause greeted a performer who was playing a duck when he appeared wearing yellow tennis shoes and a white baseball hat with a yellow bill. A few scenes later, he appeared as a jungle explorer wearing hiking boots and a pith helmet. In both cases, the audience appreciated the choices and immediately had all the information it needed. The basic white costumes were attractive and the changes were inexpensive yet very effective.

✳ Properties

Performers often have to handle or use objects. Properties can be problematic. They have to be the right object—the right period, the right size, the right shape—and the right object is often hard to build, impossible to locate, or expensive to purchase. As with all the other visual elements, we first evaluate the need and importance of the prop. Is it essential to the moment or to the ambiance? Even when we can justify the need, the questions of time and money are real. Is it worth the effort to have this prop? Does everybody understand how and why it is needed and used? Securing or making properties is part of making theatre.

The visual aesthetic of a production has consequences for the objects that will appear on stage. Selective realism, like that of Lee

Simonson, or unit sets, or a costume convention like the white clothing—each choice makes demands on the other physical objects.

Leader Dialogue

We have choices to make about the props. What do we need and how do we think about them? Can we use prop conventions? Dowel rods of different lengths to stand for any object we need? Small and large boxes? Balls of different sizes or pieces of paper or cardboard cutouts? Or do we wish to have selected objects that are literal reality for the use of each character? Look closely at your work and offer suggestions. Remember you must be consistent in your approach.

Advice to the Leader

When we opt for literal realism, we still have decisions to make about the visual effect of an object—its size, color, shape, weight, ease of use, or its historical or character appropriateness. The simple set or conventionalized costume draws a lot of focus to the objects used by performers. Like every other production element, these choices belong in the rehearsal process. They are decisions made by the company as the work is created.

Inexpensive Means and Creative Choices

We have an important maxim: *Make choices, don't make do.* It is not enough to provide something; it is essential to provide the right thing. Knowing the right thing is embedded in knowing the needs of the moment, in knowing the effect that any choice will have in a performance, and then imagining the most efficient way of creating that effect. Resources always have an effect on those choices. We have been exploring the idea of *sustainable theatre*.

> The set was an upscale row house with a foyer and a small table. Something was needed to go on the table and give decoration to the space. The person designated to locate this

prop began to explore possibilities. When he returned to the theatre, he had with him a scrap piece of linoleum that was being discarded by a local flooring shop. He cut the linoleum to the desired height of the vase, rolled it into the appropriate diameter, taped it along the back seam, and added several dry flowers. Placed on the table in the upstage foyer, it looked like a very expensive ceramic vase. If the director or designer had told the person to go and buy a tall ceramic vase to dress this part of the set, something much more expensive might have been purchased at the end of a lengthy shopping trip. The properties master knew the desired effect and used his imagination to save time and money.

For a production of *The Bacchae* by Euripides, in which most of the performers come to the final moment of the play covered with blood from a savage and animalistic beheading, it was necessary to discover a process by which the costumes could be covered with blood and then washed so the same costumes could be used for the next performance. After experimenting with several possibilities on the fabric, the costume group chose shampoo as the base for making the blood, to which was added red food coloring. The shampoo provided the soap needed to wash the garments following each performance. This solution to a very specific production problem also meant there was a need to buy large quantities of shampoo. Always thinking ahead, the costume crew bought inexpensive shampoo that came in interesting containers that were subsequently decorated and painted and used as decorative vases.

We call attention to the need for clarity about props and the fact that wonderful solutions can be provided by inexpensive means and creative choices. If the purpose, use, and look is understood, then providing props becomes an exciting challenge. We develop a way of coming at solutions to theatrical problems that are the right choice with limited resources. We also keep an eye on the future when we look at the present.

Lighting

Lighting can be one of the most difficult, complex, and frustrating elements of a performance. Electricity and wires can be frightening and dangerous. The lighting requirements for a production are often the last elements to receive thought and attention. They belong in the earliest stages along with everything else. It is necessary to understand why choices about lighting are made.

Lighting has certain functions to perform. Let's look at them.

1. *Illumination.* The primary function of lighting is to make it possible for the audience to see the performer.
2. *Modeling.* By the proper use of color and the positioning of lighting sources, the three-dimensional qualities of the performers and the setting can be enhanced.
3. *Mode.* Lighting can communicate the reality or departure from reality of the production.
4. *Mood.* Lighting enhances the emotional quality of the environment in which the action takes place—happy, dark, bright, etc.
5. *Composition.* By the selective use of light sources, it is possible to direct the focus of the audience to a particular spot or character.

Some performance venues will have enough instruments and dimmer control to take advantage of all lighting functions. More often than not, however, equipment will be limited. It is necessary to decide what is both necessary and possible. There is no reason to make the process of lighting complicated. Build on what is available and keep the functions of lighting in priority order.

Priority One: Illumination

Illumination is the primary function of lighting. Illumination can be provided adequately by existing overhead lighting fixtures in a room. In some spaces, there are several light switches, each controlling different parts of the space. By discovering which switches control which overhead sections of lights, it is possible to arrange the seating to conform to the way the lights are distributed. Lighting was introduced as a production concern when, during the Italian Renaissance, theatre moved indoors. Those concerned with the problems of providing illumination soon came to a startling observation. Without increasing the amount of light on the performer, the illusion of more light is achieved when the viewers are seated in less light. By reducing the amount of light in the audience area, there is an increased contrast between the audience and performance. Take advantage of this discovery. Explore the possibility of arranging the seating in the room in such a way that most of the audience can be in a space with the least amount of overhead lighting. If the performance takes place in a room with windows, the windows should be behind the audience. The audience gets the benefit from having the light without having to look into the windows against which the performers would be silhouettes.

✳ Backgrounds

The background of the performance area plays an important role in lighting. A general rule of thumb is to make the background as dark as possible.

Leader Dialogue

Experiment with your costume choices against different backgrounds. See what you find.

Follow-up Discussion

Generally speaking, the group will discover that the darker the background, the more contrast between the performer and the background. By using lighter colored costumes or costume pieces, the performer stands out from the background. The stronger this contrast, the easier it is to light. Visibility of the performer is already enhanced by this relationship and general illumination is made easier and more successful. There is nothing more straining on the eyes than being forced to watch a performer against a background that is lighter or similar in color to the clothing being worn by the performer. The most desirable background color is black. It provides high contrast with the performer and, at the same time, a neutral background to the action.

Available Equipment

If there is limited or no lighting equipment in the production space, then it is especially necessary to keep the priorities of the functions of light in mind. Something must be done to illuminate the performers. It may be necessary to secure additional light sources. Although not designed for such use, work lights that are found in local hardware or department stores at a minimal cost can work. The type that are most useful are those that have a conical reflector and a spring clamp. Colored exterior flood bulbs can vary the light effect. Such units can be attached to ladders or pipes. Stanchions used for volleyball or badminton nets can be light trees.

It is often possible to find overhead projectors. These can provide additional light for general illumination. Use colored transparencies in the projectors to give a bit more character to the light. These devices can focus the light image and give a soft or sharp edge to the light being projected. Use two or more overhead projectors and experiment for interesting results.

Special Effects from a Slide Projector

A standard slide projector is a useful lighting device. It has, after all, a fairly strong light source—a lens—and is designed to project light with or without a slide.

There are times when it might be appropriate to project an image that is created specifically for this production. You need a consistent, light surface on which to project. What about an image projected as the audience enters the space? Such projections could help establish an appropriate mood or locale. It is also possible to use a series of slides or several projectors to prepare the audience for what they are about to see.

> Prior to a performance of Athol Fugard's *Siswe Bonzi is Dead*, a story about the impact of apartheid in South Africa, the audience was presented with a series of projected photographs showing the brutality of the daily life of those living under the oppression of apartheid. Those pictures gave the audience information they might not have had about the situations presented in the production. They helped create a historical context for the piece and set a tone that supported the presentation.

Rarely is it possible to use these kinds of projectors to project scenic images as a background during the action. The light from the projector is not bright enough to hold a strong image on a surface that is also picking up ambient light from the general illumination. Under some circumstances, however, it might be interesting to explore the impact of using projected images as a transition between sections of the presentation.

Let your group experiment with slide projector spotlights. You can use a piece of sheet metal, aluminum from a disposable pie tin, or an undeveloped slide.

✳ Spotlights

Leader Dialogue

We are going to create a simple follow spot by using a piece of sheet metal with a hole punched in it to control the size of the beam of light. Take a mounted slide apart, and cut the sheet metal to fit into the mounting. The material will dictate what is used to make the hole. Paper hole-punchers might work. You might need a hammer and nail for the sheet metal. Undeveloped slides that are the first or last frames of film on the roll when they come back from being developed can also provide a base for making holes. Experiment with how big the hole needs to be.

Experiment to discover the location of the projector and the size of the beam of light. Try lighting only the head of the performer, then the torso or whole body. The closer the projector is to the performer, the brighter the light will be. Think about the fact that the projector will need to be located where the sound of slides changing and the constant noise of the cooling fan will not be distracting. The noise will limit where the projector can be positioned.

Advice to the Leader

If you create a selection of different-sized holes in several slides, it will be possible to select the right size simply by changing slides. Record the number on the slide tray and you can go back and forth between slides and select the right slide for the specific moment. With several projectors, a whole range of spots are possible.

Another simple technique for making a spotlight is to punch or cut a hole in a piece of cardboard and place it directly in front of the lens of the projector. By moving the cardboard away from the lens, it is possible to vary the size of the spot. The sharpness of the edge of the spot can be made to vary by adjusting the focus of the lens. If desired, movement patterns in the light can be created by moving fingers and objects in front of the hole in the cardboard.

Color

There are no shortcuts to the effective use of color in stage lighting and it takes experience to be able to select and use colors well. As a general rule, however, remember that the darker the color gel, the less light is available on the performer. Dark or primary colors allow less light from the light source to pass through them and, as a result, less light is going to be available for visibility.

Strong beams of color can be provided by slide projectors. Although plastic is now used, the term gel is still commonly used to refer to the color media because the first color filters were made from a gelatin product. Every theatrical supply house has gel color swatches from the manufacturers. These swatch books will have a sample of virtually every color provided by that company. From the swatch book you can cut out any color and put it into a slide mount. A strong beam of color can be provided with a soft or sharp edge controlled by the focus of the lens, either as a full slide of color or combined in a mount with the hole for the spot.

Several different kinds of lens are available for slide projectors, and it is worth checking on the effect of using a zoom lens or short throw lens. For most applications, a zoom lens will offer the most variety and control of the light.

These are simple solutions to be thought through with all the other elements of production. Lighting should also make choices, not make do. Light should serve not itself, but the artful aesthetic of the presentation. Time, thought, and experimentation make the difference.

If you have all the equipment you need, it is a matter of being able to focus and control the lighting fixtures into the best configuration. Even then, remember the functions of lighting and don't let the temptation to create lighting effects dominate the need for the audience to see the performers. Certainly, there is more opportunity to create mood and dramatic effects when the equipment is available.

Leading the Final Production

Rethinking the Hierarchies

As we look at the twentieth century closing, we realize that in our time the theatre world has developed a distorted perspective on the role of the theatre director. Legendary figures such as André Antoine of the Theatre Libre, Stanislavsky and Meyerhold from the turn of the century; and Peter Brook, Elia Kazan, Josh Logan, José Quintero, Tyrone Guthrie, and George Abbott in the middle of this century have contributed to the mystique. For anyone who was schooled in theatre in the last fifty years, conventional wisdom held that the future of art was in the hands of the director. A lot of writing and conversation reinforced that preoccupation. If we were told to draw a hierarchical chart, it would look like this:

Text (sacred and obscure to all but a few)—
Author (dead or in hiding)
DIRECTOR
(knows all, controls all, interprets text, and
tells everyone else what to do)
actors
(servants of the director for the interpretation of the text)
audience (grateful receivers)

We know we are exaggerating, but the force of the myth is strong. The director is the priest who gives the world access to the scripture, through his or her interpretation of it. The author depends on the director to know what the text is or should be about. The director interprets the work for the actors, designers, and technicians. And the critics speak of Peter Sellars' *Merchant of Venice* and not Shakespeare's.

Few really good directors behave this way, not even those who have contributed to the mythology. Elia Kazan, Peter Brooks, Anne Bogart, Josh Logan, and Jose Quintéro have always worked closely with writers and ensembles of actors, often collaborating through a whole series of productions. Nevertheless, the myth prevails and clouds our understanding of the real process.

We forget that Shakespeare and Molière were writers and actors in companies led by fellow actors or themselves. The commedia troupes of the Italian Renaissance were companies of actors, often whole families of performers, who created and acted their own scenarios. In the Kabuki tradition of Japan, actors handed down their art from actor to actor and authors were often leading performers. People like Dion Boucicault, David Belasco, and Laura Keene were actor/managers of the late nineteenth century who put together troupes. They wrote, produced, and commissioned work for themselves and for actors whom they managed.

Countering the director mystique in twentieth-century theatre are ensemble-based companies like Joan Littlewood's Theatre Workshop in England in the late forties and fifties; Mabou Mines, an American experimental collaborative of actors created in the seventies; Minneapolis' Théatre de la Jeune Lune, four theatre artists who build productions from both their own scripts and classics; The Road Company, in Johnson City, Tennessee, who began in the mid-seventies to create collaborative work out of community issues; the Performance Garage, a sixties' collaborative led by Richard Schechner; and Chicago's Second City, whose performers first gathered in the fifties as The Compass Players led by Paul Sills and who still build material improvisationally both in the studio and in performance.

The twentieth-century fascination with the hand of the director has validity, of course, even while it has been corrupted and romanticized. There is a great deal of truth in the idea that clarity of vision, a sense of the whole, a guiding principle, and a helpful and trusted mind behind the art work lead to a consistent and coordinated end product. Even books on directing that emphasize the production team and the collaborative nature of theatre also insist on the need for the director to provide the vision, to be the inspirational center of theatre work.

But this modern preoccupation with directing has had less than helpful side effects. Young actors have come to expect to be "directed" instead of taking responsibility for themselves as performers. Writers have been disenfranchised—told that they do not understand what they have written, that they need to have someone get between them and their work to bring it to the audience. They have been asked not to speak to actors directly. They have even been thrown out of rehearsals when they disagreed with a director's interpretation.

Many times now we have argued that good theatre grows organically out of the performers' desire to reach an audience. The performer may be singular or plural, the vehicle may be a text they write or one they find, and the audience may be very specific or very general. That encounter is most effective when there is a clear point of view, an established style, and decisions are made about what goes in and what remains outside the performance.

Those artful decisions are necessary, but it is not necessary to have a single person making all these decisions, nor does that person need to be the director. In fact, artistic leadership can come from any quarter—actors, writers, designers—and a solid performance will happen when all have reached a point of view that is so thoroughly understood and manifest in every aspect that participants would be hard pressed to say who decided it.

Finding Artistic Leadership

Artistic leadership is a real thing, not to be ignored. There are those who have imagination about what might happen or what should be. There are those whom others follow because their vision is compelling. Our point is that leadership does not have to be exercised in a way that renders all the other participants passive. We see value in active partnerships of writers, actors, and designers—students and teachers—in order that the work be as rich as possible. There is a role for guidance and facilitation, seeing that it all gets done, seeing that good ideas are heard and used, that good decisions are made and carried out, and that there is a sense of the whole. There is a role for the outside eye: noting gaps, reacting to rhythms, compositions, inconsistencies. There is a role for coaching, for experience passed on to help solve problems in individual cases. These roles may be shared or given to an individual. But it is important that the performers and writers and designers take responsibility for the whole and are able to contribute to its realization.

Teachers, group leaders, and theatre directors have the chance to be these facilitators. All of the exercises we have given thus far are intended to assist that role. The facilitator sets tasks, leads conversation, and helps everyone find their voices, their physical presence, their artistic unity, their point of view. The leader works to create an ensemble, a sense of community, an environment in which all participants can take what is given and respond to those impulses within a framework. A leader asks questions, poses problems, and watches for the evolution of solutions. Leadership is sometimes an arbiter of conflict. Leadership sometimes organizes and structures time. Leadership sometimes distributes work. But leadership does not have to be singular, or authoritarian, or dictatorial.

Probably the most difficult task for the teacher or theatre director who is accustomed to the "director as god" mode is to change the vocabulary from "I" to "we." Great joy and pride is gained from feeling at the center of theatre work. Sharing that center among individuals requires a particular discipline.

Guiding the Rehearsal Process

The rehearsal process has several goals. They are all important.

1. Establish and ensure the continuity of the aesthetic.

2. Determine what the piece is about, as well as what happens within it.

3. Provide focus: bringing the audience's attention to what you want them to pay attention to, when you want them to pay attention to it.

4. Reach the truth of the performance moment: making every interaction on stage commit the audience to the theatrical reality.

5. Illuminate the words and actions so the various subtle conflicts are realized.

6. Establish rhythms for highlights and low lights, accents, contrasts, momentum, and clear beginning, middle, and end.

7. Establish the visual and aural elements in harmony with the speech and action.

Everything we have said about acting, writing, stage space, and technical craft is now a part of this discussion. Rehearsing for public performance requires all the skills we have been developing. The environment is complex. You want to get everyone headed in the same direction, each individual taking responsibility not only for his or her own role but also for the whole of the work.

What the Leader Does

If you hang around directors for a while, you are bound to hear these jokes.

"Tell them to act better."

"There are only four directions to give actors: faster, slower, louder, softer."

"Tell them to be funnier."

In a very real way these quips reflect the truth. Even if we added "come closer" and "go back farther," we would still be admitting that the main thing a director does is help move people and things around in time and space. The rest of it has to do with the actor's own understanding and the designer's imagination. They do the work. The job out front is to reflect what you see, make comments, and listen to alternatives. In that way a production is shaped gradually from the interactions and activities of many people. Together you accomplish the rehearsal goals.

What gets lost in the mythos of the "director as god" is the "together." The work is richer and more people learn if everyone develops the larger concepts together. Then everyone makes his or her contribution based on common understandings. Then the person who "directs"—who sits out front, who presses people forward, who does editing or "sculpting" of the work—does it within a matrix of shared responsibility. Consequently, before anyone can sit out front, there is a lot of groundwork to be done.

Establish and Ensure the Continuity of the Aesthetic

Using Metaphor

Designer Joe Tilford approached Barbara Carlisle when she was directing at Cincinnati Playhouse with a question. "If this play were not taking place on a stage, where would it take place?" The play was *The Marriage of Bette and Boo*, by Christopher Durang. The question forced her to think through the real experience of the play, its story, its characters, and, more important, to whom they were speaking. If, indeed, the audience were not simply people in the seats of the theatre, who were they? Joe's question framed the work they were doing together, and the answers they found helped shape the production. Here was the starting place for a point of view toward the piece. In this case, they imagined that the audience and the characters might be gathered in a church basement where a Bible School class was in progress. With that image in mind, they were led to seeing the principal character as telling his story to a rather dull-witted group of adults not entirely pleased to be there. He was presenting something he had the power to call up from memory, but it was something about which he was not always clear. He had photographs as guides, mainly the photograph of his mother and father's wedding, and no matter what was happening to the characters, somehow they were always dressed just like they appeared in the wedding photo. The actors quickly accepted this set of conventions, and they then began to contribute their own attitudes—people annoyed at having to be called up to do this scene again in his memory, for example. Gradually it evolved that all the props were frozen, just like the images, so that food was formed out of plastic and not edible and the place settings were glued to the table tops. Together these ideas became the aesthetic that informed every aspect of the production.

Playfully exchanging ideas and images, Tilford and Carlisle found the metaphors for the piece. With the actors, they constructed a reality that governed the reality of the play and gave clues for all the subsequent decisions of character and design.

Metaphor is a primary means by which we learn. We take the realities of one construct and transfer them to another. We say that sound travels in "waves" because the waves of the ocean are something we understand; by using the metaphor of wave, we now can imagine the movement of sound. If you say someone "bubbles" with enthusiasm, or "steams" with anger, you use a metaphor to give us an image of the person. We call someone "a mountain of a man" or "a tiger." If we know art, we might say, "That is a Turner sky" or "He has a Jackson Pollock mind."

When we think about finding a metaphor for a theatre work, we are attempting to frame what will be new to the audience in a construct that helps them receive it. The very fact of *performing* instead of *being* on stage is a metaphoric act. The audience has certain expectations of a performer. There is a construct to the experience. But we search for elaboration of this stage event. What meanings might it have?

When Laurence Olivier directed and acted his film of *Hamlet*, he was much taken with Freudian psychology and specifically the implications of Freud's essay on the Oedipus complex. He let that set of ideas frame the film, and the scene in Gertrude's bedroom, where Hamlet confronts his mother with her offense, was designed to look like a huge mouth. Contemporary taste might find this exaggerated, but there was no doubting the artistic point of view that governed the film.

✳ *Finding the Metaphor*

When you start planning for a public performance, try to have a series of conversations involving everyone—performers, designers, directors, writers (who might be all the same people)—over a period of several weeks. These should be open-ended dialogues where a lot of ideas are thrown into a basket. People go away and come back, having thought about the work in the meantime. Only a few of the many ideas will be used, but the group will come to understand where it is headed and why. You will develop your own reasons for making choices. A lot of the conversation will be the search for guiding metaphors.

Leader Dialogue

Suppose we say to ourselves, "Imagine he is a storyteller and everyone is seated around a campfire." The campfire is a metaphor for the performance. It will guide how we talk and how we think about the audience. What if we said, "These people have stepped out of a Toulouse-Lautrec painting?" Can you picture the ambiance, a sense of color, an attitude that is implied? We wouldn't have to dress everyone as Toulouse-Lautrec characters to make that happen. We are looking for metaphors that have the power to determine behavior and create a condition for the performance. It is the "as if" statements you make about the context of the work that become its metaphor.

As we read and talk about the material we are going to perform, try to get your images going. Let us spin off each other. See where it takes us. Remember, we won't use it all. But every idea goes into the basket.

Side Coaching

Imagine that:

> *The characters exist in the mind of the author and speak only through her.*
> *The stories are told as if the characters tumbled off the pages of a child's bookshelf.*
> *The characters are toys in a shop window.*
> *The audience is a hostile group of drunken revelers in an Irish pub.*
> *The audience is a group of old women on a bus tour.*
> *The characters are workers in an automated assembly plant.*

Advice to the Leader

As soon as the performers identify a useful metaphor, they will find its implications. Think of these questions: What would be the right place for this work to take place if it were not taking place in a theatre? What are the important ideas within the work that will be illuminated by attaching them to ideas outside the play?

Side Coaching

There will be metaphors for moments within a piece and larger metaphors that guide the entire work. Let them tumble out in conversations. Some people work in concrete images. Some work in atmosphere and feeling. All these are useful. It is not important at first to categorize them, but rather to let them spin out and see how useful they are in helping a theatre piece make its statement.

The use of guiding metaphors is often the difference between a drab "putting on" of a script and a true "making of theatre." Given the elaborate instructions that come with packaged play scripts, anyone can "put on a play." No one even has to understand it! A director can tell everyone what to do, including the designers. Blocking, sets, lights, props, and costumes can be good or bad. The audience may have a pretty good time. But there is very little about the experience that is authentic. It is a "paint-by-numbers" event. No one discovers new ideas or invents a theatrical moment. Finding the metaphors forces the company to make inner connections, to discover what is in the words that leaps beyond the page and speaks about life to an audience. "If this were something else, what would it be?"

A caution: A metaphor is a *tool* for working. Any image will be useful for some things and not for others. It is a mental construct, not a blueprint. A metaphor should be discarded when it no longer provides ideas. And some that are tried will work for a moment, but will not be relevant in another spot. Playing with metaphor is a way of making lateral leaps of the imagination, feeding and nourishing creativity. When Hamlet speaks

> "O, that this too too solid flesh would melt,
> Thaw, and resolve itself into a dew!
> Or that the Everlasting had not fixt
> His canon 'gainst self-slaughter! O God! O God!
> How weary, stale, flat, and unprofitable
> Seem to me all the uses of this world!
> Fie on't! O fie! 'Tis an unweeded garden
> That grows to seed; things rank and gross in nature
> Possess it merely. That it should come to this! (Act I, sc. ii)

Shakespeare starts with an image of flesh as ice, leaves it, then calls up an image of the world as a weed-ridden garden. And then he leaves that. An actor needs to be able to see these images and use them for what they provide to the moment. The whole speech, Hamlet's lament for the early marriage of his mother to his uncle after the death of his father, might be imagined by the performer as taking place in the aches and fever of a sick bed, or in the icy chill of a prison cell, or as a swimmer drowning, or a mouse trapped in tar, or a child punished and sullen, talking to himself in a room alone. That will become a metaphor for the actor.

There are metaphors that work within a line or a scene and metaphors that work for the whole construct of a piece. The game of inventing and testing metaphors is essential to exploring the possibilities of a piece of theatre. It is a kind of fertilizer for sustained growth, offering nutrients to the imagination.

✳ Practicing with Metaphor

Leader Dialogue

Many of you have played the party game, "If you were a color, what color would you be? If you were a car, what car would you be? If you were a month, etc." Let's talk about what that game means.

Advice to the Leader

If many in the group have not done this, then you must ask them to write down the answers to those questions and talk with them about their choices. What did each image help them see about themselves? The game is essentially a game of metaphor. Each question has implications for attitudes and behavior. If they know this game, then you can go on to the visual metaphor exercise.

✳ Visual Metaphors

When your group is ready to present material (a play, scenes from a play, their own dialogues, monologues, poems), try this exercise. They should have their material in hand and be quite familiar with it.

Bring in a few art books. They can be from any period, but they need to have a lot of illustrations. Give people time to browse through the books and become familiar with the images. Using their poems, monologues, or dialogues, they find a visual metaphor, using the pictures in the art book, to frame their presentation. Provide them with the box of generic props and sound equipment. You may add a box of hats, a box of scarves of different sizes and shapes, or a box of gloves to the resources. They could use furniture, ladders, or basic set blocks as well.

Leader Dialogue

Using the paintings and sculptures in the art books, your task is to pick one image that will act as a metaphor for your presentation. Ask yourself the questions, "If our work were one of these paintings or sculptures, which one would it be?" Don't try to act out the art work or reproduce it. The job is to study the image and talk about its implications for attitude, movement, gesture, and point of view. How do you want the audience to perceive you? How do you think about yourselves? Take no more than ten minutes to settle on your choice, and then discuss its implications. Then stage the first two or three minutes of your performance reflecting your choice. You can show us the image at the beginning or at the end, but we are not going to guess. You can choose figural or abstract art, sculpture, painting, architecture, or a decorative object.

Side Coaching

Think about the implications of place, color, kinds of body shapes, vocal qualities, points of view, attitudes toward who is watching. Decide who you are within the whole construct and how you relate to each other. Are you crowded together? Are you distant? Are you friendly? Are you languid? Are you energetic? Is the audience likely to be hostile? Indifferent? Startled?

Advice to the Leader

Allow time to choose and discuss, but make each group commit early to a decision. The *choice* is *not* the issue. *The issue is discovering how a visual image can become a metaphor* for a theatrical presentation and how it guides and colors the work. When the groups appear to have worked through the ideas, ask them to present their choices.

Follow-up Dialogue

What issues did you have to discuss to make your choice? How did your choice influence what you did? What new ideas about the presentation did you get from the image? If you were to go on, would you stick with that image? Audience, what unifying features did you notice coming out of the metaphors? When you saw the art work, were you surprised? Did you see the connections? Performers, when did the image run out of steam and stop providing ideas? Did you consider working with a group of images rather than a single one? Did it ever get too literal? Did the image get in the way? Did the image teach you anything about the essence of the piece?

Deepening the Experience

Consider a whole range of metaphors for your presentations. You can borrow from science, from everyday objects, from literature, from images, from nature. Remember that everything that exists has the potential to be a metaphor for something else: "I am a camera," "I am a lightpost," "We are ants in an ant farm." The group may take a printed script or a story and look for guiding metaphors. They can make a list of possible metaphors for a particular scene or poem. They can identify a cluster of metaphors—images within the same category—to inform a work.

It is likely that different scenes within an entire play or different poems in a presentation will have their own guiding metaphors, or cluster of metaphors. It is often helpful in understanding relationships between speakers to see them in an image. "You are two overstuffed chairs." This does not mean that they try to look like two overstuffed chairs. Nor does it mean that throughout their interactions they are two overstuffed chairs. It means that they ask themselves what does this suggest for our interaction and our attitudes so long as it seems to apply.

Conveying What the Play Is About

Finding metaphors is part of the task of understanding what the theatre event is about. Art that has any lasting impact tells us about something important—not necessarily something big, but something important. One way theatre informs us is by letting us see the world askew. Like *Hamlet,* theatre is set in motion by "time out of joint," asymmetry, imbalance, too much or too little, something in the wrong place at the wrong time. Whether it is comic or tragic, it is this "out-of-kilter" quality that captures our attention and makes us look at a real human condition. What is it? Misplaced patriotism, destructive envy, excessive pride, bitter disappointment, impossible expectations, loving the wrong person, choosing the wrong moment, saying the wrong thing, loving too much, loving too little, holding on too long, growing old with regret, growing old with despair, being young and ambitious, being lost in confusion, being angry and bewildered, losing spirituality in a material world. Make your own list. You have to know what a work is about before you can explore its subtleties.

Do you have to know what the work is about before you can discover the metaphors that illuminate it? We have found that when images and ideas suggest themselves, they often help unravel questions about what the work is about. A test metaphor may not work—they often don't—and that helps affirm what is *not* in the work as well as what is.

Suppose the answer consists of reciting the actions of the piece. "The play is about a man who murders his best friend in order to get his wife, and he gets caught." Is there nothing else? Is the play about irresistible lust, about deception, about justice? Or is it truly just the story, with no exploration of the larger questions? It may not have much substance—or the reader has not yet learned how to look for it.

The company must discuss what the work is about, because it will affect the way everyone approaches their tasks. Where do you place emphasis? Which moments need to be foreground and which are the background fabric? What is the tone and atmosphere? What attitudes do performers bring to the performance persona?

A story, poem, or play can be about more than one thing.

Othello is a play about jealousy, for sure. It is also a play about the tragedy of rash actions and the capacity for evil to work its way on innocent, but self-doubting, persons. What will be the emphasis in our performance? If we focus only on Iago, then it is a play about revenge for slights, real and imagined. If we focus on Desdemona, then it is a play about innocent victims of distorted passions. But either of these points of view would diminish the rich texture of the piece. How do we let these elements be seen and, at the same time, decide on the perspective with which we color the whole production? The nature of the performers, the situation of the times, and our own artistic visions will help us decide. Why are *we* doing this play now? What is *our* performance about? If we cannot answer this question, we should probably be doing some other piece of theatre.

As the rehearsal period goes forward, it is the job of the person out front to help everyone see that each piece of the work contributes to a cohesive vision. The group has to establish the tone of an element, shape the emphasis, reexamine the language, look for the threads and links to the whole. The group must take responsibility for the temperature of the work. The leader acts as its thermostat.

Establishing Focus

The leader must be sure there is an eye and an ear out front—a surrogate audience member—acutely aware of the intention of the production. To a large degree, the job is establishing focus. Focus is partly visual. We have done focus exercises and "dressing the stage" exercises that help performers become aware of themselves on stage in relation to others, and to give and take focus. Visual focus is critical to understanding the meaning of the scene.

In the "chair dance," we tested the emotional impact of compositional devices. Part of the performer's job is to help each stage composition give the right emotional impact and draw the audience's attention appropriately. The leader helps the performers keep that in mind. Someone out front must critique the focus constantly, and prod the actors to revise when a pose or a movement interrupts the picture, distracts, covers, or gets boring.

This is not the conventional notion of blocking, which is a director working out the stage movements and setting them. Rather, we agree on furniture and spatial arrangements, having discussed them in conversations about space and design. We talk about what is going on in a particular moment. Then actors improvise within those conditions until they find a set of movements or relationships that do the job. You note the choices in scripts or in a prompt book. As better ideas come along later, they replace the first ones. Focus, then, becomes a goal of the entire ensemble.

We discussed *variety* as an important aesthetic element. As the actors work, they may tend to favor particular compositions or physical attitudes. These have to be balanced with the need to have variety in the look of the stage and to use repetition for specific purposes. The leader warns actors when things are getting monotonous or unclear and calls for better ideas. Here are some strategies to get people sensitive to focus:

> Rotate actors who are not performing into the audience so eventually all get a good sense of the visual impact of the work.
>
> Ask for comments and discussion from these "designated observers."
>
> Freeze moments so that performers can test the focus.
>
> Ask where the focus ought to be at a given moment.
>
> Ask where it actually seems to be.

Focus is also aural—what is heard. Aural focus is accomplished by variations in volume and tempo of speech and by changes in emotional intensity ("faster, slower, louder, softer"). The listener out front calls attention to changes or the lack of them, to things missed or overlooked, to things inappropriately emphasized.

Performers may have clever ideas about how to do something, but the action may be too small or too obscure to be picked up by the audience. Only out front can we see this clearly. Likewise, actors may want to make a big performance out of something because they have a great idea about how to do it, but it overshadows an important plot or character detail and pushes the audience's focus to the wrong issue.

In the end, we need to know where to look and what we have seen and heard. The leader must take responsibility for assuring everyone's understanding of focus.

✳ Five Frames

Go back to the "Five Frames" we played earlier and play it again for issues of composition and focus. To practice the five frames, you could review a familiar play—we have used *Romeo and Juliet*—or simply go to the piece you are working on. Divide into groups of four or five. Each group selects five key moments and does its own five freeze frames telling that story.

Advice to the Leader

Don't worry if all the groups select the same scenes or not. They will not come up with identical compositions. The variety contributes to the discussion. Get them on their feet, working quickly, responding spontaneously to the choices of others. Ask them to consider where the audience will be, since focus depends heavily on the relationship of stage and seating. Show them with the "eyes closed, eyes open" method.

Follow-up Dialogue

Let's talk about the choice of scenes. Did they tell you anything about what is important in the story? What elements of focus worked for you? Could you see the critical action? What about others in the scene? Can there be shared focus? Primary and secondary focus? Shift in focus? Did you get any scenic ideas from doing these? How did they suggest blocking within the scenes? What did you pay attention to when you were adding yourself into the scene?

Advice to the Leader

Listen for an understanding of the way composition tells its own story. Listen for recognition of the responsibility of each person to contribute to the focus of a scene. This technique teaches people how to contribute to the total picture on the stage and helps them determine the key moments that need to be captured in performance. It can also be a simple teaching tool to see how a group has grasped a work . . . what is it about? The five frames can help establish the blocking. They may also be used as a basis for choreography.

✳ Deepening the Experience with Convention and Metaphor

Once each group has done its five frames, offer them a choice of embellishments to work into their performance. The embellishments might include a set of rhythm instruments; a set of bells or whistles; a set of fans; a long string to be stretched taut as a frame or sort of giant "cat's cradle" around the action; a set of baseball caps; a set of simple black half-masks; a set of dowel rods; a set of gloves; a large rectangular piece of cloth; a set of empty picture frames; or whatever your imagination can provide from the generic props and sound equipment that the group is collecting. Lay out the embellishments in sets or categories.

Leader Dialogue

Your group must choose an embellishment or a category of embellishment and use it throughout. Here are bells; here are rhythm instruments; here is the string. Give a style or flavor to your version of the story. It is critical that within a group you do not mix up embellishment categories —not one dowel rod for a sword, and a glove for one character and a hat for another, not something to be used to substitute for some actual object. Resist the literal when you can. What you are doing is exploring the idea of a convention or a concept, a simple stylistic thread that will run through your work, giving it a particular flavor.

Advice to the Leader

To use their embellishment, they will have to think and talk about what is important, what is the character of the piece, what should be emphasized and how. That is why "making do" with a substitute prop adds nothing to their understanding. The use of a convention —a single element or category of elements—requires the players to consider metaphor and to imagine a "look" or a device that gets to the heart of their piece. If three or four groups work on the same piece and each group chooses a different kind of embellishment, everyone will learn a lot more about the piece itself.

Follow-up Dialogue

Talk about the process. Ask, "How did you choose? What did you have to think about to use the embellishment effectively? Audience, how did the embellishment focus on the critical action? How did it express a point of view?"

For many people, this movement to the abstract, to the use of convention rather than literal representation, is difficult. It is important to struggle with it in the context of preparing for the finished work. Understanding abstraction is critical to discovering elements of focus and design. What is essential in our work? How do we attend to that? Moving to abstraction and convention helps the group go beyond the ordinary in imagining the stage space. It is the key to the group's internalizing the style of a production.

Realizing the Truth of the Performance Moment

Remember that we are always searching for honesty on the stage, for the audience to believe that what they see is really happening, to real people, in a real situation—no matter how fantastical the context. Whether we are speaking a poem or playing a scene, speaking directly to the audience or among ourselves, every word has to come from a real place in the mind and body of the performer. Then the audience will participate with it.

When a group is working toward a public performance, they will need to work on the truth of specific moments, segments they have memorized and are ready to bring to life. The leader may also have to be an acting coach.

A great deal of the work in this area goes back to the patience exercises, taking the time to let the reality of the interactions come into the mind and out through speech and action. Inexperienced performers read or recite memorized speech with stilted expression. At other times, people work at "acting." They put on facial expressions or meanings that are superficial, mere indicators of the content, but not truthful portrayals of anything. These habits can be broken.

In order to free performers from dull patterns, or to stimulate their imaginations about a scene or a monologue, it is necessary to break into their thought processes, change their concentration patterns, create new synapses. Think of human behavior in the brain and nervous system as rivulets in a soft clay bed. If a thing is done once, it lays down a small track, twice, and the groove gets deeper. The only way to stop the groove from becoming a rut is to block its path, put a rock in the way or dig a trench and force the water to find a new direction. In doing that, performers find spontaneous understanding. They drop deeper into the moment. They become more honest.

✳ The Balls

You will need a dozen soccer-sized balls. (They are available cheap in toy departments, drugstores, and discount marts.) We carry them around in a big black plastic bag and call them "the acting teachers." For these exercises, the participants have learned lines—dialogue or monologue or sections of poems. They may be working with segments of Shakespeare speeches. If they are working on dialogue, they should pair up with their scene partners.

Leader Dialogue

We are now on a discovery mission to find new layers in the text. Not everything you find will be something you can use. But there are texts and subtexts. We have to find a lot of possibilities before we can settle. You need your scene partner or a partner who also has a memorized monologue. Begin your scene or monologue. Take this ball and throw it back and forth with your partner as you talk. Keep the ball in play. If you have a monologue, the partner is a silent but active player. If you have a dialogue with your partner, do your scene forgetting all the blocking and business you have rehearsed and just focus on the ball. Repeat the dialogue several times. Let the dynamics of the ball throwing break up and change the spoken interaction. You are free to pause or play with the ball any way you like, but keep the ball in play. Keep the ball active, even if you throw it up in the air or bounce it. If it gets dropped, keep the scene going and go after the ball.

Side Coaching

Keep the ball going. Keep the scene going. Now, one of you hold on to the ball and the other try to get it. Make it the intention of your scene. "I want it." "You can't have it." Go after it or try to keep it from your partner. Do not "act" like you want the ball, really want the ball. Work to get it. Work to keep it away and keep the scene going.

Now, imagine that the ball is extremely fragile and valuable. You still want it badly, but both of you know that if you break it, you both will be in terrible trouble—or neither of you will have it. Switch intentions with your partner.

Advice to the Leader

Continue each segment for as long as you can see people working at it and getting something out of it. Switch so that people can try both sides of the intentions. You can do this with a group of people at one time, if everyone in the group is working on scenes in pairs, or you can do it with individual pairs. Even if the noise level is high and they have to shout, it will help free them from stiffness and awkward speaking. If you don't have a supply of balls, try throwing a sheaf of papers on the floor and have people pick them up while doing their scene.

Side Coaching

Try pleading, try shouting, try throwing the ball on particular words or lines. If your partner holds on to the ball, take it away from her. If it falls on the floor, keep the scene going as you go to get it. Try coaxing if you need to, or scolding; try to deceive, be coy, try teasing, anything to get the ball, and always respond honestly to what your partner does. Throw the ball, bounce it to each other. Use the interaction of the ball to interact with your partner. But keep the scene going. Stay in the scene. If you laugh, make it the character who is laughing. If you get annoyed, let the character get annoyed.

Deepening the Experience

Take the scenes with the ball and experiment with them one at a time in front of the group—the whole cast or a class. Encourage the subtext of keeping the ball in play. Take the scene back to early moments if it hasn't come alive. Stop it when the players have learned to really interact around the ball. Look at several sequences. Encourage physical touching, honest work to get the ball.

Follow-up Dialogue

Audience, when did the scene really come alive? Actors, how did the ball force you to be more honest? Did anything change? What did you find? What underlying relationships did you discover? What did you see in other people's work that was new or exciting? What did you find in your character that you didn't know was there? Did you discover the power issues in the scene? Who has the power? Who tries to get it? When did the ball help uncover the power relationships? Remember that this is exploration. Not everything you discover will be useful to you.

What we are trying to do is to get deep inside the honesty of the moment. You have something to say. What is it? Why are you saying it now? Suddenly, when you have to focus on fighting over this object or keeping it in play, you uncover layers of meaning. You ignite fires, set off explosions. Most good theatre is negotiation, around ideas, around objects, around power relationships. The power question becomes manifest when you translate it into the ball.

It is the job of the leader to help performers uncover their connections to the material. Open-ended exercises like the balls put the power of that discovery in the mind and body of the performer. The leader's job is to set the conditions for exploration and call attention to new moments of honesty when they happen. Actors will sense them as well. Together you work toward the performance. You may discover you actually want a ball in the scene!

✳ More Discovery

Try any or all of the following. Work simultaneously, enjoying the chaos and the need to concentrate within it.

Leader Dialogue

Stand in two lines about ten feet apart with your partner opposite, and speak across the void trying to make your partner listen over the distance and really attend to what you mean.

Do it again, trying to keep others from hearing what you are saying. Or, in the two lines, sing your speeches as if they were grand opera. Sing them simultaneously, outdoing each other.

Spread out around the room. Now dart quickly into an empty space and say a line.

Dart quickly into another space and say another one. Sit down on the floor suddenly and speak. Then jump up and say something else.

Run around the room, playing tag, and speaking your dialogue.

Lie on the floor all by yourself and close your eyes. Speak your words quietly to yourself, convincing yourself of what you are saying.

Lie on your backs, head to head with your scene partners, looking up at the ceiling (or the sky), and whisper your dialogue or monologue as if you were speaking to each other across a secret space. Form each word carefully, completely, enjoying the value of the words themselves. Since you cannot look at each other, use this time to listen carefully and to speak to someone who is present but invisible.

Try the next ones working simultaneously, then perform in pairs so others can learn from watching.

Rearrange the chairs in the room while you exchange dialogue.
Take your partner by the shoulder and guide him along while you speak.
Take a stone out of your shoe while you talk with your partner.
Look through the pages of a newspaper as you talk.

The whole idea is to give the performers something demanding to do around which they have to shape the speech. Instead of thinking what to say next, they are now engaged in something physically real. In staging the actual scene for performance, it may then be useful to take the discoveries of the games right into production, putting elements of the activities into the scene as texture.

Follow-up Dialogue

Did you discover anything new? What happened to the relationships? Is there anything you can use from these exercises?

Deepening the Experience

Go back to your scene. This time, one of you has the task to try to speak directly to the other and look directly into his or her eyes. The other person does not want to look directly at the partner and continually tries to get away. As you play the scene, keep insisting on your task—to look into your partner's eyes or to avoid looking into his or her eyes.

Move into physical contact. *One of you wants to leave and the other wants you both to stay. Play that in your scene. Grab hold of the person; pull away. Step in front of the door; do whatever you have to insist on your own desire. Be careful not to hurt your partner, but do not hesitate to be firm.*

One of you performs some small comforting physical task for the other while you speak—combing her hair, buttoning up a sleeve button, massaging his shoulders, brushing lint off a coat lapel, helping your partner on with a coat, tying a tie, tying shoes. Get imaginative, but don't try to embarrass and never hurt your partner. *The partner can give in to the action or resist.*

All of these can be done with monologues, dialogues, poems, songs, or any performed moment. Actors can take these exercises into their individual preparation. They are all potentially self-guided. The goal is to break out of flat, memorized patterns and find human textures. These exercises help people find out what they are listening to, and it gives them comfort in their bodies so that the dialogue is released into a natural framework.

Illuminating the Truth of the Internal and External Dialogue

Eventually everyone has to deal with more complex exchanges, with sustaining the truth of performance through long segments. Skilled professionals are still studying and practicing their art. In the chapter on acting, we mention some texts to keep you going. But here are a few well-tested techniques that may prove helpful within the production phase.

Every line of dialogue is important and conveys meaning. Short interactions that ask and answer questions often have their own rhythms that play off each other and help performers react honestly. When someone must deliver a long poem, or a long section of dialogue, it takes some skill to keep the speech continuously interesting, to the actors and to the audience.

✳ *Image, Metaphor, and Condition*

Just as images and metaphors help find the meaning in the piece as a whole, they help a performer explore an individual moment. Added to them is the idea of condition or situation that informs the way one sees a speech or relationship. A coach can suggest images, metaphors, and conditions as part of the texturing of scene work or speeches.

Leader Dialogue

Your task is to think up conditions that give context to the work you are doing or that provide an insight into the true relationships within the moment being rehearsed. Here are samples:

> *Imagine yourselves marching along side by side where you are not supposed to be talking and you are afraid of being overheard.*
> *Imagine yourselves trading childhood secrets.*
> *Imagine yourselves quarreling over a favorite toy.*
> *Imagine yourselves only half listening, but rather absorbed in your own inner vision.*
> *See yourself as inside a dark room and worried that something else might be there with you while you talk.*

Advice to the Leader

This work is intended to probe a theatrical moment for its contribution to the whole of the performance and to arrive at its textures. Some things will work and some will not. Helping people imagine conditions, images, and metaphors is a road to their doing this kind of work for themselves. Part of the leader's job is to see when the images work in the whole and when they are interesting but distracting excursions and need to be dispensed with.

✳ *Intentions, Motivations, and Objectives*

Different acting theorists have used the terms intentions, motivations, and objectives to get at the problem of meaning. Going back to Stanislavsky and his interpreters, these terms are about driving the acting through real meaning. There is meaning in words—definitions—and there is meaning in context. Actors must be clear about both. There is also the critical question of "Why am I saying this to you now?" Most credible acting has to do with being able to answer that question.

Advice to the Leader

If a performer is having difficulty making a scene make sense, he or she may not really have decided what it is the words are supposed to do; that is, what effect they are supposed to have on the other person(s) in the scene. The leader poses such questions to the actor about a specific piece of dialogue.

Side Coaching

What effect are you trying to have on your partner? Are you trying to make him jealous? Are you trying to pay her back? Are you trying to explain yourself? Are you trying to make them think something different from what you are actually saying?

✳ An Exercise for Practicing Intentions

Leader Dialogue

Find a partner. Your task is to improvise a scene based on two conflicting sets of intentions. One of you plays this basic intention: I want to get out of here. *The other plays:* I want to keep you here. *You and your partner decide on who you are and where you are. What is the condition of your situation? Then start the scene going. Improvise the dialogue you need. Keep it going. Keep the intention going. You may use words and action but you may not hurt each other. You can move or sit. Don't stray from either of your intentions. You will leave if you are not stopped. You will not let him leave.*

Advice to the Leader

These scenes can get started around the room simultaneously. Don't let the actors take too long deciding who they are. Let them work simultaneously for a minute or two, once they get going. Then freeze the group and ask pairs to work before the group. Let the improvisations go on for a time until the intentions are really working. Freeze them before they dwindle out.

Side Coaching

Consider any kind of pair in any suitable situation—parent/child, lovers, friends. Make them real. Avoid clichés or stereotypes. Get in the moment and stay there. Use silence. Be patient. Take your time. Find the real words. Stay true to the intentions. Keep it going. Don't stray from the intentions into the reasons. Keep her here. Try to leave. Don't let him go. Get out of there.

Follow-up Dialogue

How did the intentions help keep the energy flowing? What were really true moments, for performers and for the audience? What happens when you stray from your primary intention? What did you learn about honest acting from watching this? From doing it?

✳ Using Subtext

Subtext is a very rich well from which to draw. Subtext is the idea that there are deep conflicts, deep relationships, deep desires among characters that affect the words but are not spoken in the words. A character may say, "You didn't water the chrysanthemums," but the subtext is anger over a failed relationship. The dialogue may be, "You didn't eat your breakfast," but the subtext is a struggle to see that one child gets punished and the other knows she is Mother's favorite. Subtext may be revealed by talking about metaphor. If you perform "Humpty Dumpty" with the subtext that two performers are in contention over political power, the piece will be a political metaphor and all the lines will gather new meaning.

Leader Dialogue

Now we are going back to the scene of leaving and staying. Both of you have an underlying subtext, I could hurt you if I wanted to, and you know it. Make the tension between your two sets of meanings, text and subtext, work for you. You want to go, but you could get hurt. You want to keep her here, but you could get hurt.

Follow-up Dialogue

How did the subtext affect your behavior? Every word spoken on the stage has meaning. It is our job to give it the right meaning for this production. We do this by knowing the text—what the author wrote, the intentions, what the character wants to be the result of what is said— and the subtext—what is really going on between these characters that drives the whole conversation. This is true in dialogue and monologue, whether you are speaking to someone else on stage or to the audience. We have to know these things and use them.

✳ What Does the Leader Say?

The goal of the leader is to help performers find the meaning and play it. The trick is to ask the right question and provide the right stimuli. When there does not seem to be real truth or when the intentions seem to be heading the scene in a direction that distorts the larger meaning, it is necessary for the leader to intervene. *It will not be useful simply to tell people what to do,* but rather to help them find out what they are really doing, and help them redirect their own paths in a more productive way. The process is *questioning.*

Leader Dialogue

Why are you saying that? What do you really want him to think? If you said what you actually mean, what would you say? Why are you stopping there on the middle of the stair? What stopped you? What made you turn around? Why didn't you just go on out of the room? What reaction do you have to what she just said? What is your real inclination? Why do you suppress it?

Advice to the Leader

As you ask these questions, the actor is obliged to go under the words of the text to the truth of the situation. It is critical that we perform the meaning and not try to perform the emotion. In life we don't try to be angry. Rather, when we are angry, we try to get even with someone, or punish someone, or escape, or hurt someone. These are our intentions and these are the things that actors play. This is basic Stanislavsky theory, and no one has written better about it. From the point of view of the leader, it is essential that we not focus on "How are you feeling?" but rather on "What are you trying to do?"

Deepening the Experience

Ask the performers to prepare detailed descriptions of their characters including their personal histories, relating exactly what they have been doing just before the moments happen on stage. Ask them to write undermeanings for their lines; that is, what is going on in their minds as they say the written words out loud. They may speak the undermeanings at some point as a way to understand better what it is they actually say. (See *An Actor Prepares,* by Stanislavsky and Charles McGaw's, *Acting is Believing.*) Ask actors to improvise unwritten scenes between these characters.

✳ A Task for Attacking a Complex Speech

Each performer has a long memorized monologue with which he or she is very familiar and is carrying a copy of the printed text.

Leader Dialogue

Your task is to find all the possible thought patterns going on within that speech—all the times you and the character sense a new question or have another idea. This is sometimes called the "beats" of a speech. Take the speech apart and put in a mark whenever any new thought enters your mind. What is it? Try thinking of a new thought on every phrase. Let the idea of continuous inner dialogue work overtime. Imagine that a new question, or a new intention, or a new image forms with each three or four words, and then read through the speech aloud, allowing for each of those new thoughts to take place. Remember, each of us is really a multitude of voices competing in our heads. Be patient and take the time to hear those competing voices. Consider again all the changes in "To be or not to be." Hamlet ponders suicide, rejects it, ponders it, rejects it, runs through a list of life's calumnies about which he has ironic and grievous thoughts, fears life after death, ponders action, ponders inaction, and comments on his own ponderings. What inner dialogue breaks up your speech? How many sides of your character can you find there?

Sometimes it is useful to play the conflict, that is, to work on the place where conflicting ideas and needs of the character meet, the "yes, but" aspects of life. Find those in your character. When you have completed your work, present these studies to each other in their highly divided state.

Side Coaching

There may be long pauses, even between words. Let that happen. What are all the possible connotations of each word? Each phrase? Which ones are you choosing? Examine everything.

Follow-up Dialogue

Listening to your fellow actors, which breaks are effective, which are confusing? What new things did you hear? A pair of actors can do the same thing in a dialogue. Once you have tried this, go back and decide which are the really important new thoughts, and group the dialogue back together.

Caution

Audience. Your job, always, is to tell what you saw, what you heard, what you missed. Do not tell the other person what they should do. *Let your fellow actors decide how they want to solve the problem.*

Sharing the Job

Acting is hard work. Some people have a gift for it, but that doesn't mean they don't still have to work at it. The leader can recognize when a performer is shortchanging a piece of dialogue. Actors can become sensitive to the same things. It is important to let actors question themselves and each other. "Why did you do that? If you say that to me like that, I'm going to react this way, and then the next thing you say doesn't make sense." Actors gain by referring questions back to themselves rather than relying on a director to answer all the questions. If the writer is present, he or she may illuminate something. Likewise, performers may illuminate weaknesses in the writing by pointing out more direct lines of action, more honest lines of emotional drive. Writers can learn better sequence from following the impulses of disciplined actors.

Establishing Rhythms, Highlights, Accents, and Contrasts

Just as each speech has units, highlights, and pulse changes, the entire piece will have divisions, connections, and accents. We spoke about the need for variety when we talked about building a whole work from various parts. We also talked about beginnings, middles, and ends, about the need for development time, and the need to identify when the moment is over. Any whole work needs its rhythm, its variations in tempo and meter. There may be lulls and bursts, periods of steady complication and tension building, playful interludes, rowdy intrusions. Even comedy must have its quiet moments for the audience to rest from the laughter.

A lot of the rhythmic arrangement is intuitive. You feel that a certain section goes "rat-a-tat-tat" while another section is a steady "hummmmmm." You also know that one "hummmmmmmm" after another may lose people's attention and that a constant barrage of "rat-a-tat-tat" will wear them down. The job is to make the right changes at the right time.

Tools for Establishing Rhythm

✳ Pace

Pace can be the actual speed of speaking the words, the time between the sentences, and the time between different persons speaking. Actors can practice the technical demands of varying pace. This is the "faster/slower" part of directing and acting.

Leader Dialogue

To discover some new possibilities in your speech, speak as fast as you possibly can, allowing no time between sentences. Speed through and try to keep the basic intentions. Jump in on top of each other's lines almost before they have ended.

Advice to the Leader

People will forget lines and laugh. Have them go back over sequences until they can actually perform the moment at high speed. Like the earlier exercises, this is a discovery technique. It helps performers find what they can use.

Leader Dialogue

This time, vary the speed as you work. Take some lines very fast, then switch to very slow speaking. Explore and discover what is contained in your work.

✹ Dynamics

This is the "louder/softer" part. Loud and soft are ways of underscoring the energy of a scene. They can be arbitrary and without meaning, but they can also help with texture and variety.

Leader Dialogue

Go through your speech and choose loud and soft sections. Try building from soft to loud. Try making sharp cuts from loud to soft and vice versa. Use this as a discovery technique. Everyone work simultaneously. Top your partner by coming in loud. Undercut your partner by coming in soft. Reverse the roles. See what you can find.

✹ Movement

The speed, the amount, and the quality of movement affect the rhythm of the stage. The art of dance teaches us that movement speaks volumes by itself. We have been working on movement as part of acting and as part of defining space. Movement is also a big tool in establishing pace, dynamics, and focus. You need two perspectives: the internal energy of the performers and their own body awareness, and the eye of the viewer out front to test the effectiveness of movement in the whole. There are choices to be made: one person remaining still and others moving, two moving simultaneously, moving in different directions, moving at different speeds, moving curvilinearly or angularly—thousands of possibilities. Walking and talking simultaneously are sometimes difficult for beginning actors. They need to discover their capacities for experimenting with movement.

Leader Dialogue

With your scene partners, play the section again, this time changing your movement on each line. Each time you speak, move with a different quality. You might skip, roll on the floor, crawl, run, fall, or freeze in a position—whatever you like. When you are not speaking, give your partner focus either by freezing or by following them around.

Side Coaching

Make your movement decisive. Stop when it is over. Go directly to a place. Do not wander. Move with intent.

Advice to the Leader

You can do this exercise with specific scenes or with a group of individuals who have short monologues. They should practice jumping up on benches, turning around, running, sitting—all the time keeping up their talking.

Side Coaching

Repeat what you did in slow motion. Alternate slow motion with drops, falls, stretches. Come to a full stop between moves. Shift direction clearly. Make every choice decisive. Keep the dialogue coming.

✳ Entrances and Exits

Each time a new person comes on or off the stage, the dynamic changes. That is how the "French scene" concept developed. The French were right. The departure or arrival of a person creates a new physical energy, a new set of tensions, a new visual composition. This is true in normal conversation, and it is especially true in the theatre. What is also true is that the quality of the arrival and departure—quick, noisy, quiet, stealthily—makes its own statement. Variety, contrast, continuity, accent, and focus: they all apply.

Leader Dialogue

Let's go to the entrances and exits for your scene. Use all the choices you tried in the movement experiment. You can crawl in, run in, skip on stage, side step to the exit, dash out, walk deliberately, or leap off. Test the movement dynamics of the entrance and exit. Choose what you need to move the piece along.

✳ Music and Sound as Part of the Rhythm

Human beings respond to music without knowing they are doing so. Music occupies the center of our rituals and celebrations. Merchants play music to make people buy more of their products. Even in the era of silent movies, musicians sat in the pit and accompanied the action on the screen. Music and theatre are children of the same family. All performers can make music in some way. It belongs in your theatre.

You might begin your sessions together with songs. You may have favorite music that accompanies your warm-up. You may use music to motivate your space explorations and body sculptures. We have already suggested using bells, drums, sticks, and tambourines to embellish readings of poetry or telling of stories.

In a few months of collecting, your musical instrument bag will contain drums, clavés, rattles, bells, cymbals, whistles, ratchets, kazoos, maracas, castanets, penny whistles, and recorders. You may even have marimbas, a piano, an electronic keyboard, and any of the string, wind, or brass families available to you.

Try this exercise to integrate music into your performance.

Leader Dialogue

Throughout the rehearsal of this section (a scene, a poem, a monologue, a narration, or a collection of quotes), *each of you will have an instrument. Your task is to play whenever you can underscore, accent, or help a moment. It may be part of your own speaking or in response to someone else. Remember that you have to give and take focus in the scenes, so whatever you do musically must contribute to the moment. Your job is to augment. Be careful not to distract or draw undue attention to yourself—unless it is* your *moment. Silence is also valuable. Use it well.*

Side Coaching

Comment with your sound. If you find a sound you like, use it again in a similar situation. If someone else has something going, let it happen. Don't let the sound get muddy. Speaker, let the sound happen. Use it; become a part of it. Interact with it. You can pause and let it finish. Players, you can stop your sound when it has made its point. If someone establishes a tempo, go along with it. If you and another person work together, stay with them. But keep your ear on the text and where it is going.

Follow-up Dialogue

What worked? How can you refine it? Let's do it again and see how it develops.

Advice to the Leader

Music, including rhythmic and melodic sound, will probably become part of most of your theatrical presentations. You can use recorded music from the standard world's repertoire. You can sing. You can use an electronic keyboard that can imitate acoustic instruments and make a whole range of its own sounds. You might use music created by the performers on traditional instruments, folk instruments, electronic instruments, or rhythm instruments, or music created by a composer in response to a performance.

Music and sound can drive a theatre piece, not simply as interludes, but as a focusing element, as a reference to ideas or places, or as character embellishments. Selecting and using music belongs in the earliest stages of creating the work. It is a part of hearing the language of the whole. It will grow as the work grows. Performers must be involved because the music will become an essential element in their work.

Leader Dialogue

We have played with the music we can make on the spot. Now consider a broader range of musical sources. Identify music that might work within your piece. It can be music that underscores, that introduces, that accents, or all of the above. Talk with your partners. In the end you may not use the music, but your job is to identify music that can make a significant contribution and determine how you could incorporate it. Bring musical sources of your own. Go to music libraries. Identify musicians who might play or compose music for you.

In the end you want to encourage performers to listen, play, sing, and dance. You want them to absorb music into their bones, to hear music in words, to sense music in the interplay of characters. We cannot take up here all the ways that music might come into the life of your theatre group, but we believe you will grow together through including music in your work. It is a basic human activity. No culture seems to be without it.

Scenery, Costume, and Properties Contribute to the Rhythm of the Whole

When you watch a production, you see how each visual element contributes to the rhythm. An orange scarf, a pink hat, a yellow pillow, a striped shirt—anything can take focus or provide an accent. People appear, carry things on, leave them, move them around. The flow of energy rises and falls. You have to decide whether an object fits or not. Any item works by its contribution to the whole, not by itself. As the company understands the whole aesthetic, it will make better choices about each object. A hat that overshadows a person, a pair of socks that is too bright, a prop that takes too long to open, a box that is too big or too small—these are things that have to be fixed.

The right or wrong visual element can sustain or kill a performance. In earlier chapters, we discussed making simple, generic set elements both for exercises and for performance. We have described simple means for neutralizing space and for providing background. We also tried to encourage the use of found spaces for performance. We hope people will see the merit in setting work around existing doors and windows, hallways, archways, stairs, platforms, balconies, and other architectural frameworks, eliminating the necessity for elaborate set construction. We have experimented with staging theatre events in people's homes, in churches, in stores, in bars, in park shelter houses, in clearings in the woods, in dance studios, and on the fire escapes and rooftops of downtown alleyways, to name a few of our favorite experiments. But whatever the venue, each visual element in a space will make its claim, positively or negatively, on the performance. We can learn to make good choices.

✳ Learning to See

With a group of people learning to become aware of the value of visual elements, try this experiment. Over time your group will collect some vests, sweaters, sweatshirts, scarves, hats, jackets, and coats for basic costume pieces. Set out a group of them.

Leader Dialogue

Look around. Someone select three people who, because of the way they are dressed now, seem to belong together on the stage. Put these people up in front seated on three chairs, arranged any way you like. Now, take these clothing pieces and give them a unity in appearance. Now, someone arrange them in the space like the chair dance (e.g., seated, standing, kneeling) and audience, comment on the effect of the compositions as they change. Someone give them a simple change—like take off a hat, unbutton a coat, tie a scarf around the hips or shoulders or head. Now make them have unity but one stands out as more important than the others. Dress them so that they are clearly in three different plays.

Side Coaching

Talk about the choices. What else do you see? What happens when you make that little change? Is it really a "little" change?

Deepening the Experience

Try combining different kinds of fabric—polyester knits, woven woolens, bright prints, muted cottons, placing them side by side, and noting issues of contrast, complement, dissonance, harmony.

Try the same exercise with performers holding different props—a glass, a basketball, a flag, a large stuffed animal, a small stuffed animal, or other large and small elements. Comment on issues of focus, color, size, and character delineation as properties change hands. Discuss the way types of properties seem to belong in the same play while others do not.

Return to the idea of "the look" in the previous chapter. What does it take for a look to become realized? How can you create different rhythms in a similar look? How can you accent a look by creating a person or an object that is clearly not in it? How do visual elements punctuate a thought?

Refining the Rhythm

Everything that happens on stage contributes to the transitions from thought to thought, from moment to moment. Smoothing, adding, and eliminating tiny elements become the clockwork balancing of the final piece. How many heartbeats are needed? How many do we have?

When a group becomes increasingly aware that all elements have theatrical value, and that the meaning of the piece and the aesthetic of the whole drive these choices, then they are able to create art together. They have gone beyond putting on plays to making theatre.

Problem Solving

All theatrical endeavors run into problems as they come into the last stages of production. All have holes in imagination, unintegrated elements, incomplete resolutions, dead spots, technical confusion, inadequate preparation in some quarters, limited abilities in others.

The scheduled performance time will come, and everyone wants the piece to work. Decisions have to be made. There is a great temptation to resort to single-minded, if incomplete, solutions, out of desperation. However, a group that has learned to be creative, responsive, and responsible can solve problems itself rather than surrender its capacity to think intelligently to a single individual. As tension mounts, the leadership needs to help everyone work efficiently, to move the project forward without cutting off useful creative energy.

If a group sets the aesthetic of a work clearly, defines the tasks, and establishes the conditions, the performers are in a position to achieve their goals. From the beginning, the leader works on problems with the group as a whole. If no one is fully satisfied with the responses, the leader has to work to elicit a good range of new ideas. After working through the solution or solutions, the best ones will be those that satisfy the performers and the director, or whoever is accounting for the eyes out front. The leader or director should be a passionate participant, putting forth as many ideas as he or she can. The context is a problem that everyone is working on. Even then, people have to make choices. Someone will have to discard her favorite idea. The stronger the sense of the whole within the group, the easier it is to make final choices that everyone understands.

✳ Put Leader Dialogue into the Form of a Problem to Be Solved

From the beginning, even the most rudimentary tasks can be set as group problems.

Sample Leader Dialogue

Our task with this scene is to take the group from a tight, clustered group at the beginning to a broken, disparate group at the end. First create a tight group up right, giving focus to X. As your piece of dialogue comes up, or in response to someone else's line, take yourself out of the group and find your own spot down left, closed off enough so that Y has focus alone. Everyone give the speaker focus, or close yourself out so you don't take focus from the speaker.

Side Coaching

A, hold up halfway, and then find your settling spot later. B, we need a higher level position from you at that spot. Let's repeat it and see if it works. Clarify your moves. Don't lose focus. Now that works for me. Is anyone having a problem? Let's have A come out and watch while we do it again. Now that it's set, let's repeat it to fix it in our minds.

Sample Leader Dialogue

I can see that we have a transition problem here. There is an awkward pause. Can we either close it up or fill it? What are you doing during that time? Propose a solution.

The same problem-solving approach works for changing the dynamics of a scene. It is the leader's job to find language that makes the performers go back in and work, language that tickles the imagination, that provides images or possibilities. If the leadership is really working, a proposal to solve a problem can come from anyone in the group.

Deepening the Experience

Let each group determine the basic stage configurations for the piece they are working on. They improvise within the picture to determine individual sets of movements. A group designates an observer to watch from out front (saying their lines out there, if necessary) to test various propositions. In the exercise above it may be that the group needs to be diffuse at the beginning and clustered at the end. Allow the working group to come up with various suggestions, and then work them out in practice. Out-front observers comment on what seems to work best. Within a given scene, the leader may need to help the performers find actions that suit them.

Sample Leader Dialogue

Let's go back into the scene with a new task. Find a moment when you (X) physically take hold of him, and then find a moment when you (Y) break away. But play the quarrel as if you did not want someone in the next room to hear you arguing.

Or: Imagine that what she says actually has the effect of paralyzing you. You can't think or speak or move. You hear her but you can't respond. You just want to disappear.

Or: Imagine that you like words so much that when you speak them you cannot help but taste each one and savor it separately, both for what it means and the way it rolls around on the tongue. Then imagine that the flavor of the words causes you to move about, changing the character of the moves as the taste demands. Jump, hide, sit, loll, stand. Then select the two or three that suit you best.

Useless Directions to Avoid

There is some behavior that on the surface seems expedient but rarely is. It is the leader's obligation to inspire and open up possibilities. These behaviors tend to do just the opposite. They shut down creativity and inspire fear. This is our list of things to avoid.

Never give line readings. That is, never tell people how to say a line and expect them to imitate you. Why? It seems like a quick way to get something done. But if the person does not say the line properly because he or she does not understand the real intention of it, a mimicked line reading will not stick in the memory. Old habits will creep back and everyone will be frustrated. A good line reading comes from a full understanding of what the character is trying to do in the situation. That is the actor's job. Ask instead, "Why did you say that that way?" or "If you didn't say those words, what else might you say in this situation?"

Never ask, "How are you feeling on this line?" That implies that trying to feel something is useful. Trying to *accomplish* something *is* useful. Use instead, "What are you getting at?"

or "What is your reaction to what she just said? What does it make you want to do?"

Never say, "Say it with more feeling" or "Use more expression" or "Put more feeling into it." *Feeling* and *expression* are very general terms. Help the performers work out what is going on in the scene—the full background, the condition, the relationships, the past experiences, the intentions, the objectives, the subtext. Use the exercises with objects and physical action, if you need to get past flat readings. You may find directions like: "Enjoy the fact that you are tormenting him" or "Does that frighten you? How can you let us know that?"

Never say, "Use more facial expressions." Facial expressions must come from the inside, from getting at the honesty of the work. Telling people to use facial expressions does not help them identify what they are missing in the scene. An expressive face will come with being in the moment, finding the truth of the scene, finding the real meaning of the words, and finding the point of view toward the words and the actions.

Never push people around physically to get them to a spot. If your verbal instructions are not clear, you may wish to stand by them and demonstrate a turn or a backing-up motion. But it is better to set the problem: "Try to get there by the shortest means possible in the quickest time" and then critique the choice. "Turn to your right rather than to your left as you exit." "Turn down stage rather than upstage when you sit. It is more efficient. It appears more natural."

A movement, like a line reading, must come from an intention, a need to do something specific. "I have to get out of here fast." "I can't face her while I say this." "I need to move around because my foot is going to sleep." Instead of thinking of blocking and movement as driven solely by composition, think of them as driven by intentions and needs. Then the movement will feel right. Then it is possible to fix composition or timing problems.

Choosing Performers

A great deal of theatre happens backward. A group gathers because they want to do plays. Then they ask themselves if anyone knows any good plays. They get a script and then discover they have to go find other people to perform that script. They hire a director, a designer—and altogether disenfranchise themselves from the process they began. There are too many things wrong with this picture, not the least of which is the unlikelihood that anything artistic will come of it.

Conventional Wisdom and Casting

By now it is apparent that we strongly believe theatre should be made out of the group of people who have come together to do it. The conventional system of choosing a work and holding an audition requires something quite different.

No matter how it is handled, an audition is a competition. If we are not careful, winning the competition becomes more important than performing the work. Some actors spend more hours of their time practicing their audition monologues than they do developing the art of performance. Before we reject this process altogether, we should examine its constituent parts.

There is a saying that casting is 90 percent of directing. That is probably true. If the performers are talented and understand the roles, if they are people the audience will accept in the parts, then the directing job is easy. If the casting is bad—the actors are not skilled or gifted and are not believable in their roles—the director cannot save the performance. The director who signs on with an unknown group goes through a nightmare of doubt casting a script. How to audition? How to know if the person will come through? How to get a good pool of actors to audition? More experienced directors have casting directors, and still more experienced directors cast only from a pool of people they already know.

To be sure, there is no substitute for knowing performers, for having worked with them or seen their work, or both. All actors have their quirks and their ways of being on stage. It is part of what they bring to the art. The better each actor is known, the more likely it is that the production can be strengthened rather than weakened by their idiosyncrasies.

Another cliché of casting is, "Typecasting is the best casting." It is a cliché because it is true. If you want the audience to accept that a character is a certain kind of person, then it is a good idea to cast that kind of person in the role. Authors write for certain performers because they know what they can do, and people imagine a role with a specific performer in mind because it brings the script to life in a particular way.

These truisms have developed around the process of identifying a play that is a known quantity, picking a director to be in charge, and then searching for actors to fill the roles. We are proposing that theatre be made from different starting points. Then we can reexamine the truisms.

Thinking Differently About Casting

Let us return to Hi Concept - Lo Tech Theatre and its premises. Our goal is to make theatre with a group of people, children or adults, who want to make theatre together and have a reason for doing so. We may also want to help those people grow in their capacity to do theatre work. The first step of casting is for the group to choose or develop the piece with the group in mind.

In that way casting is never an afterthought. Casting is part of developing the work itself. If we are twenty women aged twenty-four to fifty, we may have no reason to do Tennessee Williams or Arthur Miller. Their plays have been done by others for their own reasons. We ask ourselves, "What is it *we* want to do, what do *we* want to say, what can *we* express most effectively?" If the answer comes up Tennessee Williams or Arthur Miller, then we have to ask, "How can twenty woman between the ages of twenty-four and fifty structure that work so that we can do it?"

Secondly, casting should show off people to their best advantage. Success builds confidence and skill and allows individuals to take chances. A newcomer with little experience needs a chance to do something of substance, on a modest scale, in a limited range. More experienced people need bigger and bigger challenges to their imagination, their flexibility, and their physical and emotional skills. No one needs to fail.

Theatre performers are extremely vulnerable creatures. No other art form requires that the person's entire being be used as the material for making art. Not just the body, or the voice, but the entire summary of experiences, memories, and physical attributes becomes the medium of expression. No one should ever be exposed to humiliation. Consequently, assignments need to be accomplishable—given work, rehearsal, and help. We want to cast ourselves to type where it makes sense, and we want to explore and challenge ourselves and our fellow artists everywhere we can.

Thirdly, there is no reason to have ageism, sexism, or racism enter the casting process as long as we keep our eyes on the performance reality. Remembering that the audience is always part of the performance equation, we need to ask the question, "Can we develop our work in a way that our audience will accept our casting even if it goes against their immediate expectations? What conventions do we establish to create the frame around our production so that what we do within that frame is consistent?" Audiences will buy anything presented to them in the right package—a young boy as an old man, a girl as a boy, an old woman as a young child, a black as a white, a white as an Asian. That is the magic of the theatre. It is a world of pretense. All we have to do is give the audience the right clues to pretend with us and it will do its part.

Some Casting Guidelines

Do not rush into casting.
Explore a work with a lot of different possibilities.

Allow people to find the things they are passionate about.

Allow relationships to develop and be tested.

Allow voices to be heard doing a variety of things.

Consider developing the company before casting the roles.

Decide together on a point when roles will be set for performance.

Establish a procedure for the casting of each given piece.

Making Casting Serve the Group

Do enough different kinds of work to make the casting of any given piece of minor importance. There will then always be more opportunities.

Vary responsibilities from work to work, to share the limelight and help people grow. Unless you are a very small company, where everyone will perform a great deal, it is good to be sure that no single person is on stage significantly more than others.

Do not violate a person's basic nature. Not all people can do all things. A highly physical person may not be highly verbal and vice versa. There is a difference between stretching people and forcing them into painfully uncomfortable situations. In the first case, they can develop the skills to satisfy the basic expectations of the audience. In the second, they will always feel out of place and both they and the audience will know it.

Help individuals find realistic goals and identify their limitations. Enjoy both.

Keep in mind the pros and cons of the cliché, "Typecasting is the best casting." Typecasting does some of the theatre work for us by creating and fulfilling expectations. Casting against type, or ignoring type, opens our minds to alternative understandings. With a number of performances, a group can exploit the tension between stretching people's capacities, both audience and performer, and working with the benefits and limitations of casting to type.

Creative Casting Alternatives

1. The casting is part of the creation of the work itself. Casting evolves through the developmental process, as people improvise and contribute. Some authors may wish to perform their own work. Some people will write for others. Some pieces will be chosen with specific people in mind. Some people will claim something and ask others to participate in it.

2. A single person or a small group is given the authority to make the choices for a particular work. They may do a casting workshop or hold readings, either on an open basis or in a closed setting.

3. The group discusses casting and decides together.

4. The casting is deliberately random—drawn from a hat.

5. The casting is deliberately against type in some way decided by the group—men play women, women play men, or other choices.

Here are some possibilities:

Cast everything against age, or gender or race. Establish the convention that in this performance, all the women will be played by men, or all the whites by blacks, or all the old people by young, or all the young people by old, or everything will be played by its opposite, however you determine that. Deliberately force an audience to play along with you, thereby giving your performers tasks they will not otherwise encounter. The trick to success with this is simple and powerful: Everything else must be done absolutely straight. Everyone must take their work completely seriously and do everything *truly*, no indicating, no gags. "I play this character as if it were me. I use no funny gestures, no fake voices. I am now (even as you see me something else) fifty years old. By what I say and do you will know me—not by what you think you see."

Divide up large roles among several performers. Establish a convention that the character passes from actor to actor. This is a great trick for working with Shakespeare or other literary classics where a few people have all the important things to say. Cast five or ten people in each of those major roles, and move them through the performance. They might trade off or they might appear together as a group. A group of ten or twelve people might be Alice in a setting of *Alice in Wonderland*. They can divide up lines the way the group worked to divide up poetry—some spoken singularly, some in unison. They could work in pairs. Some simple costume device identifies them. The only limits are one's imagination.

Use people in several roles. A small group of people may wish to take on a large project. Figure out how to spread the people out so that all the words get said. It may take some cutting or some combining, but if you establish the convention from the outset that one small group will do all the roles, then the audience will accept it. It will be tricky for this not to be funny if you are not careful. Of course, if you want it to be funny, then that's no problem. However, if you want it to be taken seriously, you will need an establishing device so that there is no joke in people appearing and reappearing and there is not too much running around from place to place. All the performers could be on stage at the beginning, or they could sit at the sidelines throughout, and some may participate as voices from the group. A small group could play one set of roles and another group another set. Once again, the task is to establish the device and stick to it. Here again, gender, age, and race need play no role in determining role choices.

As a group determined to create a meaningful performance as well as to improve your theatre skills, keep this in mind: You are doing *your* performance of X, not the Broadway version or the version someone else did somewhere else. The whole point of creating theatre is *creating* theatre. What the audience sees will be what *you* thought and what *you* wanted them to think.

Final Words to the Leader

Probably the hardest job for a leader is to let go of that centrality, the "I-ness," the "my-ness" of making art. The great fear in opening the process to the group as a whole is that certain things will not get done a certain way. That fear is based on two assumptions: there are specific things that must get done and there is a certain way to do them. It could be that neither is valid. It could be that letting go of some of the agenda opens up the importance of the rest of it. It could be that the best way to do something has not been thought of yet.

Time has taught us a few things. Here are some of them.

> *The more people participate in realizing a shared vision, the greater the chance of the vision being artistically satisfying.* Time and again in these pages we have insisted that the first goal is to establish an aesthetic, a shared vision, a sense of the art in the artfulness of the theatrical venture. Without this center, there is only "connect-the-dots" theatre. It is not an evil thing, but it lacks the vitality of creating one's own theatre. Therefore, artistic leadership must put a great deal of energy into developing the shared vision of the group. It is worth the time it takes.
>
> *The more creativity you demand of everyone, the more they are likely to give.* People who have been taught to be automatons, to give right answers on tests, to do things the correct way, are often slow to trust their individual ideas. They are reluctant to give way to spontaneity. Their first efforts may be trite and trivial—and discouraging to them and to the leader. They may be resistant to their fellow performers' unsuccessful attempts, and impatient with waiting for others to "get it." They are certainly fearful of "making a fool of themselves," and may want desperately to be told how to do it right the first time.

It takes time to get people to use and trust their imaginations. It is harder work for people to solve their own problems than to get answers from others, but there is a great deal more learning that happens. The second time they try, they have made giant leaps. In the end, the group has exponentially increased capacity.

Persistence and insistence pay off. After learning that they are expected to be inventive and to put forth their ideas, and after practicing, people get better ideas. Patience is required to get through the first phases of the process. If there is anything to remember about learning, whether it is among adults or children, it is that frustration is natural. Short tempers are part of the process. Your job is to take people through their frustration to the next step. If leadership has earned its right to lead, it can endure a little bad temper.

The more power you give away, the more there is. If you keep all the artistic decisions to yourself, you are limited by your own limitations. If you give the power to others, the creative possibilities are immediately multiplied by the number of participants. Then, as the organizer or leader of the event, you have the combined power of the entire group at your fingertips. The final result will be that leadership will emerge from many directions. The work is easier. The possibilities enlarge. The end is far greater than any individual imagining.

The key ingredients are trust and patience. Both are both huge factors and both are difficult. Trust means trusting the process, trusting the participants, trusting one's own ability to guide, listen, lead, invent, stimulate, modify, and organize. And patience means taking the time to let things happen: waiting for responses, listening to ideas. It means not jumping in with solutions before others have a chance to play theirs out. It means taking the time to develop skills in others when you already possess them. It means trusting that the growth and learning that happens is worth the tension and difficulty people encounter. Every good teacher knows this. The leader of a theatrical endeavor must also be something of a teacher. And a good teacher always learns from his or her students.

The Payoff

Those of us who have made theatre a part of our entire lives obviously have a vested interest in the future of the art form. When we look at history, when we look across world cultures, when we look at cultural life in the United States, we have no reason to fear that theatre is doomed or that it is even in danger. We see that it is as natural as smiling for Grandma, as preening for an object of affection, as rehearsing an interview or playing out a fantasy in front of the mirror. But we also know that like any human endeavor, theatre can be institutionalized, conventionalized, codified, regularized, and can drive as many people out as it invites others in.

We have created this book out of two lifetimes of experience and the help of a thousand others whose books, articles, projects, productions, and experiments have gone before us, in order to recapture for another generation something of that fundamental naturalness of the art form.

Theatre is complex and subtle. It has possibilities unique to its nature. It requires practice and artful consideration. But it is not mysterious. It is not limited to an anointed few. It can be used by tiny children and aging adults with honesty and integrity.

Moreover, theatre is not a fixed body of work or practices. It is not a building or a space or a facility. It is not a set of techniques. It is rather a phenomenon that is constantly redefining itself in that basic encounter of performer and audience.

When a group of people has made theatre and has manipulated the entire process, they understand and believe in what they are doing. They are keenly aware that they have done it themselves. They are artists expressing what they think about the world. They might not have done it without leadership. And they might not really know what the leadership has done. That doesn't matter. To have helped people get themselves to this point is the ultimate triumph of leading the theatre experience.

Fully empowered theatre artists communicate honestly, out of their own experience. They can never again be simple tools of some-one else's imagination. It may not be too much to say that as artists responsible for what they say and think, for what they communicate to others, for how they communicate it, and for the wholeness, the artfulness of that communication, they are being responsible adults whatever their age. They are being courageous, strong-willed, and fully participating citizens in a complicated world. Hi-Concept - Lo-Tech Theatre could seek no more glorious tribute.

Conclusion

We don't expect this book to make you a theatre professional. That takes long days and years of training and experience. Teachers, mentors, masters, apprenticeships—these help us develop our art. But we hope that you have found here new ways to start, new images of theatre, new encouragement to be at the center of this powerful form of human expression.

We hope that our message of *hi-concept - lo-tech* will inspire you to invest in your own creative spirit and the creative spirit of those who gather with you. We hope you will have new confidence in the essence of the art and not in its temporary trappings, and a new conviction that this essence must guide you. We hope that you will remember a few of our basic premises.

> Trust the art that comes from your community of theatre workers and be driven by what they need to say.
> Make learning and growing in the art a force in all your work.
> Know your audiences and engage with them.
> Consider the power of the words you use on the stage and choose them well.

Make artistic choices that depend on having and understanding a guiding aesthetic.

Make choices, don't make do. Let artful decisions determine the use of limited resources.

Understand and use theatrical conventions to engage all in the unique magic of the stage.

Choose your space and embellishments from the center of the art itself.

Aim for sustainable theatre. Do not deplete the native soil of your art.

Work for honesty and truth in all your artistic communication.

Trust your community of workers to provide artistic leadership.

Believe in the essential nature of theatre and use it.

Appendix: Drawings for Cubes and Platforms

List of Drawings

Sheet	Drawing Title
1	List of Drawings
2	4'-0" x 8'-0" Platform
3	4'-0" x 4'-0" Platform
4	4'-0" x 4'-0" Diagonal Platform
5	Platform Construction Notes
6	18 Inch Cube
7	18" x 18" x 30" Cube
8	Cube Construction Notes
9	Rehearsal Furniture – Basic Units
10	Rehearsal Furniture – Basic Lids
11	Rehearsal Furniture – More Lids
12	Rehearsal Furniture – Dining Table Lid
13	Rehearsal Furniture – Chair Backs
14	Rehearsal Furniture – Couch Back

Virginia Tech – Theatre Arts Dept.

SCALE : N.T.S.

DATE: 6/16/91

List of Drawings

DRAWN BY: DAVID A. WEDIN

SHEET 1

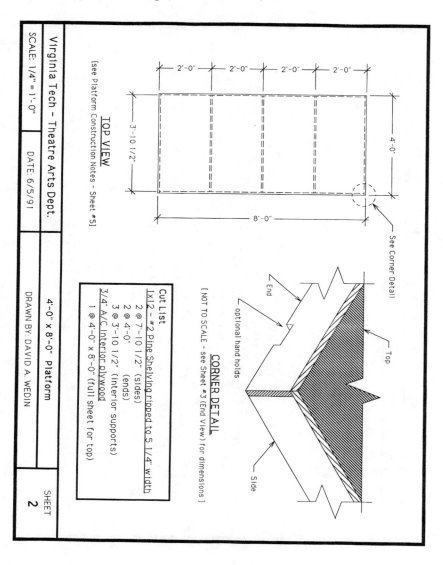

TOP VIEW

[see Platform Construction Notes – Sheet #5]

2'-0"   2'-0"   2'-0"   2'-0"

3'-10 1/2"

4'-0"

8'-0"

See Corner Detail

CORNER DETAIL

[NOT TO SCALE – see Sheet #3 (End View) for dimensions]

End

optional hand holds

Top

Side

Cut List

1x12 – #2 Pine Shelving ripped to 5 1/4" width
    2 @ 7'-10 1/2" (sides)
    2 @ 4'-0"   (ends)
    3 @ 3'-10 1/2" (interior supports)
3/4" A/C Interior plywood
    1 @ 4'-0" x 8'-0" (full sheet for top)

Virginia Tech – Theatre Arts Dept.

SCALE: 1/4" = 1'-0"

DATE: 6/5/91

DRAWN BY: DAVID A. WEDIN

4'-0" x 8'-0" Platform

SHEET

2

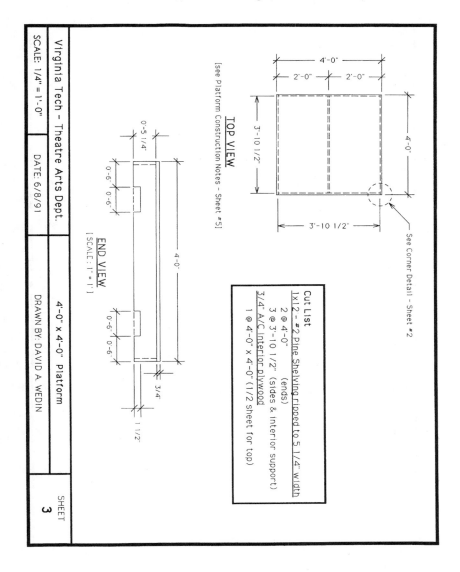

TOP VIEW
[see Platform Construction Notes - Sheet #5]

4'-0"

2'-0"   2'-0"

3'-10 1/2"

4'-0"

3'-10 1/2"

See Corner Detail - Sheet #2

END VIEW
[SCALE : 1" = 1']

0'-5 1/4"

0'-6"   0'-6"

4'-0"

0'-6"   0'-6"

3/4"

1 1/2"

Cut List
1x12 - #2 Pine Shelving ripped to 5 1/4" width
    2 @ 4'-0" (ends)
    3 @ 3'-10 1/2" (sides & interior support)
3/4" A/C Interior plywood
    1 @ 4'-0" x 4'-0" (1/2 sheet for top)

Virginia Tech - Theatre Arts Dept.

SCALE: 1/4" = 1'-0"

DATE: 6/8/91

4'-0" x 4'-0" Platform

DRAWN BY: DAVID A. WEDIN

SHEET
3

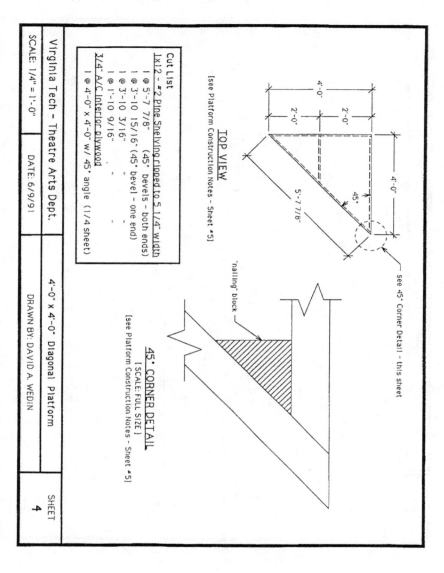

TOP VIEW

[see Platform Construction Notes – Sheet #5]

4'-0"
2'-0"
2'-0"
4'-0"
5'-7 7/8"
45°

see 45° Corner Detail - this sheet

"nailing" block

45° CORNER DETAIL
(SCALE: FULL SIZE)

[see Platform Construction Notes - Sheet #5]

Cut List
1x12 - #2 Pine Shelving ripped to 5 1/4" width
1 @ 5'-7 7/8"   (45° bevels - both ends)
1 @ 3'-10 15/16" (45° bevel - one end)
1 @ 3'-10 3/16"   "
1 @ 1'-10 9/16"   "

3/4" A/C Interior plywood
1 @ 4'-0" x 4'-0" w/ 45° angle (1/4 sheet)

SCALE: 1/4" = 1'-0"	Virginia Tech – Theatre Arts Dept.			
	DATE: 6/9/91	4'-0" x 4'-0" Diagonal Platform		SHEET
		DRAWN BY: DAVID A. WEDIN		4

SCALE : N.T.S

DATE: 6/16/91

DRAWN BY: DAVID A. WEDIN

Virginia Tech – Theatre Arts Dept.

Platform Construction Notes

Platform Construction Notes

1)   Although platforms constructed with 1x6 may be assembled using box nails it is preferable to use 1 1/2" to 2" drywall screws. Using screws allows for easy replacement of damaged parts in the future. Use 3 fasteners per joint and space fasteners 8" to 10" apart around the platform lid edge. Do not forget to screw the lid to the interior supports – this not only provides added strength, but also prevents the lid from bouncing on the supports.

2)   You may use 1x6 purchased from the lumber company rather than ripping your own, but note that 1x6 as it comes from your average lumber yard will vary in width from between 5 1/4" to 5 1/2". If you decide to use pre-ripped 1x6 make sure that the interior supports are the same width or smaller than the exterior framing pieces and that the exterior framing pieces are all the same width. This will help prevent the platform from rocking on a piece that is wider than the rest.

3)   It is often desirable to cut hand holds in the end pieces of platforms. These hand holds provide an easy way to pick up a platform that is lying on the ground and also can guard against smashed fingers when putting platforms in place. The hand holds are most easily cut using a sabre saw BEFORE the pieces are assembled.

4)   Note that if you cut a 4' x 8' sheet of plywood in half you will NOT end up with two pieces that are EXACTLY 4' x 4'. Each side will be a little shorter due to the saw kerf (the amount of material lost in the cutting process due to the thickness of the blade). If you need to use such a piece remember to adjust the lid on the frame in order to minimize the effect of the smaller lid.

5)   When making a 45° joint with 1x6 it is best to add "nailing" blocks to the corners. This provides added strength to an otherwise weak joint. "Nailing" blocks of this type can be made by ripping a piece of 2x4 at a 45° angle and then cutting each piece to length.

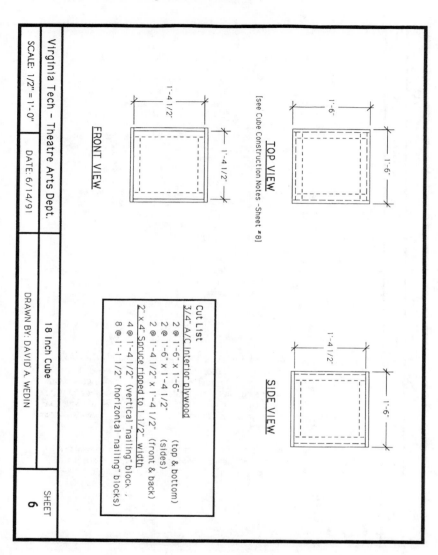

TOP VIEW
[see Cube Construction Notes -Sheet #8]

1'-6"

1'-6"

SIDE VIEW

1'-4 1/2"

1'-6"

FRONT VIEW

1'-4 1/2"

1'-4 1/2"

Cut List
3/4" A/C Interior plywood
2 @ 1'-6" x 1'-6"   (top & bottom)
2 @ 1'-6" x 1'-4 1/2"   (sides)
2 @ 1'-4 1/2" x 1'-4 1/2"   (front & back)
2" x 4" Spruce ripped to 1 1/2" width
4 @ 1'-4 1/2" (vertical "nailing" block ,
8 @ 1'-1 1/2" (horizontal "nailing" blocks)

Virginia Tech – Theatre Arts Dept.

SCALE: 1/2" = 1'-0"

DATE: 6/14/91

DRAWN BY: DAVID A. WEDIN

18 Inch Cube

SHEET

6

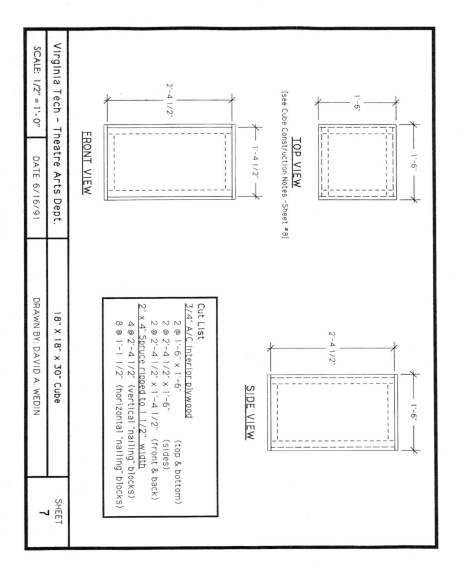

FRONT VIEW

TOP VIEW
[see Cube Construction Notes – Sheet #8]

SIDE VIEW

Cut List
3/4" A/C interior plywood
2 @ 1'-6" x 1'-6"   (top & bottom)
2 @ 2'-4 1/2" x 1'-6"   (sides)
2 @ 2'-4 1/2" x 1'-4 1/2" (front & back)
2" x 4" Spruce ripped to 1 1/2" width
4 @ 2'-4 1/2" (vertical "nailing" blocks)
8 @ 1'-1 1/2" (horizontal "nailing" blocks)

Virginia Tech – Theatre Arts Dept.

SCALE: 1/2" = 1'-0"   DATE: 6/16/91

18" X 18" x 30" Cube

DRAWN BY: DAVID A. WEDIN

SHEET
7

SCALE : N.T.S.

Virginia Tech – Theatre Arts Dept.

DATE: 6/16/91

DRAWN BY: DAVID A. WEDIN

Cube Construction Notes

SHEET

8

Cube Construction Notes

1)   Although scenery constructed in this manner may be assembled using box nails it is preferable to use 1 1/2" to 2" drywall screws. Using screws allows for easy replacement of damaged parts in the future. Space fasteners 8" to 10" apart around each face of the rehearsal cube.

2)   The order of assembly is important. First- frame the interior face of the front and back pieces with two vertical and two horizontal "nailing" blocks each. Second- attach the sides to the front and back making sure that the four sides are each 1'-6" in width. Third- add two horizontal "nailing" blocks to each of the side pieces, trim the length of these "nailing" blocks if necessary. Finally- attach the top and bottom pieces. Throughout the process make sure that the best side of the plywood faces out.

3)   It is often desirable to cover the surface of a rehearsal cube with muslin. Such a covering provides a smooth surface for painting and eliminates the need for excessive sanding. If you decide to cover the rehearsal cube with muslin use a mixture of white glue (Elmer's) and water. Add just enough water to the glue to allow the mixture to be easily spread with a brush. Take care not to add too much water because if the mixture becomes too thin it will not adhere the muslin to the wood. DO NOT attempt to use the fabric's selvage edge (a factory edge which is significantly thicker than the fabric itself) because it WILL NOT adhere to the wood surface!

4)   The "nailing" blocks are NECESSARY because driving a fastener into the end grain of plywood will almost always split the plywood layers. The "nailing" blocks are most easily made by ripping construction grade 2x4 spruce to 1 1/2". The resulting strips are 1 1/2" square and can then be cut to length. If you find significant variation in the width of the "nailing" blocks do not hesitate to adjust their length to compensate.

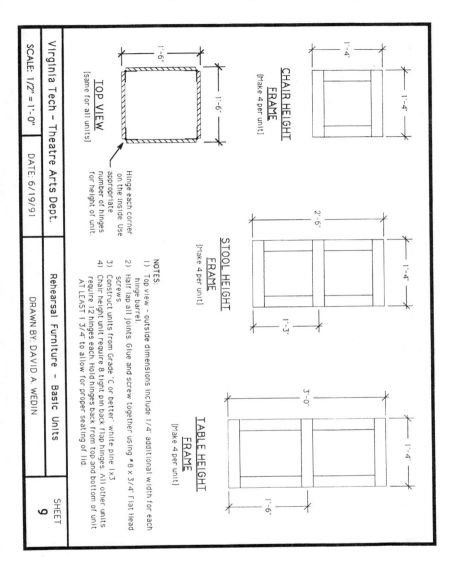

CHAIR HEIGHT FRAME
[Make 4 per unit]

1'-4"
1'-4"

STOOL HEIGHT FRAME
[Make 4 per unit]

2'-6"
1'-4"
1'-3"

TABLE HEIGHT FRAME
[Make 4 per unit]

3'-0"
1'-4"
1'-6"

TOP VIEW
[same for all units]

1'-6"
1'-6"

Hinge each corner on the inside. Use appropriate number of hinges for height of unit.

NOTES:

1) Top view - outside dimensions include 1/4" additional width for each hinge barrel.

2) Half lap all joints. Glue and screw together using #8 x 3/4" Flat Head screws.

3) Construct units from Grade "C" or better white pine 1x3

4) Chair height unit require 8 tight pin back flap hinges. All other units require 12 hinges each. Hold hinges back from top and bottom of unit AT LEAST 1 3/4" to allow for proper seating of lid.

Virginia Tech – Theatre Arts Dept.

SCALE: 1/2" = 1'-0"

DATE: 6/19/91

Rehearsal Furniture – Basic Units

DRAWN BY: DAVID A. WEDIN

SHEET
9

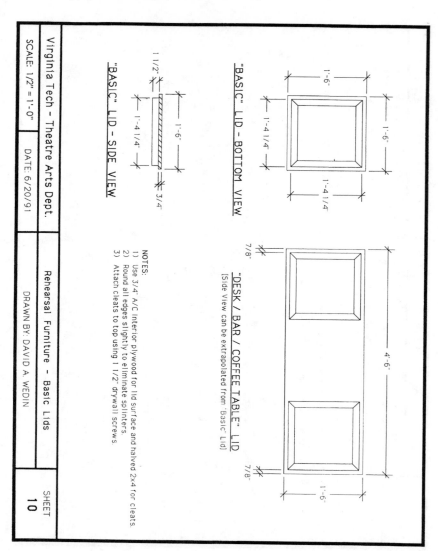

"BASIC" LID – BOTTOM VIEW

1'-6"
1'-4 1/4"
1'-6"
1'-4 1/4"

"BASIC" LID – SIDE VIEW

1 1/2"
1'-6"
1'-4 1/4"
3/4"

"DESK / BAR / COFFEE TABLE" LID
[Side View can be extrapolated from "Basic" Lid]

7/8"
4'-6"
7/8"
1'-6"

NOTES:
1) Use 3/4" A/C interior plywood for lid surface and halved 2x4 for cleats
2) Round all edges slightly to eliminate splinters.
3) Attach cleats to top using 1 1/2" drywall screws

Virginia Tech – Theatre Arts Dept.

SCALE: 1/2" = 1'-0"

DATE: 6/20/91

Rehearsal Furniture – Basic Lids

DRAWN BY: DAVID A. WEDIN

SHEET
10

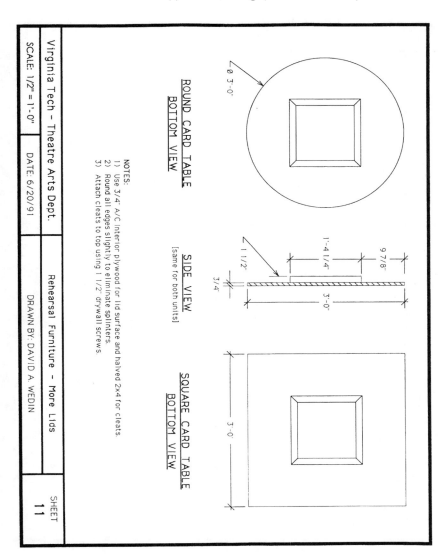

ROUND CARD TABLE
BOTTOM VIEW

Ø 3'-0"

SIDE VIEW
[same for both units]

1 1/2"
3/4"
1'-4 1/4"
9 7/8"
3'-0"

SQUARE CARD TABLE
BOTTOM VIEW

3'-0"

NOTES:
1) Use 3/4" A/C interior plywood for lid surface and halved 2x4 for cleats
2) Round all edges slightly to eliminate splinters.
3) Attach cleats to top using 1 1/2" drywall screws

Virginia Tech – Theatre Arts Dept.

SCALE: 1/2" = 1'-0"

DATE: 6/20/91

Rehearsal Furniture – More Lids

DRAWN BY: DAVID A. WEDIN

SHEET
11

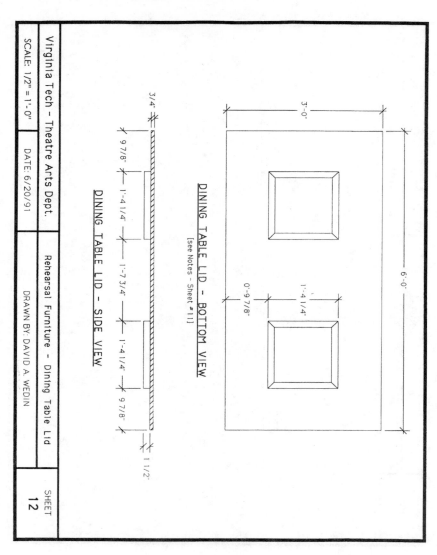

DINING TABLE LID – BOTTOM VIEW
[see Notes – Sheet #11]

6'-0"

3'-0"

0'-9 7/8"

1'-4 1/4"

DINING TABLE LID – SIDE VIEW

3/4"

9 7/8" 1'-4 1/4" 1'-7 3/4" 1'-4 1/4" 9 7/8"

1 1/2"

Virginia Tech – Theatre Arts Dept.

SCALE: 1/2" = 1'-0"

DATE: 6/20/91

Rehearsal Furniture – Dining Table Lid

DRAWN BY: DAVID A. WEDIN

SHEET

12

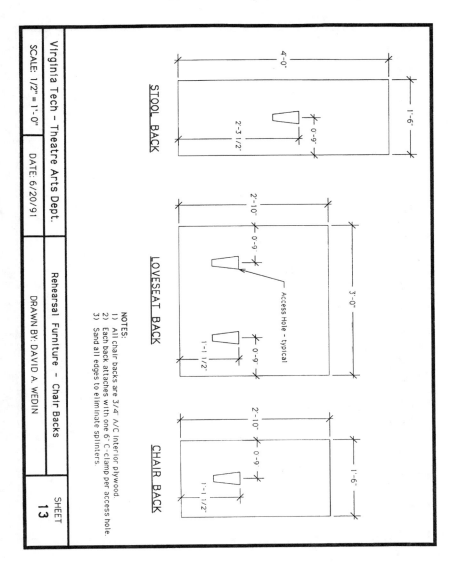

STOOL BACK

4'-0"

1'-6"

2'-3 1/2"

0'-9"

LOVESEAT BACK

2'-10"

0'-9"

3'-0"

Access Hole – typical

1'-1 1/2"

0'-9"

CHAIR BACK

2'-10"

0'-9"

1'-6"

1'-1 1/2"

NOTES:
1) All chair backs are 3/4" A/C Interior plywood.
2) Each back attaches with one 6" C-clamp per access hole.
3) Sand all edges to eliminate splinters.

Virginia Tech – Theatre Arts Dept.

Rehearsal Furniture – Chair Backs

SCALE: 1/2" = 1'-0"

DATE: 6/20/91

DRAWN BY: DAVID A. WEDIN

SHEET

13

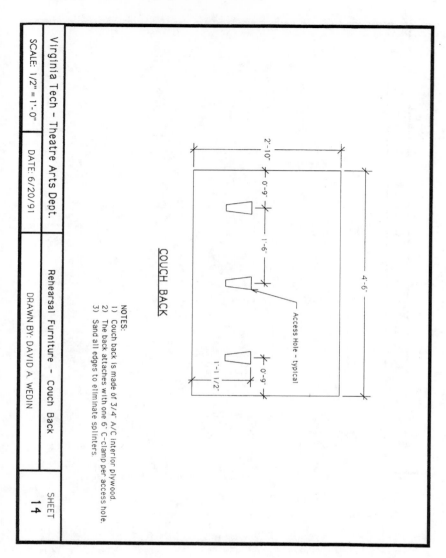

COUCH BACK

2'-10"

0'-9"

1'-6"

4'-6"

Access Hole - typical

0'-9"

1'-1 1/2"

NOTES:
1) Couch back is made of 3/4" A/C interior plywood.
2) The back attaches with one 6" C-clamp per access hole.
3) Sand all edges to eliminate splinters.

Virginia Tech - Theatre Arts Dept.

SCALE: 1/2" = 1'-0"

DATE: 6/20/91

Rehearsal Furniture - Couch Back

DRAWN BY: DAVID A. WEDIN

SHEET

14

References

Benedetti, Robert. 1993. *The Actor at Work*. 6th ed. Englewood Cliffs, NJ: Prentice Hall.

Boal, Augusto. 1985. *Theatre of the Oppressed*. New York: Theatre Communications Group.

Chaikin, Joseph. 1991. *The Presence of the Actor*. New York: Theatre Communications Group.

Cohen, Robert. 1992. *Acting One*. 2nd ed. Mountain View, CA: Mayfield Publishing Company.

Humphrey, Doris. 1987. *The Art of Making Dances*. New York: Grove/Atlantic.

Jones, Robert Edmond. 1987. *The Dramatic Imagination*. New York: Routledge Chapman & Hall..

Lessac, Arthur. 1967. *The Use and Training of the Human Voice*. Mountain View, CA: Mayfield Publishing Company.

Linklater, Kristin. 1985. *Freeing the Natural Voice*. New York: Drama Book Publishers.

Schechner, Richard. 1988. *Essays on Performance Theory*. New York: Routledge.

Simonson, Lee. 1975. *The Stage is Set*. Salem, NH: Ayer Co. Publishers, Inc.

Spolin, Viola. 1983. *Improvisation for the Theater: A Handbook of Teaching & Directing Techniques*. Rev. ed. Evanston, IL: Northwestern University Press.

———. *Theater Games for the Classroom: A Teacher's Handbook*. Evanston, IL: Northwestern University Press.

Stanislavky, Constantin. 1989. *An Actor Prepares*. New York: Routledge Chapman & Hall.

States, Bert. 1985. *Great Reckonings in Little Rooms: On the Phenomenology of the Theater*. Berkeley, CA: University of California Press.